Entrepreneurship for Everyone

Entrepreneurship for Everyone
A Student Textbook

Robert Mellor with Gary Coulton, Anne Chick,
Antonia Bifulco, Noha Mellor and Alan Fisher

Los Angeles • London • New Delhi • Singapore • Washington DC

First published 2009

SAGE Publications Ltd
1 Oliver's Yard
55 City Road
London EC1Y 1SP

SAGE Publications Inc.
2455 Teller Road
Thousand Oaks, California 91320

SAGE Publications India Pvt Ltd
B 1/I 1 Mohan Cooperative Industrial Area
Mathura Road, Post Bag 7
New Delhi 110 044

SAGE Publications Asia-Pacific Pte Ltd
33 Pekin Street #02-01
Far East Square
Singapore 048763

Library of Congress Control Number: 2007942373

British Library Cataloguing in Publication data

A catalogue record for this book is available from the
British Library

ISBN 978-1-4129-4775-6
ISBN 978-1-4129-4776-3 (pbk)

Typeset by C&M Digitals (P) Ltd., Chennai, India
Printed in Great Britain by T J International Ltd, Padstow, Cornwall
Printed on paper from sustainable resources

Mixed Sources
Product group from well-managed
forests and other controlled sources
www.fsc.org Cert no. SGS-COC-2482
© 1996 Forest Stewardship Council
FSC

Contents

About the authors

Polyglot and polymath **Robert B. Mellor** holds earned doctorates in various academic disciplines including innovation, computing and biology and is amongst the Directors of the Faculty of Computing, Information Systems and Mathematics at Kingston University, London. He is author of over 120 scientific publications in reputable journals, including *Nature* and has previously written 10 books, including 4 on innovation and entrepreneurship. His activities include being a successful serial entrepreneur across Europe.

Dr. Gary R Coulton, (Reader in Medical Biomics and Education) has more than 25 years experience in biomedical research, teaching and knowledge translation in biotechnology. He is the Director of the St. George's Medical Biomics Centre and Associate Dean for Enterprise and Innovation at St. George's, University of London. He is also a London Technology Network Business Fellow.

Anne Chick is Reader in Sustainable Design and Director of the Sustainable Design Research Centre in the Faculty of Art, Design and Architecture at Kingston University. She is Adjunct Professor in the Faculty of Environmental Design at the University of Calgary, Canada. She has managed funded research and knowledge transfer programmes worth over £1.5M and consistently publishes her research.

Antonia Bifulco is Professor of Health and Social Care at Royal Holloway, University of London and directs the Lifespan Research Group there, researching and publishing for over 25 years on psychosocial risk factors in psychological disorder. She and her research team undertake commissioned research from health and social services, evaluating service provision for children and families. In recent years she has become very involved in entrepreneurship, and she also runs CPO training courses and workshops for practitioners.

Noha Mellor is Senior Lecturer in Media and Cultural Studies, Faculty of Arts and Social Sciences, Kingston University. She is the author of *The Making of Arab News* (2005) and *Modern Arab Journalism* (2007).

Alan Fisher is currently Head of department of Music and Fashion at the University of Westminster, he qualified as an architect at the University of Sheffield in 1983 and subsequently went on to sign for Virgin records as part of the seminal electronic group Cabaret Voltaire. He moved into production, engineering, company directorship, and label management with Fon records working with artists as diverse as Take That, Bjork, Boy George, Sparks, Inspiral Carpets, and 808 State, succeeding in promoting and engineering numerous top-ten hits, in both the album and singles charts. He is a Westfocus Fellow working on industry knowledge transfer events such as the Art of Record Production conference, now in its third year of international delivery.

List of abbreviations

4Cs	Consumer wants, Convenience, Cost and Communication
4Ps	The 4Ps of innovation: Product, Process, Position and Paradigm, or the 4Ps of marketing: Product, Place, Price and Promotion
ACE-Chase	An action audit tool
A-I	Adaption-Innovation
ALUO	Advantages, Limitations, Uniqueness and Opportunity
BA	Business angel
CDA	Compact Disk Audio
CEO	Chief Executive Officer
CGI	Computer Generated Images
CPS	Creative Problem Solving
CSF	Critical Success Factor
DoI	Diffusion of Innovations
DRM	Digital Rights Management
DVD	Digital Video Disk
FFF	Friends, Family and Fools
GM foods	Foodstuffs produced from genetically modified sources
HOTPLOT	See SWOTPLOT
IPO	Initial Public Offering
IPR	Intellectual Property Rights
ISP	Internet Service Provider
M&A	Mergers and Acquisitions
MALDI-TOF	Matrix Associated Laser Desorption & Ionization-Time of Flight
MBA	Master of Business Arts
MPG	Moving Picture (Experts) Group
MTFC	Multidimensional Treatment Foster Care
NGO	Non Governmental Organization
NHS	National Health Service
OHP	Overhead Projector
PCR	Polymerase Chain Reaction
PLC	Product Life Cycle (not to be confused with plc, public limited company)
PR	Public Relations
QoS	Quality of Service
R&D	Research & Development
RiP	Research in Practice
RoI	Return on Investment

SDS-PAGE   Sodium Duodecyl Sulphate-Poly Acrylamide Gel Electrophorsis
SEARCH   Scan, Expand, Adapt, Revise, Create and Harvest
SELDI-TOF   Surface Enhanced Laser Desorption & Ionization-Time of Flight
SGM   Strategic Group Mapping
SIP   Session Initiation Protocol
SLC   Social Learning Cycle
SLEPT   Social, Legal, Economic, Political and Technological
SME   Small and Medium-sized Enterprise
SWOT   Strengths, Weaknesses, Opportunities and Threats
SWOTPLOT   A development based on SWOT
TBL   Triple Bottom Line
TD   Trickle Down Theory
TQM   Total Quality Management
TROTPLOT   See SWOTPLOT
TTM   Time To Market
UGC   User Generated Content
UNIX   Software commonly used as a server platform
USB   Universal Serial Bus
USP   Unique Selling Proposition
VC   Venture Capitalist
VHS   Video Home System
VoIP   Voice over Internet Protocol

Introduction

Why entrepreneurship?

Robert B. Mellor

Entrepreneurship gives birth to new commodities, techniques and goods, booting human progress forward and rendering the old obsolete, leading to the extinction of whole branches of industry and the creation of new ones. It is the use of innovation that makes many of our goods today not only better, but also cheaper, than they were even a decade ago. This process is so powerful that many large corporations are beginning to ask how they can use their employees' talents for innovation.

Innovation and the evolution of business

Existing large firms are seldom capable of using innovation, e.g. of the largest ('Fortune 100') companies from 1930, only one – General Electric – still exists. New industries evolve out of start-ups. Few succeed. As new industries arise, they displace the old. The 'first world' technologies are being copied globally, meaning that 'first world' countries must constantly improve efficiency and create new industries in order to survive. In order to succeed, companies must constantly change and innovate; this is not impossible, but examples are few, e.g. the Preussische Bergwerks und Hutten Aktiengesellschaft (Prussian Society for Mining and Steel) became tourist giant TUI and the Nokianvirta Paper Mill became the mobile telephony giant Nokia.

Traditionally, the focus of classical microeconomics is price; capitalists, owners and other businessmen choose labour-intensive production when labour is cheap and interest rates high, or capital-intensive production techniques in the opposite circumstances. Guided by price, then they can choose to make fewer goods, or more. However, they rarely invent new goods or radicalize production; those who use innovation to introduce something new are often called entrepreneurs. But introducing new products is a risky business; experience shows that less than 10 per cent of all inventions will result in a product and indeed only 0.5 per cent will return a significant profit. Clearly this is not an area that interests a manager of any traditional company, where stability, smooth adjustments and uninterrupted production are of the utmost priority. Most organizations or individuals do not want to change unless forced to – and logical, rational reasons alone are certainly insufficient to generate and sustain change. It is mostly the entrepreneurs, following their visions, who are ready to tackle such odds.

If entrepreneurs – using innovation – take this step, then the question may be 'How can we get more of them?'. That is the aim of this book – to teach and inform about entrepreneurship both those who wish to start a business, large or small, and those who wish to work in innovative companies. Fortunately, however, learning entrepreneurship goes further than that; entrepreneurship training teaches you how to be more enterprising, more creative, more innovative, more commercially aware and more self-motivated. These are skills that can have a profound positive effect on your employability, as well as on your private life.

Some years ago there was a debate among academics about whether entrepreneurs are 'born or made'. Obviously, if entrepreneurs became so by virtue of their genes, then there would be little point in trying to teach it – one cannot teach blue-eyed people to have brown eyes! However, as I discussed in one book (Mellor, 2005: Chapter 1.4), entrepreneurial behaviour does not follow Mendelian inheritance patterns and I believe that the data in question (for review, see Bridge et al., 2002: Chapter 3) can best be explained by social imprinting – similar to a Pavlovian reflex – from entrepreneurial role models during childhood.

Entrepreneurship during one's early twenties is also relatively popular; 'nothing ventured, nothing gained' is an attractive philosophy when you have little to lose. However, there is a dip in numbers of new entrepreneurs in their thirties and forties; risking everything is less attractive when your house and family are part of the stakes. A relatively recent noted phenomenon is later-life entrepreneurship among the 45+ age group ('senior entrepreneurship'). Such mature people often have some financial resources, but more importantly, they master their subject with massive competence and expertise, are psychologically very stable and have realistic expectations. Companies started by entrepreneurs in this category show a higher average success rate and above-normal growth rates. Indeed, the Australian organization EGC (www.egc.net.au) specializes in venturing with mature and experienced returning ex-pats.

Thus it can be seen that anybody can be an entrepreneur at any stage in their life and indeed it could be argued that learning the tools of business creation is a skill that, if learnt now, may come in useful if not in the immediate future, then perhaps in 20 years time. Indeed, one factor this book expressly covers is entrepreneurial management; the overlap between entrepreneurship and management, in the realization that individuals can shift from one to the other (Figure 0.1).

To illustrate its importance, 1,500 colleges and universities in the USA offer some form of entrepreneurship training. Growth in the UK has been even more explosive, with over 500 courses being offered at over 100 UK universities and interest in entrepreneurship education spreading to non-business disciplines, where students in engineering, life sciences and liberal

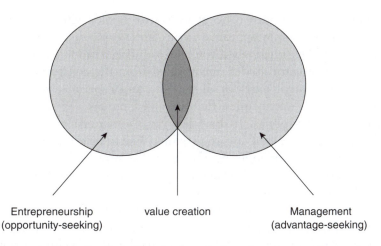

Entrepreneurship   value creation   Management
(opportunity-seeking)   (advantage-seeking)

Figure 0.1   A Venn diagram illustrating that efficient value creation often occurs at the overlap of entrepreneurial and managerial behaviour (often called 'strategic innovation', 'entrepreneurial management' or 'strategic entrepreneurship')

arts are interested in becoming entrepreneurs, fostering a 'comparative entrepreneurship' approach. This module will give you a good grounding in entrepreneurship, regardless of your background.

A sound mastery of technical fundamentals is needed for success and the core competencies for new ventures must include the technical skills involved. This has led to a bit of a quandary, because the Business Schools claim 'ownership' regarding the teaching of the commercial activity called entrepreneurship, but unfortunately the Business Schools – per definition – are incapable of teaching the wide variety of deeply technical skills needed for successful entrepreneurship. These technical skills are provided by what I call 'the ABC Schools' e.g. Architecture, Biology, Chemistry, etc., where A, B and C can be any academic discipline. Thus this book is aimed at technical experts learning technical 'ABC' subjects and it is hoped that the number of disciplines covered will expand with subsequent editions, so 'A' may cover Aerospace, Architecture, Art and Archaeology; 'B', Building, Beauty and Biology; 'C', Chemistry, Cloning and Clothing, etc. We call this approach 'Embedded Entrepreneurship' and feel that only in this way – offering optional modules as 'Entrepreneurship & X' – can we ensure that aspiring student entrepreneurs possess the required technical background.

Teaching innovation, like innovation itself, flourishes on discontinuities, e.g. sudden unemployment. For final-year students one major discontinuity involves 'employability'; leaving the cosy education system behind and graduating into the cold harsh world. Experience shows clearly that – especially for non-business students – entrepreneurship courses are by far most effective in the final year, or final semester and this module will help prepare you as a new graduate for this large discontinuity. The module instructor will guide participants through the course in such a way that you, upon graduation, will be in a better position to be able to see more clearly the choices and paths open to you.

This book follows the European concept of 'course book', with a chapter for each class lesson. To Anglo-Saxons this may appear as lecture notes expanded into a standalone text and indeed optimal value will be gained when you read it during a module where your lecturer uses the presentations and instructor guides downloaded from the companion web site. The text itself is divided into four generic parts for all students, and a specialist part. This structure uses the first three generic parts – Principles, Practice and Context – to introduce concepts common for students of all disciplines. In Part IV, you then concentrate on the chapter most related to the discipline you are studying and you may like to read the extra case studies related to the specialist chapters in Appendix B. The specialist strands re-join in Part V ('Action'), which is about the young venture and academically forms a connection between the disciplines of entrepreneurship and small business research.

There is much to learn, so you must read the appropriate chapter before each class lesson; first, Chapters 1–9, then the chapter on your specialist discipline, then Chapter 16. If you are not certain what an acronym stands for, look it up in the list of abbreviations. If you do not understand a piece of jargon, e.g. 'market shakeout', 'entropy' or 'goodwill', then Google it and try find out before asking your instructor. The text is sprinkled with 'think boxes' containing cases, definitions, etc. that illustrate the surrounding text and prompt you to investigate the subject further. This is also the point of the references, the further reading lists and web links contained at the end of every chapter. It is a challenge, but only by reading around the subject will you master it!

Part I

Principles

1 Developing People and Competencies

Robert B. Mellor

Introduction

In this chapter the need for an entrepreneurial team is put forward, as is the need for a concrete strategy (normally documented in the form of the business plan) and a network. The latter part of the chapter introduces how these and related topics are further developed in this book.

Capitalizing on a bright idea

The concept of 'the entrepreneurial inventor' does not hold much water and indeed only a few of the classical 'engineer entrepreneurs' like Robert Stephenson, Isambard Kingdom Brunel and Alexander Graham Bell have received both honours and economic reward for their efforts. But the majority of the great scientific inventive minds have not managed to make a lasting financial profit (e.g. Curie, Einstein, Marconi, Pasteur and Whittle) and today a pop star probably makes more money than 50 Nobel Prize laureates (see Chapter 15). Even Thomas Edison, founder of the Edison Electric Light Company (later to merge with the Thomson-Houston Company and be called General Electric), like many scientists and engineers, was not a good financial manager and despite all his incredible energy he managed to bankrupt several – if not most – of his ventures despite the fact that he held 1,093 US patents and 1,239 foreign patents, including those on the phonograph, motion pictures, the alkaline storage battery and synthetic rubber, as well as the first practical incandescent light bulb (note that the 'incandescent filament lamp' was invented by Joseph Swan, Edison bought the rights and made the process practical). Technical competence – the ability to make new things – can be plotted against managerial competence – the ability to get things done and products sold (Figure 1.1).

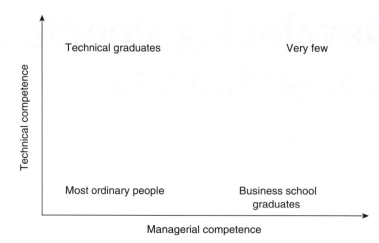

Figure 1.1   Plot of technical versus managerial competence. Very few inhabit the top right quadrant, although the multi-skilled (e.g. an engineer with an MBA) will tend away from the axes towards the middle and thus may be more innovative (see Chapter 2)

In contrast to inventors, the entrepreneurs often mentioned in connection with entrepreneurship, e.g. the late Anita Roddick (the Body Shop), Marks & Spencer, Tesco and Richard Branson (Virgin), achieved fame and fortune not by applying new technological inventions at all, but by using creative business models.

So having a bright technology-based idea is only the first of several factors needed to form a successful enterprise. The second factor is the other people involved in the business aspects of a technical idea and who can bring it forward, while the third factor is most often called 'the network'. The combination of the second and third factors, judiciously applied, can go a long way to solving the budding entrepreneurs' major problem, namely finding finance.

The entrepreneurial inventor

The career of Elmer Sperry offers an excellent example of the entrepreneurial inventor. Sperry was born into a New York family of modest means and after attending public schools, decided that he wanted to be an inventor. He tried to learn as much about electricity as possible from the library and courses, including attending lectures at nearby Cornell University. Acting on the suggestion of one of the professors there, he designed an automatically regulated generator capable of supplying a constant current when the load on its circuits varied and then immediately started to search for a financial backer. In 1880, he was taken in by the Cortland Wagon Company, whose executives included both inventors and investors and which provided him with the services of a patent lawyer, as well as money to live on and a workshop. In this 'incubator' Sperry not only perfected his dynamo, but over the next two years developed a complete system of arc lighting to go with it. Thus the Sperry Electric Light, Motor, and Car Brake Company was formed in 1883, with Sperry (who owned a large part of the company's stock) serving as 'electrician, inventor, and superintendent of the mechanical department'. Although the company was not a financial success, it launched Sperry's career. He would go on to write more than 350 patents and found nearly a dozen companies including – with the help of a wide assortment of financial backers – the Sperry Electric Mining Machine Company, the Sperry Streetcar Electric Railway Company, and the Sperry Gyroscope Company. Although Sperry often played an active role in these companies in their early stages, he typically downgraded his role to the position of technical consultant and went on to a new project, once they were reasonably well established.

Sperry focused on ensuring that his inventions were commercially exploited as best possible and consequently sold many of his inventions to companies better placed to put them to productive use. Indeed, one of his firms was the Elmer A. Sperry Company of Chicago, formed in 1888 as a vehicle for his research and development activities and whose output was patented technology. Interestingly, this firm also advertised its business as helping inventors 'develop, patent and render commercially valuable their inventions'.

(*Source*: Further researched from Hughes (1971))

How, then, can you combine excellence in technical subjects, with excellence in business? Clearly it is advantageous if you have a large family consisting of marketing people, lawyers, accountants, etc. and in the early 1990s it was rumoured that the single largest success factor for new start-ups was a high-earning spouse! Most individuals wishing to start up, however, are not in the privileged position of being able to surround themselves with the necessary expertise from their immediate family. As a consequence of this – and as illustrated in Chapter 6 – investors strive to surround the inventor with bought-in professionals possessing these skills.

Covering the business side

Another method is to team up with people possessing complementary skills from the start. This involves teaming up 'content people', often real experts in their field, with 'structure people', who can sell – no matter what it is. The right person may not necessarily be someone

Table 1.1   Illustrating the 'Hewlett-Packard' effect; 'content' people team up
with 'structure' people to form a winning team

	Inventor (Content)	Business (Structure)
Bolton and Watt Pattern Store and Erecting Shop	Watt	Bolton
HP	Hewlett	Packard
Genentech	Boyer	Swanson
Wolffolins	Wolff	Olin
The Beatles	George, Paul, John and Ringo	Epstein
Apple	Wozniack	Jobs

already known, or even liked (indeed taking best friends or family on board can lead to excru-
ciating conflicts). It must, however, be someone that the inventor can trust to make good business decisions, to be highly motivated and someone who can work towards a common goal.
This mixing factor has been a feature of leading undergraduate courses for some years (e.g. at
the University of Nevada, Reno – see Wang and Kleppe, 2001; and at the IT University of
Copenhagen, Denmark – see Mellor, 2003, 2005). The very positive effect of these synergies is
often called the 'Hewlett-Packard' effect after the huge success of the Hewlett-Packard
Company, which combined the technical brilliance of Hewlett with the business brains of
Packard (see Table 1.1).

Entrepreneurship is often wrongly perceived as a solitary activity – this misconception is
actually reinforced by terms such as 'sole trader'. However, not only the high-profile examples
cited in Table 1.1 but also the results of recent surveys e.g. *Entrepreneurship and Local Economic
Development*, by the OECD (OECD, 2003) indicate that team-based business start-ups fare
much better than individual start-ups. Specifically:

- In micro enterprises, partnerships exhibit higher rates of survival than individual firms.
- Investors are more likely to approve financing to team-led start-ups in early-stage
  venture capital assessments.
- The success of the firm and client satisfaction correlate well with the degree of social
  interaction in entrepreneurial teams.

And, indeed, many of today's leading corporations, like General Motors, DuPont, Coca-Cola
and McDonald's, were all set up by teams and not by individuals acting alone. Although not all
business ideas will result in a new Hewlett-Packard or Apple, a strong sales team can sell most
things, so investors can expect some Return on Investment (RoI). Unfortunately most new
businesses are weak on the business side; whereas 91 per cent of high-tech start-ups are confident in their technical ability, only 27 per cent of high-tech start-ups are confident that they
can get their product to the market on time (Mellor, 2003). This lack of proper management is
seen as a major drawback by investors – who invariably know their business very well. It cannot

Table 1.2   Number of business plans receiving funding in some common venture capital areas

	Ideas	Plans	Funds
US Biotech	1000	100	56
EU 'Hi-Tech'	182	20	5
EU Internet	400	25	12

Source: Modified from Mellor (2003).

Table 1.3   Commonly cited reasons for rejecting business plans

Reason for rejection	Number
Weak management	52
Not market driven	38
Timeframe too long	31
Investment too large	25
Lack of patent/protection	15
Lack of technical expertise	12
Other	17

Source: Modified from Mellor (2003).

be stressed enough that the business objectives are of paramount importance in setting up a business. One major indicator of the quality of the business acumen is the business plan. Table 1.2 illustrates that typically only few business plans receive funding and Table 1.3 illustrates that the reason for rejection is most often a poor management team.

Since usually 100 ideas are needed to generate one business plan, the business plan needs not only to be excellent but must also address both technical and managerial issues.

The essential social and business network

The third ingredient for success is having a network. Networks are also useful in starting new companies as they provide a knowledge background. Since growing a company is full of uncertainties, it is not possible in advance to know which expert tips are going to be needed (i.e. heterogeneous knowledge is needed). Those entrepreneurs with an extensive network are therefore in a much stronger position to reply to external threats, changes in the market and similar challenges. They will be in a stronger position to innovate and overcome obstacles. This is the social capital that adds value to the company. Such social capital can be accessed formally or informally, e.g. on the web there exist many networks (communities) specifically to create this type of social capital, and where membership gives one the 'right' to approach others.

Network, finance and technical ability: the case of Silicon Valley

The importance of networking is perhaps best illustrated by the example of Silicon Valley. Silicon Valley is contained by the San Francisco Bay on the east, Santa Cruz Mountains on the west and the Coast Range to the southeast. Once – when fruit orchards predominated - it was called the 'Valley of Heart's Delight'. The San Francisco Bay Area has traditionally been a major site of US Navy work, as well as the site of the Navy's large research airfield – including anti-submarine warfare rockets and torpedoes – at Moffett Field. A number of technology firms had set up business in the area around Moffett to serve the Navy. However, the Navy moved its west coast operations to San Diego and, in 1935, Moffett Field came under the control of the US Army Air Corps and later NASA took over portions of Moffett for aeronautics research. Many of the original companies stayed, while new ones moved in. The immediate area was filled with aerospace firms and the Air Force Satellite Test Center was created adjacent to Moffett. By this time a large pool of highly skilled knowledge workers were living in the 'Valley of Heart's Delight' and, despite closures, many wished to stay in the area. Both from changing jobs and working in large bases, they often knew each other (network), had hard-to-imitate know-how (expertise) and some had significant cash lay-off settlements from the Government (finance).

Given the vivid social network and access to capital, the area was already on its way to becoming a technology hot-spot (the software firm Novell pays tribute to these early days by retaining a section of the railway track to the military base in the reception of its Silicon Valley office). But the enormous expertise the area had accumulated in radio and microwave technology, microelectronics, etc. (and later semiconductors, the example of Intel is probably the most famous) also made the area attractive for more established players, who were looking for something in short supply – competent suppliers. The more established players, however, were having difficulty moving in due to lack of space. Serendipitously and due to unrelated finance problems at Stanford University (who own large portions of the estate), Professor Fred Terman had the idea of building an industrial park and raising finance by leasing land out to commercial companies. In 1951, Varian Associates signed a lease, and in 1953 the company moved into the first building in the park. Others, including Eastman Kodak, General Electric, the Admiral Corporation, Beckman Instruments, Lockheed and Hewlett-Packard, followed suit soon after. Today some 2000–4000 electronics and information technology companies, along with numerous service and supplier firms, are clustered in the area.

Building the right strategy

But is entrepreneurship only about building a team of at least two, possibly up to four or five 'core' entrepreneurs with different but complementary skills and experience that will pay attention to networking? The answer is not so easy. The other side of the coin is working out what the entrepreneur wants. Common aims for entrepreneurs are:

1   Some wish to open their own business or company immediately and head for an initial public offering (IPO). This involves writing an excellent business plan and showing a high degree of business acumen because it entails targeting providers of fairly substantial amounts of financing.

2   Establishing social enterprises like charities or other forms of 'social entrepreneurship'; non-profit and not-for-profit enterprises. Nuffield, Carnegie, Rockefeller and others (probably including Bill Gates) all returned their enormous profits to society by way of such constructions. Major differences include tax laws and the use of capital (e.g. social enterprises often rely on voluntary labour).

3   Some want 'organic growth' starting with a micro-business and invest some low level of resources – like evenings and weekends – to see if the concept will work. Examples include Lovereading.co.uk and Totstofrance.co.uk. Here a business plan can function as a personal 'roadmap' but will also be needed to attract investment should the concept begin to take off.

4   Some want to be employed in an 'innovative company' (which could be big or small). Large companies may try to act like a collection of small innovative companies and working in such an environment has significant differences to working for more traditional companies. It is becoming more common for employees in innovative companies to be asked to make a 'business plan' concerning proposed reorganizations, new workflows, product improvements, etc. Indeed, innovative companies may even put up the resources needed for employees to spinout their own ideas, like Rob Hamilton did with 'Instant Offices'. This is often called intrapreneurship or corporate entrepreneurship.

After having read and performed the exercises in this book, you should be in a good position to prepare the following:

- a business plan;
- a more (or very) concrete 'central business proposition';
- an elevator pitch.

Supported, where appropriate, by:

- posters;
- press releases;
- consultancy reports or other presentations.

However, reading on its own is not sufficient. For knowledge to be understood and used, the individual must be involved in its active construction. You must have opportunities to answer questions, to discuss (heatedly) and debate meanings, strategies and implications, thus engaging authentic problem solving in near-real situations. Thus your business partner (ideally an inventor, if you are a business person, or a business person, if you are a more technical person) and your network should become your sparring partners in order to get first-hand experience of 'decision-making' and 'action' and thus to gain a real benefit that can be used in entrepreneurship.

Choosing a topic

The subject of these debates should ideally be a business idea that you and your business partner (or partners, if you have several) have agreed upon. The objection to this is that you may not have a fully finished idea right now. Those who have the germ of an idea may find the creativity techniques described in Chapter 3 useful. Using these techniques, your idea can be modified or polished and thus can be used as a vehicle of entrepreneurship. Those who have no idea at the present time can choose between those presented shortly below – a fuller description is included in Appendix C – or your instructor may have created some other examples for you.

- Euroflorida: This involves a scalable model of advertising and selling to other people over the web. The core is communicating Italian real estate to north Europeans, but could just as easily be e.g. Trinidad real estate to US Americans and involves globalization and legal, as well as trans-lingual, aspects. Furthermore, the idea is scalable, and could include not only selling retirement-quality estates to 'grey gold', but also e.g. integrating early retirees with useful skills into their new community, keeping in contact (clubs, newsletters), providing them with local services, etc., and thus the 'product' can contain considerable 'added value'.
- Gnashes: A simple Internet supply chain, trying to extract value from a service (comparison of dentists' prices) by e.g. advertising related goods on the web site or by sponsoring. Extra spice is added because the service suppliers and service receivers may not share common interests, i.e. dentists providing high-price services may drop out of the system unless some motivation is added.
- LP2CD: This involves making a gadget to record CDA and/or MPG-compatible CDs from LPs. Thus it incorporates technical aspects and would be well suited to those with IT technical hardware/software patent-like ideas and interested in researching demographics as well as IPR issues or advertising and distribution channels.
- WFYK Holdings: A simple financial construction concerned with preserving knowledge assets. However, large degrees of complexity can be added, e.g. taxation issues and the project is aimed at those interested in venture creation, accounting and business economics.

Your instructor will also give you templates for the confidentiality agreements, etc. that you should exchange with your business partner(s).

The development of a start-up

In the course of this module you will learn many things. However, covering everything is not possible. In principle, the stages a classical start-up goes through are: Idea, Proof of Concept, Strategic Planning and Development, Venture Creation, Business Growth, Maturity and finally Exit. Your final report (the 'business plan') should cover these areas, although if you are heading for a try-it-and-see 'organic growth' strategy, then Exit may not be very relevant.

In this book we shall cover the 'Idea' area in a comprehensive fashion:

- Your motivation and creativity (Chapter 3).
- Fitting your ideas to the market (Chapters 3 and 5).
- Looking at emerging strategy (Chapters 3 and 4).
- Starting your planning and operations (Chapter 7).
- Your abilities and skills (Chapters 7 and 8).
- The resources available to you (Chapter 9).

As for the next stage, proof of concept, we will look into a more detailed marketing plan (Chapter 5) and the business plan itself (Chapter 6). However, if you have hard-to-imitate know-how and/or previous relevant experience, then you may wish to include more background. What this is depends to some extent on your specialist area.

Table 1.5 points out what factors are important for which branch of industry and these, where appropriate, could be highlighted in the final version of the business plan.

Table 1.5   A matrix plotting the importance of various background factors in the specialist areas covered in this book

	Knowledge barriers	External network	Financial and legal barriers	High-end IPR patents, etc.	Low-end IPR copyright, etc.
Technical	High	Low	Low	High	Low
Biotech	High	Low	High	High	Low
Green	Medium	Low	Medium	Low	Low
Health & Social	Medium	Medium	Medium	Low	Low
Journalism	Low	High	Low	Low	High
Arts & entertainment	Low	High	Low	Low	High

Chapter summary

Inventors and innovators can experience difficulty in bringing new products to market because they often lack the business skills needed to introduce new products to the market. Conversely, management specialists can only rarely invent breakthrough devices. Forming partnerships between business-minded people and technical-minded people can rectify this. This is the reason why group work is favoured.

A good marker for possessing a high degree of business expertise is being able to produce a good business plan. Most business plans fail to attract funding and the major reason is because they reflect the lack of managerial and business ability of the authors.

Business plans are needed not only by entrepreneurs – including entrepreneurs in the social sector – but also increasingly often by employees, especially in more innovative companies.

An extensive network – 'social capital' – can help enormously both to produce the business plan, as well as to realize its aims, including raising finance.

References

Hughes, T. P. (1971) *Elmer Sperry: Inventor and Engineer*. Baltimore, MD: Johns Hopkins University Press.

Mellor, R. B. (2003) *Innovation Management*. Copenhagen: Globe.

Mellor, R. B. (2005) *Achieving Enterprise: Teaching Entrepreneurship and Innovation in Business and Academia*. Cologne: Eul Verlag.

OECD (2003) *Entrepreneurship and Local Economic Development: Programme and Policy Recommendations*. Available at: www.oecd.org/document/27/0,3343, en_2649_33956792_2502299 _1_1_1_1, 00.html.

Wang, E. L. and Kleppe, J. A. (2001) 'Teaching invention, innovation, and entrepreneurship in engineering', *Journal of Engineering Education*, October: 565–70.

Further reading

De Bono, E. (1996) *Serious Creativity*. London: HarperCollins.

Drucker, P. F. (1999) *Management Challenges of the 21st Century*. Oxford: Butterworth-Heinemann.

Kirby, D. A. (2003) *Entrepreneurship*. Maidenhead: McGraw-Hill.

McDonald, M. (1999) *Marketing Plans*. Oxford: Butterworth-Heinemann.

Mellor, R. B. (2003) *Innovation Management*. Copenhagen: Globe.

Web links

The Financial Times. www.ft.com/businesslife/entrepreneurship

The National Council for Graduate Entrepreneurship: www.ncge.org.uk

Global Entrepreneurship Monitor: www.gemconsortium.org

What's happening in the EU: http://ec.europa.eu/enterprise/entrepreneurship/index_en.htm

Suggestion for exercises

Google the terms 'added value', 'organic growth', 'grey gold' and 'elevator pitch'.

2 The Economics of Entrepreneurship and Innovation

Robert B. Mellor

Introduction

In this chapter, entrepreneurship is introduced in its economic and academic setting; an economic theory and practice outside the perimeter of classical input-output economics. By the beginning of the twentieth century, neo-classical economics had refined the theory of the capitalist economy to one where the central concept is market equilibrium, and where market supply equals demand in a perfectly competitive market. In this scheme there is little place for innovative entrepreneurs and, interestingly, communist theoreticians also belittled entrepreneurs as merely being factors adding to the 'background noise' in the grand historical imperative. The benefits of economies of scale, i.e. the supremacy of the large corporation, remained the dominant theory (see e.g. Galbraith, 1967) for much of the twentieth century. However, several scholars, including Schumpeter, insisted that the equilibrium could be radically disturbed by the introduction of innovative products or services.

The evolution of innovation and enterprise

In the 1960s, uncertainty in the 'smokestack' industries led to widespread diversification among large companies. The strategy was that if you had a finger in many pies, then nothing much could go wrong. This went so far that many giant corporations ended up with divisions in rubber, in electronics, in chemicals, in steel, in coal, etc. However, it soon became obvious that quite different sets of skills were needed to run each division profitably. This led to a process of divestment, where the new mentality dictated 'do what you are good at'. This shift meant that each industry had quite a narrow focus. It was built on the assumption that there only are a certain number of industries and that therefore understanding and controlling these will lead to optimal performance (for review see e.g. Mellor, 2003, 2005). Many scholars believe that this break-up of markets – the so-called 'post-Fordist era' – was actually the natural result of the downswing in the last Kondratieff cycle (Kondratieff, 1935), which introduced a period of 'creative destruction' (Schumpeter, 1942). This process has cast new light on the role of the entrepreneur, the force that rearranges the market into new and more efficient forms (e.g. Drucker, 1985).

Value chains

The IT and Internet revolution of the 1990s focused attention on the possibilities of opening up new business areas, it showed that – against existing dogma – it was possible to make new business where there no previous industry or business existed: the so-called 'sunrise' industries (e.g. Microsoft). However, it also cast just as much attention on the fact that existing business process can be recombined to form new 'value chains', involving the faster delivery of products that were both better and cheaper. This is the basis of entrepreneurship. Innovation and entrepreneurship are often associated with the terms 'value chain' and 'creative destruction' (note that disruptions are for companies, and that customers should experience progress, not disruptions). The value chain represents the value of a product in an unfinished state and increasing in value as it reaches the customer. The expression 'value chain' is also used in an intra-organizational sense, referring to a bundle of factors affecting value, from when a product enters the firm, to when it leaves it. Several 'value chains' may make up a 'value system' (e.g. Porter, 1990). Disruptions or discontinuities in the value chain cause a disturbance in the manufacturing or marketing equilibrium, leaving previous processes or intermediaries stranded outside the value chain. This is referred to as disintermediation or 'creative destruction' (Figure 2.1 overleaf).

Entrepreneurship is a topic largely overlooked in classical economics and indeed Schumpeter (e.g. 1939, 1942) is hardly mentioned in the standard textbooks, probably because enterprise is not amenable to mathematical modelling, and thus is often regarded by academics as, at the most, an interesting exception to neo-classical economic theory. However, Joseph A. Schumpeter introduced entrepreneurship theory and practice and Schumpeter's book *Theorie der wirtschaftlichen Entwicklung* (1912) directed the attention of economists away from static systems and towards economic advancement. Schumpeterian rents are those arising from innovation, they are by their nature dynamic and transitory, and occur in the time between the initial innovation and the rise of imitation. Nevertheless, they may generate high returns for considerable periods of time.

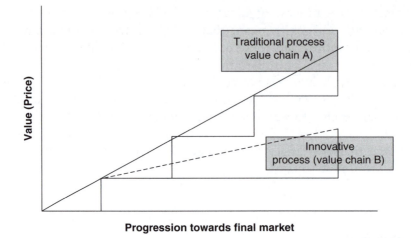

Progression towards final market

Figure 2.1   In traditional processes, value is added in a series of steps; as illustrated in value chain A a company may e.g. make pig iron from iron ore (the first triangle) then sell their product on to the next, who may make steel, then sell their product on to the next, who may make steel sheets, then sell their product on to the next, who may press sheet steel to car bodies, then sell their product on to the next, who may make automobiles. This is classically the realm of Input-Output Economics and the value increases as one progresses along the links of the value chain until a 'final price' is reached. In value chain B innovation (e.g. a new smelting or cheaper rolling process, or novel materials) is used to construct a new value. The old intermediaries are stranded ('creative destruction') while the entrepreneurial innovator can vary the final height of the stippled line to share more or less of his 'Schumpeterian rents' with the final customer

Types of economic returns

In economics, types of economic returns are called 'rents' and may sometimes be synonymous with profits. Some of the major types are listed below:

- *Porterian*. Named after Michael Porter, these are rents returned from monopolies or monopoly-like situations.
- *Ricardian*. Named after David Ricardo, these are rents returned by 'supply and demand' trading.
- *Schumpeterian*. Named after Joseph Schumpeter, these are rents returned from using innovation and improved techniques.

Schumpeter believed that the innovation practised by entrepreneurs allows economic systems to avoid repetition; especially repetition of old mistakes, and thus can progress on to more advanced states.

Economic cycles

Schumpeter (1939) also popularized the work of Nikolai Kondratieff. Kondratieff (1935) developed the theory that technology stimulates industries in waves lasting approximately 50 to 60 years (the 'Kondratieff cycle'). Each cycle consists of around 20 years to perfect and use a series of related technologies, followed by 20 years where the growth industries appear to be doing well, but what look like record profits are actually repayments on capital in industries that have ceased to grow. This perilous situation can turn to crisis, often precipitated by a relatively minor panic, and crash. There follows a long period of stagnation during which new, emergent technologies cannot generate enough jobs to make the economy grow again. Completed Kondratieff cycles include the 'steam and agriculture' cycle (1820–1870), 'rail and coal and steel and textile' cycle (1870–1930) and the 'electrical and auto and rubber and petroleum' cycle (1930–1980). Kondratieff also predicted that the content of previous cycles couldn't be repeated, thus earning himself execution at the hands of Stalin, who had just instigated an 'agricultural renewal' in the USSR.

Some believe that the present Kondratieff cycle is based on microelectronics and IT; others add space travel and biotechnology. Critics point out that IT is just an 'enabling technology', and not in itself a major new industry, and that the new cycle is best characterized by the rise of the service sector. This sector is centred on the knowledge areas, e.g. architecture, consulting, design, education, finance, publishing, research, etc., surrounded and supported in turn by communications, distribution, health, leisure, transport, etc. Conversely some writers believe that the move away from manufacturing and towards service industries is merely the result of basic needs being successively met, and that this development is simply part of the evolution of economies from agrarian to industrial to service activities. Others argue that this is not a new type of 'late capitalism' economy, but that manufacturers have simply had to contract out services in order to cut costs, increase flexibility and thus remain competitive. The most correct analysis will probably be published around 2080.

The works of Schumpeter and Kondratieff were popularized by Peter F. Drucker, in his influential text *Innovation and Entrepreneurship* (1985). Drucker contrasted the employment situation in Europe and in the USA, because at that time the USA was booming, while Europe showed the symptoms of being at the stagnation end of a Kondratieff cycle. While there could be little doubt that the western economy had entered the 'post-Fordist' stage (the end of the 'smokestack' industries and beginning of the 'sunrise' industries), Drucker argued that the difference was due to the entrepreneurial culture in the USA, which was more flexible and thus better able to take advantage of the change. The effect was that within five years most European governments (and the EU itself) had passed legislation setting up initiatives to promote innovation and entrepreneurship. Entrepreneurship has been a recognized independent discipline of management science in the USA since 1987, and since 2000 in the UK.

Focus on entrepreneurship

Classically, economics recognizes three factors in production: raw materials, labour and capital. All products, both goods and services, are a mixture of these three components. Value is created by combining these factors in such a way that human needs can be satisfied. Since the Industrial Revolution this process has taken place in organizations. Under these circumstances, entrepreneurship is sometimes referred to as the fourth factor, the way of organizing the other three factors. Thus entrepreneurship (classically) means:

1   Finding new products or combinations in order to satisfy needs (to innovate).
2   Organize resources effectively (to create organizations).
3   Create wealth by adding value (to generate employment).

The word 'entrepreneur' comes from the French *entre* meaning 'between'. The root of the verb *entreprendre* can be traced back to around 1200. By 1500, a noun form appeared and soon thereafter both the verb and noun entered the English language. Already in 1730, 'entrepreneur' was used to mean a self-employed person with a tolerance for risk. Already here there exists confusion between the concept of 'middle man' or intermediary (the 'between' part) on one hand and, on the other hand, the concept of an innovative businessperson using superior managerial ability, new and improved methods, etc., to achieve commercial growth.

As a broad generalization, classical economics focuses on the creation of demand, then satisfying this with a slightly lower supply (i.e. reaping Ricardian profits, or 'rents'). This is in contrast to an entrepreneur, who today would be described as a person who uses innovative methods to restructure a value chain so as to reap an entrepreneurial (or Schumpeterian) profit, see Figure 2.1.

However, on a note of caution, innovation and enterprise are not equal to exploitation and capitalism. Innovation is anti-totalitarian; see, for example, the persecution of innovators like Galileo through the ages. Indeed, diversity and incremental innovation have their base in solid communities and helpful personal interactions. Furthermore, the great role of social entrepreneurship cannot be overlooked and indeed the Peter F. Drucker Foundation (www.pfdf.org) has the express mission: 'To strengthen the leadership of the social sector'. Thus innovation and enterprise actively erode class distinctions and are by nature anti-war. As Mellor (2003) puts it, 'Innovation is essential to development and human progress. Innovation builds on education and intellectual freedom.' Indeed, one can pose the question, what would the status of innovation be in a society if that society were based on a static source like the Bible or the Communist Manifesto?

Enterprise can be defined broadly as activity that raises the capacity (attitude, skills and competencies) for:

- invention
- innovation
- commercialization
- technology acquisition
- founding new businesses (business creation).

Thus, an enterprising person is:

- creative
- innovative

- commercially aware
- entrepreneurial
- self-motivated.

This is thought to mean that enterprising people are continuously employable, even in times of high unemployment, because an enterprising person would rather be self-employed than unemployed. This is thought to lead to a sustainable advantage, also at the national economic level (Porter, 1990).

Some important basic definitions

Entrepreneurship is an academic discipline in management and economics. In the framework of economics, entrepreneurship is an exception to classical input–output economics. In a social and management framework the entrepreneur is often an active 'change agent'. The entrepreneur consciously uses innovation and creativity as tools to achieve enterprise.

The formalization of innovation into forms that can be patented is a relatively new phenomenon. Thus the term 'entrepreneur' is today used differently from earlier terms like 'trader' and 'merchant', even though Marco Polo and the other merchants who plied the Great Silk Road were acting in an entrepreneurial fashion, for their time. These words and their meanings have simply evolved. Unfortunately many terms are still used interchangeably. These may be enterprise, invention, innovation and creativity. They may also be owner, entrepreneur and capitalist. Among the unfortunate lack of clarity when dealing with this topic is that a plethora of names and definitions abound. For example, there are many people who own their own businesses. These represent an enormous and hugely diverse range of businesses from being a plumber to being a lawyer. Clearly all (successful) business are mercantile and thus to some extent must add value. However, not all of these businesses or owners are entrepreneurial.

Owners, capitalists and entrepreneurs

For this reason the owner of a small business (small and medium sized enterprises, SMEs) is defined as: 'an individual who establishes and manages a business for the principal purpose of furthering personal goals ... The owner perceives the business as an extension of his or her personality, intricately bound with family needs and desires' (Carland et al., 1984).

Similarly, a capitalist has the will, ability and possibly the technical knowledge to produce wealth, but this wealth is normally personal, and should preferably be produced at minimal risk. In contrast to these, Schumpeter saw the entrepreneur as a person who implements new combinations of the means of production, including:

- creating new products;
- altering the quality of an existing product;
- developing new processes of production;
- opening new markets;
- capturing new sources of supply;
- developing new forms of organization or industry.

Some of the differences between owners, entrepreneurs and capitalists are listed in Table 2.1.

Table 2.1   The mercantile uses of innovation: classification of owner, entrepreneur and capitalist according to their use of different types of innovation

	Owner	Entrepreneur	Capitalist
Invention	Clearly an inventor is an owner (they own their inventions) and may even set up a business on the basis of this. But a glance at the Yellow Pages will reveal that the overwhelmingly vast majority of small businesses are not based on technical breakthroughs	The entrepreneur may well work closely together with an inventor to bring a new product to market, however, entrepreneurs are more inventors of e.g. business processes and are rarely inventors of concrete technological products	May seek to invest in others' inventions, but rarely is an inventor
Creativity	The process of forming a business is by definition a creative act, and quite often the original business idea from an owner will involve a reasonable degree of creativity (theme restaurant, etc.)	The entrepreneur is often creative	May seek to invest in others' creativity, but is most often a fairly mechanical profit maximizer rather than being creative
Innovation	Owners may well use external innovation (the newest tools, etc.) but will rarely innovate or use innovation in systematic way to improve their product	The entrepreneur is often highly innovative or open to innovation and it is this innovation, which drives the entrepreneurial process	May seek to invest in others' innovations, but is rather a risk-minimizer than an innovator

Invention is not innovation

At this point, it is appropriate to take a closer look at innovation. Often one hears the terms discovery, invention and innovation used as synonyms, however, they are quite distinct. Discovery is a new addition to knowledge. These are (normally) in the physical, biological or social sciences. Theoretical knowledge is obtained from observations and the experimental testing of hypotheses while practical knowledge is obtained from practice, e.g. the practical knowledge acquired by a workforce in making new machinery operate well. Invention is a new device or process. Most inventions are minor improvements and do not qualify as patents. To qualify as a patent, an invention must pass a test of originality (i.e. is different from previous inventions). Only a small percentage of patents have any economic value. Those that do, tend to be those which are immediately applicable. An example of this is the Phillips screw which made two crosswise grooves in a screw head instead of only one. Robot arms can grip this screw and this opened whole assembly lines to automation. Innovation is a better way of doing things. An innovation improves performance in goal-directed behaviour (e.g. re-election politics, personal lifestyle) as measured by any applicable or relevant criterion (e.g. profit maximization).

Invention is not innovation. One simple example of this difference could be spreadsheet programs like Excel. The invention is the computer and its various parts, including the software (e.g. Excel). However, using spreadsheets to plan hourly work in an office is an innovation. Invention is promoted by discovery (especially in biology) whereas innovation is promoted by invention (especially in industrial engineering and business). Thus it also becomes obvious that innovation is time and context dependent; clearly in the eighteenth century inventing the steam engine and applying it to the cotton industry was an innovation, but today it would not be so.

Prescott and Van Slyke (1996) refer to 'Technology Cluster Innovation', pointing out the links between discovery and entrepreneurial application (Table 2.2).

Table 2.2   Illustrating that the meta-cluster 'Aerospace' can be divided according to the inventive character (e.g. based on patents) on the left, the mostly innovative in the centre, and the entrepreneurial applications on the right. Even this superficial overview shows a meta-cluster consisting of three overlapping clusters, ranging from mostly inventive, through mostly innovative, to almost purely entrepreneurial

Branch	Products	Application and exploitation
Aerodynamic and engineering research performed at e.g. universities	Producers (e.g. Boeing) of many different types of aeroplanes, helicopters, rockets, etc.	Many different airline companies with different target groups, e.g. Ryanair

Types of innovation

Radical innovation is an intellectual jump, which changes a whole area. An example of this is the steam engine of the 1770s, which revolutionized industrial production, resulting in the price of cotton cloth falling to 0.1 per cent of what it had been. Vertical innovation reflects the mobility of ideas at a systems level, i.e. between the social strata of a society. By 8000 BC, humans had begun to use agriculture, as opposed to being purely hunter-gatherers. For the first time people were able to use relatively permanent settlements, and this, together with the greater productivity of their efforts, enabled them to devote more time to non-subsistence activities. As the population grows, more hands are available for labour tasks and, as Adam Smith pointed out, division of labour involves specialization. Specialization leads to greater efficiency and technological progress. Indeed, pottery, requiring less labour to produce than stone containers, was in use around 2000 years later. However, hunting, gathering and farming were complementary activities for many generations. Perhaps migratory bands or hunting expeditions would replace shelters of skins and tree branches with dugouts or wooden shelters, followed by sod houses and eventually houses of sun-dried mud brick (see e.g. Cameron and Neal, 2003). Experience in making bricks may have been cross-fertilized with pottery skills. As potters refined their art, they invented the potter's wheel, preceding the use of the wheel for transport. Such invention and innovation progressed by almost-imperceptible increments. This type of progress is thus called 'incremental innovation'. In spreading from farmer to farmer, we can also speak of 'horizontal innovation'; innovation spread between peers, i.e. people with common problems, and without large differences in social status. However, incremental innovation can also be vertical: Henry Ford copied production processes that he had seen at Chicago meat plants and 'simply' applied them in the motor industry (Chaston, 2000), creating an assembly line out of a disassembly line with huge ramifications (Figure 2.2).

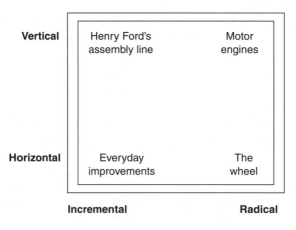

Figure 2.2   The dimensions of innovation

Some authors refer to the '*4Ps of innovation*': Product, Process, Position and Paradigm (note that this is not the same as the '4Ps of Marketing'), even constructing 3D relationships. In principle, vertical can refer to Paradigm and the assembly line example above to the process part, the motor engine to the product part. The 4P model suffers from being rather blurred, especially with respect to services.

The traditional economic perspective of the Schumpeterian hypothesis (see Schumpeter, 1942) addresses the relationship between company size and the efficiency, or productivity, of the innovative process, especially as to whether there are economies of scale in innovation. For example, Palmer (2004) reports that L'Oréal have 28,000 patents, Proctor & Gamble have over 30,000 active patents and that IBM applies for typically more that 3,000 patents each year. Clearly this is a pipeline production where a few patents more or less may not matter. So there appear to be economies of scale in invention.

To add to this concept, Utterback (1994) showed that companies often start with a 'product innovation' (possibly invention) but after introduction, the impact of the 'product innovation' grows less, and 'process innovation' becomes more important (Figure 2.3). An example is the invention of the light bulb, a great breakthrough where the first light bulbs were produced by craftsmen using a process involving many hundreds of steps. Clearly 'process innovation' was an important factor in automating this process so as to ensure that satisfactory light bulbs could be produced to an acceptable price.

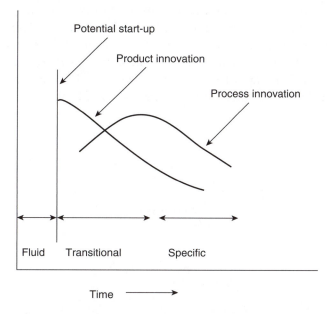

Figure 2.3   Change in type of innovation with time: Ideas in a 'fluid' phase crystallize into an innovative product. If appropriate, a company can be set up at this point. However, the effect of product innovation decreases and the focus shifts to process innovation in a transitory stage. Eventually the two curves come closer and parallel, the so-called 'specific phase'
Source: Modified from Utterback (1994)

Process innovation is often driven by diversity innovation (as opposed to e.g. invention). Diversity innovation is most often a peer-to-peer phenomenon, i.e. horizontal and incremental innovation. It can be best summed up as 'sometimes the answer just falls into your lap'. A typical environment could be simply an informal talk with someone from a different background.

Sources of innovation

In sum, it appears that significant progress stems from invention, but inventions are few and far between (look through the Yellow Pages and try to estimate how may companies are founded on the basis of patents or inventions). New business models can spring from a middle layer of innovation ('creativity innovation'), and there exists a layer below, which depends on the simple diversity existing between humans ('diversity innovation') (Figure 2.4). To put it simply, talking to somebody with a different background may deliver the problems solution right in your lap, without any significant degree of invention and/or creativity.

However, diversity innovation is hard to provoke and control. Also there cannot be economies of scale in diversity innovation. Quite the opposite; if x is the number of two-way communication connections and y the number of nodes (people involved), then $x = y * [y-1]/2$, or that for a company with 120 employees, 3,540 communication possibilities exist. Taking 5 minutes each, talking continuously and without any break, this would take 595 hours or 16 man-weeks of working time, and this is just for employees to talk to each other for 5 minutes, excluding that any employees got a chance to repeat conversations or do any work. Each further employee would take 10 man-hours to talk to existing employees for 5 minutes each. This is called the transaction costs for communication and the consequences of this are discussed further in Chapter 8 (Knowledge Management).

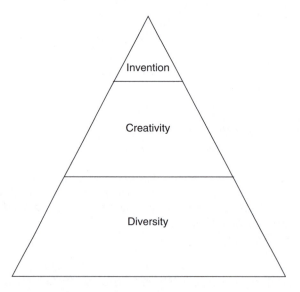

Figure 2.4   Illustrating that innovation can come from three sources, the application of invention, the application of creativity, and the application of diversity, where the 'mundane' diversity is responsible for the majority of everyday problem solving (incremental innovation) and invention is responsible for the few radical innovations

Chapter summary

The two classically known sources of innovation are the applications of either invention, or of creativity. These are important factors in large companies that have e.g. an R&D department. However, a third source exists: a kind of mutual inspiration derived from the application of diversity. This 'diversity innovation' (largely) and 'creativity innovation' (to some extent) are major contributors to 'incremental innovation', most often progressing horizontally, but sometimes vertically. Thus, this third kind of innovation is the most important when companies are small.

Entrepreneurs are different from owners and capitalists in that they seek to use innovation as a tool to achieve shorter-term advantage. Improved processes result in 'creative destruction' and new value chains being formed.

The result is better products and services – often at lower prices.

References

Cameron, R. and Neal, L. (2003) *A Concise Economic History of the World*, 4th edn. Oxford: Oxford University Press.

Carland, J. W., Hoy, F., Boulton, W. R. and Carland, J. A. C. (1984) 'Differentiating entrepreneurs from small business owners, a conceptualisation', *Academy of Management Review*, 9: 354–9.

Chaston, I. (2000) *Entrepreneurial Marketing*. London: Macmillan.

Drucker, P. F. (1985) *Innovation and Entrepreneurship*. Oxford: Butterworth-Heinemann.

Galbraith, J. K. (1967) *The New Industrial State*. Boston: Houghton Mifflin.

Kondratieff, N. D. (1935) 'The long waves in economic life', *Review of Economics and Statistics*, 17: 105–15 (originally published in 1926 in *Archiv für Sozialwissenschaft und Socialpolitik*).

Mellor, R. B. (2003) *Innovation Management*. Copenhagen: Globe.

Mellor, R. B. (2005) *Achieving Enterprise: Teaching Entrepreneurship and Innovation in Business and Academia*. FGF Entrepreneurship Research Monographs, 49, Cologne: Eul Verlag.

Palmer, A. (2004) *Introduction to Marketing Theory and Practice*, 2nd edn. Oxford: Oxford University Press.

Porter, M. E. (1990) *The Competitive Advantage of Nations*. London: Macmillan.

Prescott, M. B. and Van Slyke, C. (1996) 'The Internet as innovation', Industrial Management & Data Systems, 97/3: 119–24.

Schumpeter, J. A. ([1912]1952). *Theorie der wirtschaftlichen Entwicklung*, 5th edn. Leipzig: Duncker and Humblot.

Schumpeter, J. A. (1939) *Business Cycles: A Theoretical, Historical, and Statistical Analysis of the Capitalist Process*. New York: McGraw-Hill.

Schumpeter, J. A. (1942) *Capitalism, Socialism and Democracy*. New York: Harper.

Utterback, J. M. (1994) *Mastering the Dynamics of Innovation*. Boston: Harvard Business School Press.

Further reading

Mellor, R. B. (2005) *Sources and Spread of Innovation in Small e-commerce Companies*. Copenhagen: Globe.

Ormerod, P. (2005) *Why Most Things Fail*. London: Faber & Faber.

Von Stamm, B. (2003) *The Innovation Wave*. Chichester: John Wiley & Sons, Ltd.

Web links

EU articles on innovation: http://ec.europa.eu/enterprise/innovation/

The Ewing Marion Kauffmann Foundation: www.kauffman.org

Harvard Business School On-line: http://harvardbusinessonline.hbsp.harvard.edu

Suggestions for exercises

1   Explain what a 'value chain' is and what is meant by 'creative destruction'.
2   Look up the Kondratieff cycle. Do Kondratieff cycles drive the whole of society or do a few industries drive the economy as a whole?

3 Promoting Creativity

Robert B. Mellor

Introduction

New and entrepreneurial companies are formed on the basis of someone having an innovative, novel or creative idea. This chapter explores what creativity is, starting with some of the more accepted thoughts on the subject.

Defining creativity

'Creative' refers to novel products of value, as in 'The airplane was a creative invention.' 'Creative' also refers to the person who produces the work, as in, 'Picasso was creative.' 'Creativity,' then refers both to the capacity to produce such works, as in 'How can we foster our employees' creativity?' and to the activity of generating such products, as in 'Creativity requires hard work…'.

(Weisberg, 1993: 4)

'Creativity is defined as the tendency to generate or recognize ideas, alternatives, or possibilities that may be useful in solving problems, communicating with others, and entertaining ourselves and others. Three reasons why people are motivated to be creative are the:

1   Need for novel, varied, and complex stimulation
2   Need to communicate ideas and values
3   Need to solve problems

In order to be creative, you need to be able to view things in new ways or from a different perspective. Among other things, you need to be able to generate new possibilities or new alternatives. Tests of creativity measure not only the number of alternatives that people can generate but the uniqueness of those alternatives, the ability to generate alternatives or to see things uniquely does not occur by chance; it is linked to other, more fundamental qualities of thinking, such as flexibility, tolerance of ambiguity or unpredictability, and the enjoyment of things heretofore unknown'.

(Franken, 1994: 394–6)

The psychological origins of creativity

The origins of research into creativity can be traced back to Max Wertheimer who was one of the principal proponents of Gestalt theory (i.e. behaviourism). Gestalt theory says that the characteristics of stimuli received by the brain cause us to 'group' (structure or interpret a problem) in a certain way (Wertheimer, 1923). The primary factors – called 'the laws of organization' – determining grouping are:

1   *Proximity* – elements tend to be grouped together according to their nearness.
2   *Similarity* – items similar in some respect tend to be grouped together.
3   *Closure* – items are grouped together if they tend to complete some entity.
4   *Simplicity* – items will be organized into simple figures according to symmetry, regularity, and smoothness.

Wertheimer was especially concerned with problem-solving and, in 1959, he provided a Gestalt interpretation of problem-solving episodes of famous scientists (e.g., Galileo, Einstein) as well as children presented with mathematical problems where he explained that the essence of successful problem-solving behaviour is being able to see the overall structure of the problem:

'A certain region in the field becomes crucial, is focused; but it does not become isolated. A new, deeper structural view of the situation develops, involving changes in functional meaning, the grouping, etc. of the items. Directed by what is required by the structure of a situation for a crucial region, one is led to a reasonable prediction, which like the other parts of the structure, calls for verification, direct or indirect. Two directions are involved: getting a whole consistent picture, and seeing what the structure of the whole requires for the parts'.

(Wertheimer, 1959: 212)

Gestalt principles: parallelograms

The classic example of Gestalt principles provided by Wertheimer is children finding the area of parallelograms. As long as the parallelograms are regular figures, a standard procedure can be applied (making lines perpendicular from the corners of the base). However, if a parallelogram is provided which has a novel shape or orientation, then the standard procedure no longer works and the children are forced to solve the problem by a different method, which they can only do if they understanding the true structure of a parallelogram i.e., the figure can be bisected anywhere if the ends are joined.

Source: Adapted from Wertheimer (1959)

Thus, the principles of creative problem solving were postulated to be:

1   The learner should be encouraged to discover the underlying nature of a topic or problem (i.e., the relationship among the various elements).
2   Gaps, incongruities, or disturbances are an important stimulus for learning.
3   Instruction should be based upon the laws of organization: proximity, similarity, closure and simplicity.

The relationship between creativity and other human characteristics like intelligence has been a central concern of psychology for some time (see e.g. Guilford, 1950) and much effort has been devoted towards the semi-quantitative measurement of creative potential (e.g. Guilford, 1986; Torrance, 1979). Taylor and Williams (1966) provide a survey of the relationship between creativity and instruction and there have also been many attempts to increase creative behaviours (e.g., Osborn, 1953; Parnes, 1967). Popular questions include: is there one kind of creativity, or is creativity specific to a medium? For example, are good painters also good musicians? What are the work habits of extremely creative people and can these be emulated so others can be more creative?

Arising from this intensive research, there is general agreement that the creative process involves the application of past experiences or ideas in novel ways. One example is the Creative Problem Solving (CPS) Model, based upon the work of Osborn and of Parnes (Osborn, 1953; Parnes, 1967; Van Gundy, 1987) and which refines the 'laws of organization' as suggested by Werthheimer to five major steps:

1   Fact-finding
2   Problem-finding
3   Idea-finding
4   Solution-finding
5   Acceptance-finding.

However, the situation is complicated by the general acknowledgement that social processes play a major role in the recognition of creativity (e.g. Amabile, 1983) and that certain cognitive skills that may either be instilled at an early age, or learned later, seem to underlie creative behaviour. These include fluency, flexibility, visualization, imagination, expressiveness, and openness.

Edward De Bono, like the behaviourists, argues that the characteristics of stimuli received by the brain cause us to 'group' (structure or interpret a problem) in a certain way and that this process involves the application of past experiences, i.e. that when looking at a phenomenon, the subconscious locates how this was handled in the past, and – assuming that the past experience was not so disastrous as to have impinged upon the consciousness – will try to process the new input in the same way. This appears a reasonable argument since the converse, constantly trying to find new processes for routine problems, would quickly lead to a nervous breakdown or similar overload situation.

Tools for analysing problems

Several methods exist for structured problem identification and analysis. The most common are the Pareto analysis (sometimes known as the 80/20 rule), cause-and-effect (also known as fish-bone or Ishikawa) diagrams and cognitive mind-mapping. Pareto analyses plot the cause of a problem against frequency, e.g. companies often have to deal with dissatisfied customers; there may be five causes of dissatisfaction but analysis typically shows that the frequency of complaints is not equally spread and that only one (i.e. 20 per cent of the potential causes) accounts for 80 per cent of complaints. This has led to companies recording and storing customer complaints for data-mining exercises. Cause-and-effect diagrams consist of a few simple steps and are a way of refining the search further – to arrive at a tighter shortlist of potential problems and solutions.

· Mind-mapping (more for individuals) and the related technique of cognitive mind-mapping (more often for groups of stakeholders) may be useful techniques to uncover hidden assumptions. This area borders on the discipline of decision-making and many software tools ('Decision Support Systems') have been developed to aid these processes.

Tools for promoting creativity

De Bono's best-known creative method – lateral thinking – uses Wertheimer's second law of organization ('gaps, incongruities, or disturbances are an important stimulus') to get a different perspective on a problem by breaking the elements up and recombining them in a different way (sometimes even randomly!). The actual process of lateral thinking then uses feedback iteration, or a 'harvesting' step, to take the idea through the stages 2–5 as proposed by the Creative Problem Solving Model (although note that De Bono does not acknowledge any theoretical antecedents for his lateral thinking technique).

De Bono goes on to identify four critical factors associated with lateral thinking:

1 The recognition of the dominant ideas that polarize the perception of a problem.
2 Searching for different perspectives – different ways of looking at the case ('thinking out of the box').
3 The relaxation of the 'normal' rigid control of thinking, i.e. relaxing the process pathways used for the routine handling of input.
4 Encouraging the use of chance to encourage other ideas (chance, because lateral thinking involves ideas of such low probability that they are unlikely to occur in the normal course of events).

An example of lateral thinking

A merchant (Mr A) who owes money to a moneylender (Mr B) is unfortunately insolvent and thus agrees to settle the debt based upon the random choice of two stones – one black, one white – picked by Mr A's daughter from a money bag. If Mr A's daughter chooses the white stone, the debt is cancelled; if she picks the black stone, then the moneylender gets the merchant's daughter.

However, the moneylender tries to 'fix' the outcome by putting two black stones in the bag. The daughter sees this and when she picks a stone out of the bag, she immediately drops it onto the path full of other stones. She then uses logic to point out that the stone she picked must have been the opposite colour of the one remaining in the bag. That is, the one she did not pick is now revealed as black; ergo she must have picked the white one. Unwilling to be unveiled as dishonest, Mr B the moneylender must agree and cancel the debt.

The daughter has solved a seemingly-intractable problem through the use of lateral thinking.

(*Source*: Taken from De Bono 1967) Reprinted with permission from the author.

Lateral thinking applies to all human problem-solving and involves (typically) a deliberate provocation – like a negation or wild over-exaggeration – to 'heave' the input out of the normal thinking or thought-processing pathways. For example, the statement 'cars cost money' could be negated with 'cars are free' or 'the customer comes to the pizzeria' is negated by 'the pizzeria comes to the customer'. However, ideas at this mid-point are typically of little use. From there a second round of creativity is applied to 'heave' the input into a new and innovative channel ('cars are free, if you only buy your petrol from me' or the concept of a mobile pizzeria on a truck). One often-cited example of creativity is George de Mestral's observation of how cockleburs attach to clothing, which led him to invent the hook-and-loop fastener known as Velcro®. He transformed a common nuisance into a useful product. Another is Dell computers who have created the software and service for networked printers to automatically order new ink cartridges on-line when they are running low. When one looks back in time to analyse how a creative act was made, one often finds that creators made a novel interpretation of a well-known fact or occurrence, often involving converting a disadvantage into an advantage.

Another commonly cited example of creativity is Art Fry's development of Post-It® removable notes at 3M Corporation in 1974. Conventional wisdom states that all adhesives must be strong, but another 3M scientist had developed a polymer adhesive which takes years, if ever, to set. Fry wanted a better bookmark for his church hymn book, so he used a bookmark smeared with the weak adhesive. By ignoring the conventional wisdom, Fry developed a highly successful office product by redefining the problem (i.e. to finding a use for a weak adhesive). However, not only did he need to develop the idea, but he also had to sell the idea to his management and marketing departments (points 4 and 5 of the Creative Problem Solving Model).

De Bono has discussed the application of lateral thinking both to management development and in some of his recent work, on schools (e.g., De Bono, 1991). Visit the De Bono website for up-to-date information on lateral thinking and related techniques like brainstorming and 'six thinking hats'.

From the above, it would appear that to enhance innovation anyone could simply apply creativity exercises. This idea has been important in spreading the works of Edward De Bono. For example De Bono's book *Serious Creativity* (1996) starts with the words 'If I were to sit down and say to myself I need a new idea here … I could quietly and systematically apply a deliberate technique of lateral thinking … and in 10 to 20 seconds I should have some new ideas.' All humans think and are to some degree able to solve problems. Why then are not all humans creative (by self-definition)? To postulate that they have not read De Bono's books is not a satisfying answer. The worst complication is that creativity is neither precisely defined nor measurable. Parkhurst (1999: 18) produced probably the best definition of creativity by stating that creativity is 'the ability or quality displayed when solving hitherto unsolved problems, when developing original and novel solutions to problems others have solved differently, or when developing original and novel (at least to the originator) products'. Unfortunately this definition is still imprecise because, for example, it lacks quantitative measures of how original a product (be it a poem, a painting or a patent) must be to qualify as the result of a creative process and furthermore it opens a significant overlap between creativity and 'mere' problem solving.

Creativity focused on the marketplace

It is not the aim of this book to explain phenomena such as Shakespeare, Beethoven, Michelangelo or Aristotle; creative innovation is used here in the sense of being the tool used to achieve differential advantage at the marketplace. To expand on this point, the target that being creative should achieve, in a business sense, is for the venture to be more competitive. Competition is defined as:

> Test of skill or ability; a contest, rivalry between two or more businesses striving for the same customer or market, the simultaneous demand by two or more organisms for limited environmental resources.
>
> (*Oxford English Dictionary*)

This obviously begs the question, why use creativity with the target of creating a new competition, i.e. to be one of many in an existing market? Would it not be better to create a new market, because where the market is hitherto unexplored and unexploited, then there is no other competition? Examples of such inspired creativity have been Hotmail, the bag-less vacuum cleaner and the clockwork radio. The sequence of events is summarized in Figure 3.1.

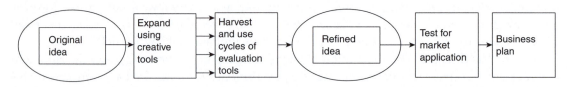

Figure 3.1   Illustrating that the original germ of an idea can be expanded upon with creative tools (provocation, negation, etc.) and after harvesting and reiteration evaluated against semi-structured tools (SEARCH, ALUO, etc.), after which they can be analysed for market applicability with tools like SWOT and SLEPT (see Chapter 4, and incorporated into the business plan (Chapter 6)

Evaluating ideas

With respect to markets, several semi-structured evaluation tools (see Figure 3.1) have been developed to help evaluate raw innovative ideas as bases for venture creation. Examples of these are SEARCH, ALUO and 'Give Me 5' (Gundry and LaMantia, 2001). SEARCH is an acronym for:

S: Scan the environment.
E: Expand on the idea.
A: Adapt the idea to the circumstances.
R: Revise components.
C: Create the business opportunity.
H: Harvest the revised idea and develop the vision.

Similarly, ALUO enables the potential entrepreneur to adopt a perspective that is slightly different:

A: Advantages: what are the advantages the proposed product or service offers to the customer, how does it build or extend something which may already be available?
L: Limitations: what elements of the idea may not work as predicted, which flaws may exist, how far does it go?
U: Uniqueness: what is unique about this idea, can it be substituted by something else already on the marketplace, can it easily be imitated?
O: Opportunity: what opportunities emerge from the unique features you have identified?

The 'Give Me 5' method is a slightly more quantitative approach, involving giving five responses to five questions:

1   Name five things you have observed as a consumer or employee in that branch of industry.
2   Name five things this branch of industry should be anticipating right now.
3   Name five things that others would tell you about this branch of industry.
4   Name five actions or types of business behaviour that participants in this industry should be considering.
5   Name five ideas that companies in this branch have not yet thought about or mastered.

Obviously answers to these five questions both test the individuals' knowledge of that industry, as well as can be compared to the original idea. By using all these techniques, the idea harvested from lateral thinking exercises can be critically illuminated from several different angles and perspectives. Further details about these and similar methods can be found in Gundry and LaMantia (2001). Furthermore, Appendix A contains a tool widely used by professionals for evaluating more strictly technical ideas.

While the above analyses normally do not comprise part of the business plan, more formal extensions of these analyses are used for testing market application (Porter's, SWOT, SLEPT, etc., as detailed in the next chapter) and these often do appear in the business plan.

Chapter summary

Both theoretical and practical studies point to the fact that all humans – to a greater or lesser degree – are creative. The correct work environment for promoting creativity is discussed in Chapters 7 and 8.

Simple techniques exist – and can be learned – which, by introducing paradoxes or discontinuities, can magnify and focus the individual's creativity.

The object of the exercise (in a business sense) is to increase competitiveness by creating innovative new products. However, a flash of insight can – even better – create new and hitherto uninhabited (i.e. competition-less) markets.

Ideas can be evaluated by a variety of methods, e.g. SEARCH and ALUO. For technological innovations, the 10-dimension scale – reproduced in Appendix A – is another example of such methods.

References

Amabile, T. (1983) *The Social Psychology of Creativity*. Berlin: Springer-Verlag.

De Bono, E. (1967) *New Think: The Use of Lateral Thinking in the Generation of New Ideas*. New York: Basic Books.

De Bono, E. (1991) *Teaching Thinking*. Harmondsworth: Penguin Books.

Ellis, W. D. (1938) *A Source Book of Gestalt Psychology*. New York: Harcourt, Brace and World.

Franken, R. E. (1994) *Human Motivation*, Third edition. New York: Wadsworth.

Guilford, J. P. (1950) 'Creativity', *American Psychologist*, 5: 444–54.

Guilford, J. P. (1986) *Creative Talents: Their Nature, Uses and Development*. New York: Bearly Ltd.

Gundry, L. K. and LaMantia, M. (2001) *Breakthrough Teams for Breakneck Times*. New York: Dearborn Books.

Osborn, A. F. (1953) *Applied Imagination*. New York: Scribners.

Parkhurst, H. B. (1999) 'Confusion, lack of consensus and the definition of creativity as a construct', *Journal of Creative Behaviour*, 33: 1–21.

Parnes, S. J. (1967) *Creative Behaviour Guidebook*. New York: Scribners.

Taylor, C. and Williams, F. (1966) *Instructional Media and Creativity*. Chichester: Wiley.

Torrance, E. (1979) *The Search for Satori and Creativity*. New York: Bearly Ltd.

Van Gundy, A. B. (1987) *Creative Problem Solving*. New York: Quorum.

Weisberg, R. W. (1993) *Creativity: Beyond the Myth of Genius*. New York: W.H. Freeman and Co Ltd.

Wertheimer, M. (1923) 'Laws of organization in perceptual forms'. First published as 'Untersuchungen zur Lehre von der Gestalt II', in *Psychologische Forschung*, 4: 301–50. Translation in Ellis, W. (1938) available at: http://psy.ed.asu.edu/~classics/Wertheimer/Forms/forms.htm.

Wertheimer, M. (1959) *Productive Thinking*. New York: Harper and Row.

Further reading

De Bono, E. (1996) *Serious Creativity*. London: Harper-Collins.
Fox, M. J. and Fox, R. L. (2000) *Exploring the Nature of Creativity*. Kendall/Hunt Pub. Co.
Gundry, L.K. and LaMantia, M. (2001) *Breakthrough Teams for Breakneck Times*. New York: Dearborn Books.

Web links

www.brainstorming.co.uk

www.creativitypool.com

www.edwarddebono.com

www.spaceforideas.uk.com

www.totallyabsurd.com/archive.htm

www.whynot.net

Suggestions for exercises

1   Go to www.halfbakery.com and find a topic that you can possibly combine with your ideas.
2   Google 'Pareto analysis' and comment on it.
3   Briefly compare de Bono's ideas with those of the behaviourists.

Acknowledgements

Weisberg quote (page 31) from *Creativity: Beyond the Myth of* Genius; R.W. Weisberg; Copyright 1993; Reprinted with permission of John Wiley & Sons, Inc.

Franken quote (page 31) from *Human Motivation* 3rd edition by FRANKEN, 1994. Reprinted with permission of Wadsworth, a division of Thomson Learning: www.thomsonrights.com. Fax 800 730-2215.

Gestalt principles (page 32) from *Productive Thinking*, M. Wertheimer (1959) © HarperCollins Publishers. Reprinted with permission.

Part II

Practice

4 Gaining Strategic Advantage

Robert B. Mellor

Introduction

Understanding what entrepreneurship (Chapter 2) and creativity (Chapter 3) are is not sufficient to succeed in business; a strategy is also needed that explains how a novel product or service can discover a market or market niche.

Positioning in the marketplace

Almost 80 years ago Harold Hotelling (Hotelling, 1929) developed a simple analogy model explaining how and why market entrants must position themselves in order to ensure some degree of success. Hotelling's model imagines a sunny beach 100 metres long and of totally uniform composition with respect to quality of sand, bathing, exposure to sun, etc., so that all of the people on the beach are distributed randomly yet uniformly along it. An ice-cream vendor arrives at this beach, which is analogous to a pristine market (assuming that all the people on the beach are potential consumers, in this case, consumers of ice-cream). It doesn't really matter where the vendor positions himself along the beach, from position 0 to position 100 since, as the only vendor (i.e. he has a monopoly), everyone wanting an ice-cream must come to him, but it would be most logical to go to the centre, position 50. Now assuming that a second vendor arrives, where should he position himself? Hotelling assumes that there is no difference between the goods on offer and that all consumers will only go to the nearest vendor. Thus, it may be that vendor 2 positions himself at point 75. In this case, vendor 1 will enjoy custom from people from positions 0–62.5, but people at position 62.5 and higher will go to vendor 2, because vendor 2 is closer to them (i.e. vendor 2 has taken 37.5 per cent of the market). Clearly, it is in the best interest of vendor 1 to rush up the beach to position 74, so vendor 1 will attract all custom up to

74.5, and vendor 2 only between 74.5 and 100 (i.e. vendor 2 is only able to take 25.5 per cent of the market). The next day is also sunny and vendor 2 arrives to find vendor 1 setting up his stall. Learning from his mistake (positioning himself at 75) the previous day he rushes out to the centre and sets up his stall at point 51 – forcing vendor 1 to move slightly to point 49 – so both vendors now control 50 per cent of the market (i.e. vendor 1 from 0–50 and vendor 2 from 50–100) each. This simple analogy tells us that, given few players in a market, they will always tend to cluster.

Now a third vendor arrives; if he does not know the market, then he may head for the logical position, point 50. In this case his arrival will affect the market position of the two incumbents only very slightly: vendor 1 will control 0–49.5, vendor 2 will control 50.5–100 and vendor 3 only 49.5–50.5, a mere 1 per cent of the market! Obviously this is not an attractive situation for vendor 3 and clearly, if vendor 3 had done his market research better, he would have chosen either point 48 or point 52 – turning the tables on one of the two existing market players and snatching their markets.

An alternative strategy could have been for vendor 3 to go for a niche market – say, position 20 – which would have immediately netted him a 'safe' 35 per cent of the market, but even after establishing himself at point 20, it would be attractive economically to move up the beach to 48. It may of course be that vendor 3 thinks he can do that since he may have time because a fourth vendor, seeing the situation, would logically move into a 52+ situation and not immediately affect vendor 3. Unfortunately the arrival of vendor 4 at position 52 could have a knock-on effect, provoking a response from vendor 2 (presently at 51 and now out-manoeuvred) who could decide whether to re-position himself either at 53+ or at under 48, the latter posing a threat to vendor 3. So how do new entrants gain a good initial position and then keep it after the existing players respond?

What Hotelling is saying is that gaining market intelligence about where the present market players are and how they can (or intend to) move, is of paramount importance so that new entrants can position themselves correctly for maximum impact (or at least avoid instant bankruptcy, taking into account that the logical maximum point for new entrants to enter may be exactly the worst point to be).

Making the connection

At this stage the creative idea emerging from the techniques illustrated in Chapter 3 can be analysed by the tools listed in this chapter and the 10-dimension rating scale included in Appendix A. This enables a 'fine polishing'. If the analyses show that there could be problems, then adjustments can be made at this stage. When completed, and when the analyses look promising, then the completed analyses can be 'imported' into the business plan (Chapter 6).

Tools for analysing the market

Several tools exist which can be used to analyse the intended market and determine what the new entrant needs in order to succeed. These include:

1   *Porter's Five Forces*: The classic analysis of how attractive a potential market is.
2   *SLEPT*: A kind of extended Porter's, dealing with the Social, Legal, Economic, Political, and Technological influences from the environment acting on a business.
3   *Strategic Group Mapping*: An extension of Porter's, used to identify Critical Success Factors.
4   *SWOT*: Estimating the proposed company's (or product's) ability (Strengths, Weaknesses, Opportunities and Threats) to conquer the intended market.
5   *Boston Matrix*: Established firms can analyse their current portfolio of products, divide them into 'Stars', 'Cash Cows', 'Problem Children' and 'Dogs' and thus decide which products should receive more or less investment.

Here we will be running through numbers 1, 3, 4 and 5; the other techniques and several more like them can easily be found on several business resource websites (e.g. www.tutor2u.net/revision_notes_strategy.asp).

In the post-war period there was a boom, creating a seller's market, but these markets gradually became saturated, consumers better informed and more demanding. In these times differentiation and innovation are critical, increasing specialization has led to hyper-fragmented markets and niches – it is therefore essential that the entrepreneur can assess if a given niche actually exists and, if so, how attractive it is. Porter's Five Forces Framework (Porter, 1980) is the name given to the tool that is used to analyse the attractiveness of a market (Figure 4.1 overleaf). The ability of a company to create and sustain profits depends upon how many other organizations are operating in the same market niche, how easy it is for competitors to invade that territory, and on the bargaining power of suppliers and buyers.

The classic 'Porter's Five Forces' consider the case of rivalry among sellers already in the marketplace and the model concludes that this depends on factors such as the number of companies already in the industry, their relative size and how hard they fight each other for market share. If only one organization exists, then a monopoly is said to exist. If two or more firms inhabit that market, then rivalry exists which will constrain the ability of firms to set prices and generate profits. Higher degrees of rivalry (more vendors) can make markets unattractive. Thus, it may be unattractive to launch new ventures in the telecom area, where companies like Vodafone, Carphone Warehouse, O2, Orange, T-Mobile, etc. are already locked in cut-throat competition, unless one specifically is aiming at being bought out in the short term by an established player.

In Figure 4.1, potential competition refers to that inhabiting a market successfully may mean the generation of above-normal profits which in turn is likely to attract potential competitors and, if new entry takes place, then prices and profits are likely to fall. However, if there are 'barriers to entry' (for example, patent rights), then profits will be easier to sustain.

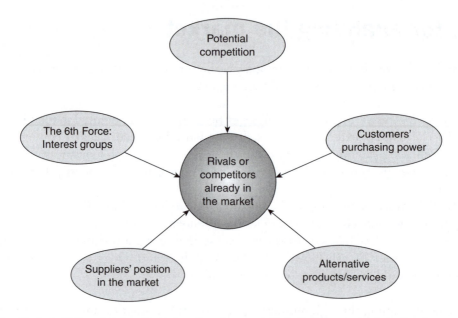

Figure 4.1   Porter's 'Determinants of industry attractiveness'. Note that the centre is both a force as well as being acted upon

Alternative products or services refer to the ability of substitutes to reduce profits. For example, manufacturers of glass bottles would make much more money if there were no plastic bottles or cans.

Customers' purchasing power refers to the ability of buyers to negotiate about purchase price. Clearly if buyers are powerful, then they may squeeze prices and profits. Similarly suppliers' position in the market refers to the ability of suppliers to negotiate prices, or even, if there are very few suppliers, terminate supply.

Industries are likely to be unattractive if they consist of many rivals, easy entry, several close substitutes, powerful buyers and suppliers. Thus, by using Porter's analysis, the entrepreneur can assess the market and avoid unattractive markets.

Porter's original Five Forces model has been modified by adding a sixth force: interest groups (e.g. Greenpeace, etc.), which can exert a powerful influence if a product is offensive to environmental, women's, etc. pressure groups.

The sixth force

Porter originally describes five forces, but a sixth has been added subsequently; the sixth force can be tortuous and a significant barrier to how attractive a market is. For example, in 2007, General Electric bowed to environmentalist pressure (a 'sixth force') and proposed introducing green policies using the slogan 'ecomagination'.

This provoked a response from the Free Enterprise Action Fund (another 'sixth force') who objected because green overheads would lead to higher energy prices that would hurt GE profits and disadvantage shareholders. Although GE hurriedly dropped 'ecomagination', the furore led the regulatory body concerned – the Securities and Exchange Commission (yet another 'sixth force') to be called in.

Although the sixth force has assumed enormous proportions, it can act – paradoxically – not only as an efficient barrier (see above), but also as a rich and constant source to be tapped; the car industry, for example, should beware, e.g. environmental groups as a sixth force, but entrepreneurs in e.g. journalism and media (see Chapter 14) can reverse this and become environmental media, producing 'green' messages. The same goes for e.g. gun owners as a force (e.g. the National Rifle Association in the USA), pet owners (and the RSPCA) and presumably by extension toy owners, etc. Pressure grouping and lobbying truly present a case where the tail wags the dog.

Successfully inhabiting the market

After completing a preliminary Porter-type analysis, more details can be obtained using strategic group mapping (SGM) – a five-step process. A valuable addition to the analysis process is that this also enables the entrepreneur to see what the critical success factors (CSFs) are. At this stage data collection is important and one should collect competitor business information from reputable sources, e.g. Yahoo! and Companies House. You can also conduct potential customer surveys on-line, do they visit the competition? Some also subscribe to competitors' mailing lists to find out what they think is new.

SGM

Step 1: Identify competitive characteristics that differentiate companies in an industry. This may also result in good clues to what the CSFs are. These are found by trial and error, simply gathering data and plotting factors against each other until significant matches are found. However, there are some 'favourites', including:

- price/quality
- geographic coverage
- degree of vertical integration
- product line breadth

(Continued)

- use of distribution channels
- degree of service.

Step 2: After you have found differentiating characteristics, use these as axes on a graph to plot where competitors are.

Step 3: Assign companies that fall into about the same strategy space to the same strategic group.

Step 4: Draw circles around each strategic group, if possible making the circles proportional to the size of the group's market share. Then it is possible to rate companies/rivals on a scale of 1 to 10.

Step 5: Weight any CSFs found by importance, multiply rate (above) by weight/weighted rate and sum the weighted rates. Repeat the exercise for your own company and evaluate where you stand competitively.

Having assessed the attractiveness of the proposed market and identified competitors and CSFs, the next task is to see if the proposed company can actually inhabit that market. To put it a different way, has the entrepreneur the appropriate competencies to pursue the opportunity? An old management adage says, 'Opportunism without competence is a path to fairyland.' To check that competencies and needs are aligned, the entrepreneur needs to perform what is called a *company situation analysis*. The key issues include: cost competitiveness, competitive position, what problems need to be addressed, market share and competitive advantage. These can be addressed by incorporating them into a *SWOT analysis* (see Glossary). SWOT stands for Strengths, Weaknesses, Opportunities and Threats. In its most simple form, a SWOT analysis consists of a matrix (Figure 4.2).

A SWOT analysis enables 'killer assumptions' to be identified in time. These could be manifested under Weaknesses or Threats. Furthermore, it should be useful in locating your company's core competencies (something a company does better than the competition). Examples could be:

- know-how
- quality control
- service capability
- product design
- marketing skills
- quality of management.

One of the subjects covered should be cost position relative to competitors, but raw materials supply, logistics, distribution, etc. may all enter the equation. Correcting a cost disadvantage may entail: tightening the budget, increasing productivity (equipment and employees),

	Positive	Negative
Internal	Strengths	Weaknesses
External	Opportunities	Threats

Figure 4.2   The SWOT matrix

eliminating cost-producing activities, relocating high cost activities geographically, redesigning the product, etc.

The beauty of SWOT analyses is that they can be applied almost everywhere. The business idea/proposed product, the individuals or team involved, individual products can be subjected to SWOT, as can competing firms, potential retailers, etc. In any situation it can be used to determine if strengths heavily outweigh weaknesses, where the competitive advantage is, and are there any weak spots in the present strategy. A particular use of SWOT in intending start-ups is in making it plain to potential investors where weaknesses lie and thus helping to justify the projected budget/expenditure. More complicated versions of SWOT are also often used and the interested reader is advised to look up e.g. HOTPLOT, SWOTPLOT, TROTPLOT and an action audit (e.g. ACE-Chase).

Formulating a mission statement

As the way forward becomes clearer – thanks to undertaking the above analyses – the path to be taken can be verbalized in a *mission statement*. This is partly a concise statement which defines the tasks of strategic management and the overall goal of the company and includes defining the main business and business mission. Hopefully the mission statement will inject the company with a sense of purpose, provide long-term direction and give the organization an identity. A good mission statement implies where the organization is, where it wants to go and in what market. An example of a mission statement is:

> Our mission is to expand our worldwide leadership in the spice, seasoning, and flavouring markets. (McCormick and Company)

Backing up the mission statement should be a programme that establishes targets and objectives because without measurable objectives, a mission statement is basically just hot air. Objectives should be measurable, difficult, but doable, and should have a time frame. Examples could be:

- Achieve a X per cent return on equity within the first three years.
- Achieve a net sales growth rate of Z per cent per year.

- Pay out between X per cent and Y per cent of net income in dividends per year.
- Within X years, achieve the largest market share in the industry.

An expanded version of this – developing a strategy and ways to implement the strategy, how and when to evaluate, review, and make adjustments, etc. – can be incorporated into the business plan. Indeed, all of the above analyses will finally find their way into the appropriate part of the business plan (see Chapter 6).

Analysing your products

The Boston Matrix is a mapping tool for use on existing products (Figure 4.3). Using historical data (market growth) and building on estimates coming from SGM-like analyses, it plots the relative market share of a product against market growth. In many ways the Boston Matrix resembles a product life cycle (PLC) because a new product introduced onto the market will have a low market share, but (hopefully) large growth.

Seen from the point of view of the Boston Matrix, the strategic stages in the PLC through which a product may progress or develop are:

1   Problem Child: Opportunistic development.
2   Rising Star: Invest.
3   Cash Cow: Maintain.
4   Dog: Kill or divest.

When a new product (occupying the Problem Child box) is launched, opportunistic development is normally the only strategy that can be applied. As its relative market share increases, the product starts to move anti-clockwise through the matrix, to occupy a position of high relative market share and high market growth. At this position (Rising Star), an investment strategy should be followed. As market growth flattens out, the product gains Cash Cow status, signifying a maintaining strategy to be able to milk the market returns. Eventually, however, the product will be superseded and the product, while maintaining low

Relative market share			
		High	Low
Market growth	High	Rising Star	Problem Child
	Low	Cash Cow	Dog

Figure 4.3   The Boston Matrix, plotting market share against rate of change of market share (i.e. growth)

market growth, will also slide down in relative market share. This is the Dog position where the product should either be withdrawn, or the company may like to divest itself of that interest.

Chapter summary

Creative ideas – generated using the techniques illustrated in Chapter 3 – have to be harvested and evaluated. One possibility is the 10-dimension rating scale in Appendix A.

However, to establish a business, other strategic considerations – like positioning in the market – have to be taken into consideration. A Porter's analysis enables the potential market entrant to assess if the market is attractive or not. This can be extended by SLEPT (if appropriate) and Strategic Group Mapping.

The ability of the product or company to actually conquer the proposed market can be analysed by various techniques, the most common being the SWOT analysis. After completing this, new companies may be able to formulate a mission statement.

Companies may also analyse and re-align existing products using e.g. the Boston Matrix. For companies with existing products, the Boston Matrix may give clues as to where products are on their PLC.

Subjecting the business proposition to analysis by these tools enables a 'fine polishing' step to take place because if the analyses show that there could be problems, then adjustments can be made at this stage.

When completed, the analyses are 'imported' into the business plan (Chapter 6).

References

Hotelling, H. (1929) 'Stability in competition', *The Economic Journal*, 39: 41–57.
Porter, M. E. (1980) *Competitive Strategy: Techniques for Analyzing Industries and Competitors*. New York: Free Press.

Further reading

Chaston, I. (2000) *Entrepreneurial Marketing*. Basingstoke: Macmillan Press.
Kirby, D. A. (2003) *Entrepreneurship*. Maidenhead: McGraw-Hill.

Web links

For SWOT etc.

www.businessballs.com/swotanalysisfreetemplate.htm

www.marketingteacher.com/Lessons/lesson_swot.htm

www.mindtools.com/swot.html

www.tutor2u.net/revision_notes_strategy.asp

For patenting/intellectual property rights, etc.

If you are interested in free advice you can get up to 45 minutes with an IP lawyer to discuss any IP issues. E-mail your advice enquiry, with as much information as possible, to info@own-it.org. They will either respond to it in-house, or recommend you to attend a free one-to-one advice session with a specialist lawyer. The Own-It Free IP Legal Advice Clinics take place at the Own-It offices at the University of the Arts London (LCC).

You can also search the Online European Patent Register at: http://www.eponline.org/portal/public/registerplus

Suggestions for exercises

1   Make a SWOT of yourself and another one of your proposed company.
2   Start identifying players in your intended market. Think about how you can collect market data. Use this to start preparing a SGM analysis.

5 The Marketing Plan

Robert B. Mellor

Introduction

In Chapter 3, your ideas for a product or service were created and/reviewed using creative techniques. In Chapter 4, these ideas, in a more concrete form, were subjected to an analysis designed to enquire as to whether the proposed market could successfully be entered both by looking at the internal organization and by analysing existing competitors. However, up to now, 'the market' has not been explained and the other inhabitants of the market – consumers/customers – have, as yet, hardly been mentioned. The marketing plan – introduced in this chapter – details how the product or service is to be brought to which customers, when and how. It is an important part of the business plan and also forms a basis for a large part of the budget.

Customer segmentation

Ideally the marketing plan will help to define primary target customer groups, secondary, tertiary, etc. and account for how the product or service, after penetrating one group, will be poised to conquer subsequent groups. For products or services which are close to market (i.e. Time To Market – TTM – is short), then the marketing plan should be very detailed, e.g. how many of what size of what adverts are to be placed in which newspapers. Conversely, new technological or pharmaceutical products may still need several years' development and clearly marketing plans for such products cannot be developed at the same level of detail. However, as a rough guide, the targets should include a three-year strategic plan and a more detailed one-year operational plan (i.e. addressing tactical objectives) in one consolidated marketing plan. In short, the aim of the marketing plan is to link the resources of the company to the requirements of the customer. Thus marketing can be defined as the identification and profitable satisfaction of a customer's need.

Examples of customer segmentation

As Evans et al. (2006) point out, as western society progresses from modernism to post-modernism, some markers of changes in social behaviour include:

- growing cultural unwillingness to commit to any single grand vision or plan;
- a greater importance given to form and style – as opposed to content – in determining meaning and lifestyle;
- an increased awareness that chaos and disequilibria – as opposed to order – are the common states of existence;
- acknowledgement that value is created not by production, but by consumption.

This underlines the point made by Kotler and De Bes (2003) that markets are becoming hyper-fragmented, meaning that economic power is being concentrated in the hands of the distributors who in turn are required to continually and rapidly re-bundle offerings according to transitory fluctuations in demand.

This transition into post-modernity is obviously a continual and gradual process, however, it has led to different generations acquiring labels according to their overall characteristics. These are:

- *War babies*, born 1930 to 1945: Meta-characteristics include an acceptance of a single grand vision or plan and a belief in community and self-sacrifice. Members of this generation are likely to do voluntary work and donate regularly to charities, etc. Having experienced frugality and rationing, high-profile consumption is unlikely. However, the post-war labour shortage meant that this generation had much more earning power than any previous generation, which did result in new fashion/lifestyle phenomena like 'Teddy Boys', etc.
- *Baby boomers*, born 1945 to 1965: The generation to grow up in the Sixties, when property was cheap and jobs plentiful and perhaps because of this affluence their meta-characteristics include a lifestyle which is less materialistic. The word 'teenager' was invented for/by this generation and they invented their own culture – rejecting that of their parents – with their own music and fashions. Anti-militarism, women's liberation and sexual 'freedom' in a pre-AIDs world are also keywords for this generation. This generation was also the first generation of 'knowledge workers' (see Chapters 7 and 8), i.e. they are the first generation not to be physically worn out upon reaching retirement and now form the 'grey gold'.
- *Generation X*, born 1966 to 1976 (or the 'baby-busters'): Meta-characteristics include a need for autonomy, leading to (in the absence of training in traditional religious values) the tendency to formulate personal religions – often a

mix of reincarnation, naturalism, karma, etc. Generation X is said to be sceptical about the future (e.g. 'Punks'), shunning long-term relationships (both professional and personal/marital) and have unrealistically high expectations of others.

- *Generation Y*, born 1977 to 1994 (or the 'N-Gen', after the Net): Meta-characteristics include concentration on their personal lives, including materialism, risk-taking (often extreme), keen on business, hedonism, brand-orientation and celebrating the cult of the celebrity as a surrogate community to make up for lack of close physical community. Generation Y, however, are not perceived as being as cynical as their predecessor, Generation X.

Conversely, other ways of segmenting the population may be more useful; common alternatives include 'yuppy' (young upwardly mobile professional), 'dinks' (double income, no kids), 'yaps' (young affluent parent), 'sitcoms' (single income oppressive mortgage) and 'skis' (spending kids' inheritance).

The form of the marketing plan

The marketing plan, like most plans, can be broken down into:

- objectives
- analysis
- strategy
- tactics.

At any point in the marketing plan the value proposition (i.e. explain how higher profits can be made) can be emphasized by e.g.:

1 Raising the price by adding value.
2 Re-targeting the market.
3 Cutting costs.

The objectives will normally be a logical consequence of the analyses presented in Chapter 4 and especially will follow on from the product SWOT analysis. This will have given clues to questions like: who are my target customers, and what differentiates them from non-customers? Through which medium can we reach them? What are the benefits my product offers the customer? What distinguishes my company from others? What approach do competitors take? Objectives can be made very tangible in the marketing plan because one can go back to SGM analyses, identify the major competing brands/companies and benchmark progress against these competing products. This can be used to build finance-related objectives (also known as 'task-related budgeting').

How to do market research

The types of analyses are often broken down into primary data collection and analysis, and secondary data collection and analysis. Primary data can consist of:

- a pilot study (small sample size);
- survey/observation/experimental research (large sample size – questionnaire, telephone, stop and speak, e.g. shopping mall interviews);
- recruiting focus groups and performing depth interviews (in-depth analysis, small sample size).

However, such market research for primary data is often very expensive and gathering secondary data is the major thrust for small companies. Secondary data consists of:

- the Internet;
- data mining (own and other people's databases);
- experience surveys (i.e. interview known experts).

The strategic section should address marketing continuity. Products can be introduced in niches, but the marketing plan should explain how they can move to larger segments. New technology, in particular, often has little problem in entering the 'venturesome' niche, but fails to cross the 'innovation chasm' (Moore, 1995) into mainstream markets. Thus, it would be logical at this point to list some alternatives to selling existing products to existing market segments (or developing modified products for existing market segments), such as how to extend existing products into new segments or how to modify or re-position existing products. Some considerations may loop-back to very basics like the product name, e.g. in planning geographical expansion, shifts in meaning between languages may become important.

Globalization means spreading into other cultures

Advertising methods must also be adapted to market (geographical) expansion. The disappointing sales performance of the Ford Nova in Spain may be attributable to that, in Spanish, 'no va' means 'won't go'. Similarly 'mist' (as in the Rolls-Royce Silver Mist) in German means 'manure'. One could imagine that drinks like 'Pschitt' (French) or 'Pocari Sweat' (Japanese) would probably fare badly in English-speaking markets, not to mention Colon washing powder (Spain), Krapp toilet paper (Sweden) and Poo tofu (Indonesia). On the other hand the 'KIA' make of automobile is pronounced 'car' in Denmark.

One US manufacturer of washing powder produced a very successful TV ad featuring the fairy tale character Snow White, who was washing spotlessly for the seven dwarves, who, following common US practice, were selected from across a broad ethnic spectrum. This ad was later aired on Egyptian TV, leaving the audience – who had no knowledge of the Snow White fairy tale – flummoxed and dumbfounded. They saw an attractive but poor single mother who had seven children all by different fathers (a rather repulsive thought for most Arab females) and, while acknowledging that the constant trek of menfolk through mommy's bedroom must be tough on the sheets, they did not find this sufficiently motivating to purchase the washing powder (and indeed did not wish to associate themselves with this image at all). Sales plummeted.

(*Source*: Washing powder case taken from Mellor and Mellor, 2004)

The 4Ps and the 4Cs of marketing

The strategic marketing plan must thus identify needs, define target segments, group customers into manageable groups of specific characteristics, it must specify how to create differential advantage (i.e. be in a different position in relation to competition) and how to make a profit. For example, McDonald's is known as a fast food retailer, but – by virtue of its promotional offers aimed at children – it is also one of the largest toy retailers in the world. Traditionally strategic marketing addresses the '4Ps' (see Kotler, 1999) (see Glossary) which is rooted in the product, but it should be noted that in recent years the 'Relationship Marketing' model, which addresses the 'Need, Wants and Demands' of the consumer, sometimes called the '4Cs model' (see e.g. Gummesson, 1999) has also gained in popularity. The two models are compared in Table 5.1.

Table 5.1   Comparison of Kotler's 4Ps and Gummesson's 4Cs models

Transactional marketing (the '4Ps')	Relationship marketing (the '4Cs')
Product	Consumer wants and needs
Place (includes logistics and distribution)	Convenience (access, availability and distribution)
Price	Cost
Promotion	Communication

Since these two models address essentially the same criteria, the 4Ps model will be presented (Table 5.2).

Presumably by this time the details of the proposed product are quite firm, so product decisions at this stage involve possible bundling – either with other complementary products or later stage products (account trade discount, guarantee, follow-up and service, help-desk, etc.) – or future modifications to the product, e.g. a different colour for a second market segment.

Table 5.2   The 4Ps of marketing: a breakdown of the 4P factors

Product decisions	Price decisions	Distribution (Place) decisions	Promotion decisions
Brand name	Pricing strategy	Distribution	Promotional
Functionality	(skim,	channels	strategy (push,
Styling	penetration, etc.)	Market coverage	pull, etc.)
Quality	Suggested retail	(inclusive,	Advertising
Safety	price	selective, or	Personal selling &
Packaging	Volume discounts	exclusive	sales force
Repairs and support	and wholesale	distribution)	Sales promotions
warranty	pricing	Specific channel	Public relations &
Accessories and	Cash and early	members	publicity
services	payment discounts	Inventory	Marketing
	Seasonal pricing	management	communications
	Bundling	Warehousing	budget
	Price flexibility	Distribution centres	
	Price discrimination	Order processing	
		Transportation	
		Reverse logistics	

How to price your goods properly

What should a good (product or service) cost? Mark up is the difference between cost to buy a good and its retail price (i.e. Cost + Mark up = Retail Price), but many entrepreneurs cannot, or will not, work this out. Most adopt an 'estimate what the market can bear' attitude and adjust the price as experience is gained (start-up entrepreneurs have a marked tendency to undervalue their time and effort). Furthermore, price conveys image, e.g. discount or upmarket, so it may not be a good strategy to automatically try to beat competitors' prices. Moreover, cutting prices by 10 per cent on a good with a 25 per cent profit margin will mean that turnover (sales) may have to be doubled to break even. Moreover, in some cases, e.g. bundled services on the Internet, price is much less important than convenience value. Various guiding strategies can also be used to price new products. These include:

1   *Penetration*: Set price just above total unit cost (usually production costs plus profit margin, although production costs may vary according to quantity produced) to quickly win a large market share.
2   *Skimming*: Set a higher-than-normal price to quickly recover initial outlay.
3   *Demand curve*: Set prices high initially and be prepared to lower prices quickly. However, one should be aware that initial ('innovator') customers on the one hand may pay high costs to possess a unique product, but also may become alienated when they see others gaining the same product at a fraction of the cost a while later.

For established goods, a whole set of strategies can be used:

1   *Odd pricing*: Merchandise with an odd-numbered price is assumed to be cheaper than one with an even price.
2   *Price lining*: Categorizes merchandise which is similar in quality, performance, etc.
3   *Leader pricing*: Temporary mark-down to attract customers.
4   *Geographical pricing*: Selling at different prices to customers in different places.
5   *Opportunistic pricing*: Raising price on articles in short supply.
6   *Discounts*: Reductions in stale, outdated, etc. goods.
7   *Multiple discounts*: Reduction for high quantity.

How to place your offerings

Place decisions address where to sell the product, i.e. concerns about where the customers are and how to get to them, because 66 per cent of all buying decisions are made at point-of-sale. Place decisions can include tricky logistics, because place includes the 'distribution channels', meaning all the different middlemen used to get the product out to the customer (including home delivery).

Promotion – effective advertising

Promotion includes any publicity, any free commercial news by the media (especially celebrities), contests, coupons, free samples, sponsoring, sending out own (or co-operative, e.g. branch) newsletter, personal selling or advertising. The objectives are to get the product accepted by potential customers, as well as to maintain or increase market share, also in the face of growing competition.

Media options

- Word of mouth: cheap and most effective.
- Newspapers: Account for 25 per cent of all advertising. Focused geographical coverage but short ad life.
- Magazines: Focused interest group coverage and long ad life, but expensive.
- TV and radio: Reaches all markets, short spots.

(Continued)

- Direct mail: High targeting potential, but high throwaway costs.
- The Internet: Excludes some segments. Viewer fatigue.
- Outdoor and transit ads: High investment for brief message.
- Directories: Yellow Pages, etc. are surprisingly effective.
- Trade shows and sponsorships: Need much preparation with potential for high waste and costs.

A successful advert should not only attract attention, but also emphasize a key benefit (or several) and incite the customer to take action immediately. To do this it may highlight the Unique Selling Proposition (USP) and prove it with facts, statistics, testimonials, etc. Especially difficult is designing a form of feedback enabling the advertiser to check if it has been a quantifiable success (otherwise failures may be expensive to rectify).

The type and content of any promotional material will be rooted in considerations of the targeted customer segment, including the following factors:

1 The size of the company's trading area.
2 Who are the target customers and what are their characteristics?
3 Which media are the target customers most likely to watch, listen to, or read?
4 What budget limitations are there?
5 What media do any competitors use?
6 How important is repetition and continuity in the advertising message?

Taking the 4Ps into consideration, the marketing plan must then proceed to do the following:

- Select the primary customer segment.
- Delegate who does which activity (including who takes and processes/dispatches customers' orders).
- Explain how the activities are to be accomplished (media, etc.).
- Account for what this costs (staff and direct costs).
- Present a logical time plan (some things can only begin after others are complete).
- Account for how the product can expand into larger markets (secondary customer groups, etc.).
- Consider critical ('killer') assumptions and sketch out a contingency plan.

Customer groups, including a typical customer profile for each group, demographics and trends in the macro-environment are referred to where appropriate throughout the marketing plan.

People: Task matrices

The marketing plan is ideally cross-linked (this can be presented in separate tables) insomuch as it will specify which person does what activity or task, plus cost per activity, resulting in cost per person. To do this you make a list of tasks and number them, then make a timetable for the tasks and then make a matrix of people versus quarter and put the numbered tasks in the cells. Attach financial values to these and thus derive cost per person per quarter and cost per task per quarter. Costs can be broken down further and cross-correlated (e.g. budget by manager, budget by market, budget by product, budget by type, etc.). Making task matrices is a bit of an art but those interested in making task matrices can find examples in the excellent book by Malcolm McDonald (McDonald, 1999). If the TTM for the product is short, then costs can be broken down further to quarters or months, resulting in cost per person, per task, etc. with time. This is a great help in making the final consolidated budget for the business plan (Chapter 6).

These outlay figures (which are minus numbers) can also be plotted against estimated revenues per quarter and the result should be a 'hockey stick' curve as in Figure 6.1.

Chapter summary

The aim of the marketing plan is to link the resources of the company to the requirements of the customer, how to fulfil the needs and desires of the customer and how to bring the product to the customer.

To do this, a written statement of the marketing strategy, tactics, timetables, objectives and goals has to be prepared. This can be about the acquisition of new customers, or the increased retention of existing customers.

The marketing plan also details the implementation of the key activities, including the roll out of the actual marketing, advertising and sales activities. These are summarized and collated – often in tabular form – along with their costs. Costs can be broken down further and cross-correlated (e.g. budget by manager, budget by market, budget by product, budget by type, etc.).

Finally, the marketing plan reviews and tries to identify possible remedial actions.

References

Evans, M., Jamal, A. and Foxall, G. (2006) *Consumer Behaviour*. Chichester: John Wiley & Sons, Ltd.

Gummesson, E. (1999) *Total Relationship Marketing*. Oxford: Butterworth-Heinemann.

Kotler, P. (1999) *The Principles of Marketing*, 8th edn. Englewood Cliffs, NJ: Prentice Hall.

Kotler, P. and De Bes, T. (2003) *Lateral Marketing*. Chichester: John Wiley & Sons, Ltd.

McDonald, M. (1999) *Marketing Plans*. Oxford: Butterworth-Heinemann.

Mellor, R.B. and Mellor, N. (2004) *Applied E-Learning*. Copenhagen: Globe.

Moore, G. (1995) *Inside the Tornado*. New York: Harper Business.

Further reading

Brooksbank, R. (1996) 'The BASIC marketing planning process: A practical framework for the smaller business'. *Market Intelligence and Planning*, 14: 18.

Evans, M., Jamal, A. and Foxall, G. (2006) *Consumer Behaviour*. Chichester: John Wiley & Sons, Ltd.

Mellor, R. B. (2003) *Innovation Management*. Copenhagen: Globe (see sample marketing plan on p. 53).

Web links

www. barclaysmicrosites.co.uk/start_up/landing_eggs.html

www.businesslink.gov.uk/bdotg/action/layer?topicId=1073858842&tc=000KW020942918

www.fsb.co.uk

www.mybusiness.co.uk

www.startups.co.uk for a list of things to consider

Suggestion for exercises

Start preparing your marketing plan.

6 The Business Plan

Robert B. Mellor

Introduction

The business plan combines many of the topics discussed up to now (e.g. idea, novelty, strategy, judging how attractive a market is and market penetration) into one easily understood document. This chapter details the use and format of that document – the business plan.

Sources of capital investment

All start-ups need money. If the time to market is short, then the amount of money will be largely that figuring in the marketing plan (Chapter 5) and the amount will be small. In this case members of the family and social circle (often referred to as Friends, Fools and Family; 'FFF') will suffice if backed up by a bank loan. Banks are getting more flexible and improving their performance in supporting SMEs, but they still reject on average 50 per cent of all such cases (as a pointer, even most established SMEs in the UK find it easier to run off an overdraft due to difficulties in securing a bank loan). However, if successful, the bank may well want security or other collateral and this can mean the entrepreneur signing over their house, etc. to the bank. Experience shows that this is a bad idea (including for the bank) because the entrepreneur, in order to make a go of the business, does not need to be awake at night worrying about the roof over the family's head!

Business angels and venture capitalists

An alternative to the bank can be a business angel. A business angel (BA) is someone who has done it before, made some money, has got a bit hooked and is open to the idea of doing it again. The difference between a BA and a venture capitalist is shown in Table 6.1.

Table 6.1   Some characteristics of business angels and venture capitalists

Business angel	Venture capitalist
Works alone, perhaps within a network of like-minded people	Works for a firm or investment trust
Invests less than £1 million	Invests more than £1 million
Does it for profit and fun	Does it for profit alone
Aims to sell their share on to a venture capitalist	Aims to sell on to an investment trust or head for an IPO
Is willing to work with the entrepreneur as part of the team (in fact, may insist upon this) and use their talents, experience and contacts to the full	Will not be part of the team but will insist on having their people in key positions

The business plan has been referred to before. Banks, business angels and venture capitalists will all want to see the proposed company's business plan. Thus it is the single most important document in attracting investors. Venture capitalists in particular like the business plan and especially the marketing and strategy aspects, banks are heavily biased towards the financials, while business angels prefer the topic and the personalities involved (Mason and Stark, 2004). However, the importance of the business plan lies not only in attracting investors (including a bank, when the company needs a loan). It also functions as a 'road map' which one always can refer back to, and is thus invaluable in keeping the company on track.

Different sources of investment have different consequences

The late Anita Roddick needed £4,000 to open the first Body Shop. The bank refused, so her friend Ian McGlinn lent her the money in exchange for 50 per cent of the company stock ('equity'). Roddick went on to establish an empire of 2,000 shops and McGlinn, who ended up owning 22.4 per cent, got £146 million when the Body Shop was sold to L'Oréal in 2006. It would have been much cheaper for Roddick to have taken a bank loan for £4,000 and paid that back, instead of giving away £146 million in shares – so experienced entrepreneurs try to borrow as much as possible and try to keep as many shares as possible. Some of the pros and cons are shown in Table 6.2.

Finance is a recurring problem with start-ups. As a rule of thumb the value of a company is 2½ times its annual turnover. So what is the value of a company started yesterday and which not only has never sold anything, but also may not even plan to do so for several years? The result of this impossible calculation determines how much stock the investor will get in return for the money needed.

Most banks will expect the entrepreneur to put up 30–40 per cent of the money needed, while most investors will not invest unless their returns (Return on Investment, RoI) are over 35 per cent. One of the most famous individual investors was Ken Olsen who invested in Digital Equipment in 1957 and made a 5000 per cent return. The most famous venture investment company – as far as technology is concerned – is probably Sequoia Capital, early backers of companies like Apple, Cisco, Flextronics, Oracle, Google and YouTube.

Table 6.2   Pros and cons of bollowing

Taking on debt	Giving away equity
Keep ownership and take on creditors	Dilute ownership by taking on partners
Low expected returns	High expected returns
Small amounts of funding	Large amounts of funding
Periodic repayments up to a given maturity date	No short-term repayments up to a negotiable 'exit' date
May need personal guarantees and pre-determined financial ratios	Few restrictions – primarily a satisfactory 'due diligence' followed by agreed checks and balances

Figure 6.1 (overleaf) shows the 'J-curve' or 'hockey stick curve' for capital demand. Entrepreneurs' cash flows move from area A to B (break-even point), then hopefully into area C (investments covered) and area D (profits).

Figure 6.2 shows a (theoretical) investment chain for a start-up. Initial investment is from the entrepreneurs' savings and those people around him/her. This stage is called FFF (see above). Seed capital (and pre-seed capital) often comes from public sources. In boom times the players will move down the curve towards the origin. In times of recession, the players will move to the upper right, leaving large 'holes' around the origin. In times of recession, business angels and venture capitalists may get together to merge 'their' companies (M&A, Mergers and Acquisitions) in order both to streamline their portfolios and to optimize benefits of scale within individual holdings.

The curve in Figure 6.2 illustrates the schizophrenic nature of a start-up, where the owners, perhaps after being immersed in technological development, have to turn their attention to selling. Quixotically this selling activity may well not be to what may be thought of as 'customers', because the major customer for the company and its investors is the next investor to the right. Thus the

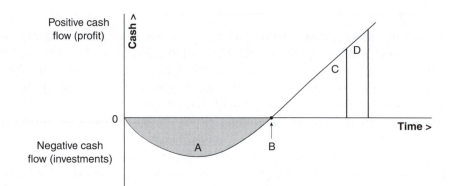

Figure 6.1   The 'J-curve' or 'hockey stick curve' for capital demand. Initial negative cash flow in amounts equal to the area labelled A is gradually offset by sales to reach break-even point (B). Thus A equals total investment needs (normally broken down by quarter, as detailed in the marketing plan). When positive returns are achieved, the company eventually reaches a point where investments have been covered, i.e. the area of A is equal to the area of C. This equates to the basic RoI time. When further profits are returned – typically when D > 35% of C – then investors are ready to sell to later investors - see Figure 6.2
Source: Modified from Mellor (2003)

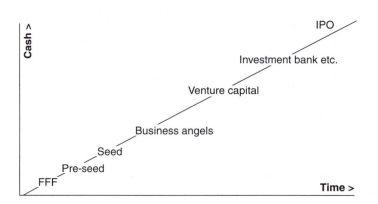

Figure 6.2   The chronological development of funding sources for a start-up company
Source: Taken from Mellor (2003)

'customers' for the fledgling company are often BAs. Their customers, in turn, may be venture cap-italists, and theirs, in turn (as proof of concept is established and risk diminished) are investment banks or the investment branch of a regular bank. They, in turn, get their return on investment from members of the public, either by selling products to the public, selling the company to a larger firm (a takeover) or selling stock on the stock exchange after an initial public offering. As if that was not enough, the types of management needed to face the different types of crises en route are quite different. At the pre-seed/seed stage the crisis is one of feasibility (and possibly market entry), where foundation-building management – implying creativity and evaluation – is needed. As the company progresses, it encounters the 'expansion crisis', requiring entrepreneurial strategies for growing a venture (normally the implementation of opportunities, creating and evolving a management team, etc.). This is followed by the 'organization crisis', necessitating a different entrepreneurial strategy of continual innovation and change to sustain growth.

The 'psychological wringer' (Mellor, 2003) described above is the reason why first-time entrepreneurs are encouraged to write an excellent business plan in order to get a seasoned business angel on board; there are many psychological obstacles confronting a first-time entrepreneur, which few can master (and those that can come through are seldom unscathed) so getting experienced help is paramount. In this respect, the business plan is also the bait on the entrepreneur's hook.

The form of the business plan

Business plans can be between 2 and 300 (typically 30) pages long, with a large margin (2.5cm) so investors have space to make notes. The font size should not be less than 11 point (max. 13, titles max. 16) with 1.5-line spacing. Tables and graphics should be very simple, preferably in monochrome because full colour can appear garish, and accepted business plans will be photocopied anyway, so you may as well get a correct black/grey/white balance from the start. Pages should be numbered, and appendices clearly labelled.

Typically the contents of a business plan will consist of the 16 classical elements:

1   Executive Summary
2   The Business Idea
3   Background*
4   Ownership ands Company Structure
5   The Team: Leadership, Board of Directors, Accountants and Lawyers
6   The Product
7   The Patent Situation*
8   The Marketing Plan
9   Sales and Distribution
10 Competitors
11 Customers
12 Agreements and/or Alliances*
13 The Budget
14 Investment Needs
15 Any Barriers
16 Profit and Exit

However, business plans will often not need all of these elements, so those elements marked with an asterisk (*) are not always applicable to every business plan; personal judgement must be used.

Is it financially viable?

The business plan should reveal if the idea can profitably be converted into reality. For example the 'Space Pen' was a triumph of engineering: US astronauts were equipped with a pressurized pen which could write in extreme conditions. The pen was made in 1965 by Fisher Pen Co. at an initial investment cost of about $1 million. NASA still buys pens for astronauts but the Russians, after buying 100, have returned to equipping their cosmonauts with pencils or normal ballpoint pens. The rest of humanity lives in a temperate gravity well (the Earth) and has no obvious use for space pens. Has the investment been returned or was the space pen an expensive marketing stunt? Writing a business plan would have given more insight into this issue.

The business plan can be compared to a dock, insomuch as much of the work covered in previous chapters (mission statement, customer analysis, SWOT, market research, the marketing plan, etc.) can simply be towed into position and afterwards reviewed to eliminate discrepancies, add missing details and ensure smooth reading. Variations on the basic template presented here certainly exist and it is up to personal taste (and judgement) to find out which one is most applicable. The business plan, when finished, must also have addressed the following:

- How the innovation is manageable and how it will be managed.
- Finding new ways to deliver customer satisfaction.
- How competitive advantage will be built upon.
- What the strategy is and why.
- How, upon success, the inevitable rise of competitors will be countered and negated.

The business plan normally starts with a cover page, stamped 'Confidential', and containing a title and the name and address of the author. One may also wish to include the mission statement on the title page and, according to length, a table of contents may be useful. In some countries (including the UK) it is usual to include a standard disclaimer at the bottom of the title page:

The contents of this business plan have been prepared by XYZ Ltd using sources believed to be reliable and accurate but which without further investigation cannot be warranted as to accuracy or completeness. Information and opinions are subject to change without notice. No director, employee or representative of XYZ Ltd accepts liability for any loss arising from the use of information provided. © XYZ Ltd: All rights reserved. No part may be reproduced or distributed in any manner without written permission. XYZ specifically prohibits redistribution via the Internet or otherwise, and accepts no liability whatsoever for the actions of third parties in this respect.

The classical 16 sections template

1 Executive Summary

Venture capitalists report that in 1999 and 2000 they were receiving 300 business plans per day. That means that the Executive Summary has to be very well written in order to get attention. It should be clear, concise and not one single word too long. Normally it is the part that is written last, since many experience that the process of writing the rest of the business plan helps formulate their ideas.

Classically entrepreneurs are supposed to practise their 'elevator speech', explaining their business proposition in the time an elevator takes to travel from the first to the tenth floor. The Executive Summary is the 'elevator speech' in writing. It contains the absolute essence of the business plan. This may take the form of:

> I have an idea. I can offer companies with up to 120 staff a system that will reduce their expenses between 3 per cent and 5 per cent. Analysis shows that profit margins will be between 45% and 55%. I can reach the target group because I worked in that field for five years and know it well. Sales are by direct marketing.

The 'elevator speech' does not mention gigabytes, server software or other details. Nor does it offer pie-in-the-sky. Without going deep into product technicalities, it outlines the answers to the following questions:

- What benefits does it offer the customer?
- What is the RoI?
- How is the customer to be reached?
- Which methods are to be used?

After carefully crafting the Executive Summary, the plan continues to outline the business idea.

2 The Business Idea

This is similar to the strategic business proposition described in Chapter 5. All change is a source of innovative opportunity and the Business Idea section must explain how processes operate normally, what the innovation is, and how the entrepreneur will take advantage of this. Changes include e.g.:

- the unexpected;
- incongruity;
- process need;
- changes in industry or market structure;
- demographics;
- changes in perception, mood, meaning;
- new knowledge.

It should start with a description of which problems the product solves and what advantages it offers to the customer, and the advantages it has over competing products/services. It includes a Porter-type analysis, a SGM and SWOT analysis, all of which can be inserted into place (see Chapter 4).

3 Background

If applicable and if it adds to the prestige, then some background information can be added. For example, if the invention was made in the research labs of a prestigious university and has won three major international prizes, then this can be documented here.

4 Ownership and Company Structure

This records the name and number of the company, the number of stock issued and their ownership, together with any other relevant information (e.g. accreditation, membership of professional organizations, etc.). There should be a paragraph detailing how many others are employed, together with a projection about the company size in the future. Employee options and warrants may be detailed here, and this is highly relevant because it affects future ownership issues.

It may also be relevant to add a paragraph about the organization or mention any other special organizational aspects. This may be, e.g., if distribution is important, that the company is located adjacent to major transport arteries; if it is a maritime company, that it is on the harbour front. Scientific companies may wish to mention that they lease premises in an incubator or science park, etc. Note that there may be overlap with 'Agreements and/or Alliances' (below).

5 The Team: Leadership, Board of Directors, Accountants and Lawyers

The leadership will probably consist of the original inventors and entrepreneurs, together with any professional help, which has been bought or borrowed. This section should list their names, what their functions are, their affiliations and a brief CV of each one. It may be useful to make a matrix of their competence profiles in order to uncover any 'holes'. This shows the investor that the company is interested in being effective, as well as providing grounds for putting staff posts in the budget. It may be useful to give an indication that the entrepreneur is aware that, at least in the start, s/he will be working long hours for little money.

The Board of Directors is extremely important. Typically they are 'bought in' experts from various fields and have excellent networks. They may work for as little as two hours per quarter (i.e. attend quarterly board meetings) bringing in their advice, network and business contacts. A good board with 3–5 well-known and reputable directors will convince the investor that you have presented convincing arguments to competent and experienced people who, in turn, are able to steer the company and sell the product. They should be listed by name, together with their affiliation and perhaps a short description of their special field and competencies.

The names and addresses of the accountants and company lawyer are appended last in this section.

6 The Product

A brief description of what the product is, what it can do and how it differs from other products. If the product is not complete, then milestones should accompany the development plan. Here product lifetime and expected frequency of buying may be relevant. It may also be the best place for pricing strategy. Note that price strategy can be different for different customer groups.

If pricing is discussed here (see Chapter 5), then it is also relevant to discuss discounts, guarantee, follow-up and service strategy, help desk, etc. if these have not been included in the marketing plan.

Drawings, blueprints, etc. of the product can be attached as an appendix and should not be part of the business plan.

7 The Patent Situation

Here the IPR situation is briefly explained, including a description of competing patents. It is an excellent idea to include the results of searches performed by patent agents. These (copies of original letters), as well as any completed patents or patent proposals should be attached as an appendix and should not be part of the business plan.

8 The Marketing Plan

The marketing plan was described in Chapter 5 and can be incorporated here in its entirety. At this point, possible product differentiation can be described, for example, if the same product, perhaps in different packaging, can be sold to different customer segments (see 'Customers' below). The marketing plan should also begin here to mention milestones.

9 Sales and Distribution

This section may include any details missing from the previous section. These may include any special advantages the company has, as well as special activities (Roll-Out, etc.). Price policy can be discussed here, if not already a part of the product description.

10 Competitors

There are always competitors (if not immediate, then at least potential) and baldly stating that competitors do not exist will, unless it is an extremely special circumstance, make the business plan appear unrealistic. Indeed, if there are no competitors, then there is probably no market! Competitors should be listed together with a mini-SWOT for each one, which realistically appraises the risks that each one poses. This will lead to a suggested positioning strategy as to how to avoid them.

11 Customers

No two customers are the same. For example, some will always go after the newest technology ('early movers'), while others are conservative and will not use a superior technology simply because it is new. Thus customers are broken down into segments according to different factors. These may be:

- geographical factors, e.g. country or population density (town or country-dwellers);
- demographic factors, e.g. age, gender, income group, profession, etc;
- life style, e.g. environmentalists or techno-freaks;
- behaviour, e.g. way of using the product or frequency of use;
- buying patterns, e.g. price-related or preference for certain trademarks.

This section should specify which customer segment is/are the primary target group(s) and which are the secondary, tertiary, etc., if possible with a time scale (if not already mentioned in the marketing plan).

12 Any Agreements and/or Alliances

This section specifies any agreements (further product development, media, marketing, etc.) that have been made with other companies, and any formal alliances (distribution, co-branding, etc.), which have been signed, or are in the process of being negotiated. This may include suppliers, agents, franchising, resellers and retailers, etc.

13 The Budget

If the company has been running for some time, then the previous year's budget and accounts can be used. In principle, this consists of:

- net turnover
- change in inventory
- other sources of income
- raw and other supplies
- other external costs (insurance, etc.)
- personnel costs
- depreciation
- other costs
- earnings versus costs
- disposition
- tax.

However, it must be stressed that legal formats change with time and with country, so an accredited accountant is really a 'must'.

If the company is new, then the budget's needs are estimated from the business plan. An accountant can help here, and there are also many types of accounting software available on the Internet and elsewhere. The running costs should ideally take cash flow into account.

14 Investment Needs

Investment needs follow logically from the budget. Figures come from two sources:

1   *Outlay*: Fixed costs (salary, rent, etc.) plus capital (e.g. buying a PC) and investments (web site, etc.). These may well come out of your marketing plan. For large and/or high tech projects, development costs are a major outlay.
2   *Income*: This is the projected income, i.e. represents your best supposition, based on the marketing plan, but is approximate by its very nature.

In short, the final budget = marketing budget (from Chapter 5) plus start-up budget plus running costs. Figures of total cost per quarter can be calculated against estimated revenues per quarter, which should give a 'hockey stick' curve (Figure 6.1), from which break-even and RoI can be calculated. To do this, one should make a graph or histogram of Outlay (minus) and Income (positive) by quarter; you should come up with an investment curve (see Figure 6.1). To get to break-even (where $O - I = 0$) you may have to project the figures over two or three years, but for small projects, annual needs may be sufficient. To project the figure to include the point of total investment return, three or more years may be needed. However, investment needs are detailed by quarter. Obviously investment needs may continue over several years, especially if breaking into different markets is envisaged (this may result in detailing the first year by month or quarter, then annually for subsequent years). Such assumptions must be explicitly mentioned and this will result in 'best case' and 'worst case' investment scenarios.

15 Any Barriers

Barriers (if any) must be openly and honestly discussed, together with rescue scenarios. Often investors are willing to find extra cash for situations that have been foreseen, but had been hoped to be avoided. On the other hand, what investors really do not like are unpleasant surprises. Unpleasant surprises may cause investors to suddenly and catastrophically withdraw their support, even where the extra amount may appear to be minimal.

Another way of seeing this is that the original plan can almost never be followed in every detail, so potential problems must be located early on and adjustments or alternatives proposed.

Barriers can be divided into two kinds: external and internal. External could, for example, be changes in national law. Other external factors could already have been discussed under risks in the SWOT analysis; these could include the factory burning down, competitors start marketing a cheaper product, the patent application fails, the major customer goes bankrupt, etc. Internal factors may be that a key worker decides to leave, or the company cannot attract sufficient personnel of the right quality.

16 Profit and Exit

An investment should be a 'win-win situation' for investor and company alike. Thus there must be a clear exit strategy from the start, a strategy that everybody knows about and explicitly approves of. While a company may have provided income, it is the exit which provides the profit. Investors are interested in selling their share in subsequent rounds of financing, so the original inventors may end up owning only 10% of their 'baby' and must realize that they will be forced to play a subordinate role (e.g. technical director) working for someone else – or even be squeezed out all together. This underlines the need for a solid valuation of the company; there are three different approaches to valuation (Market approach, Income approach and Asset approach) and entrepreneurs need to get reliable expert advice on the pros and cons of these three approaches.

Three common methods for determining the value of a company

- *Market approach*: calculates the value of a company based on the average value for several similar competitors in the marketplace.
- *Income approach*: calculates the ability of a company to generate revenue, usually by discounting a company's future income or cash flow at an assumed opportunity cost.
- *Asset approach*: calculates adjusted book value by offsetting liabilities against assets (assuming all the assets are liquidated and all debts are repaid). In this case the entrepreneur may insist on including 'sweat equity', the value of their hard but hitherto underpaid labour.

(*Source*: Modified from Fiduccia (2001) and Pricer and Johnson (1997))

Some entrepreneurs may regard their company as for sale from the first moment; others may wish to sit in the directors' chair until they are 90. The exit part of the business plan should sketch out the expectations that the author has.

Due diligence

A good business plan allows any interested investors to set 'due diligence' in motion. Due diligence is defined as an examination of the books and records of a company and interviews with officers, partners, etc. to confirm information about the company's business as well as legal and accounting affairs. Towards the end of due diligence, lawyers will move in to verify everything about the legal framework of the company, including partner contracts to date (especially schemes like shares, options and warrants), patent, immaterial and other rights (e.g. stock options and warrants) assigned to the company, contracts with employees, etc.

Chapter summary

The business plan, normally, is a quite cut-and-dried document, which often adheres to a standard 16-element format. In a logical sequence, it informs the investor as to why the project is a good idea and to the dimensions of investment and return. It goes on to describe the new product or service, as well as the market to be inhabited, plus how countermoves from competitors will be parried.

The marketing plan is described in detail in Chapter 5, which in turn allows a detailed budget and a time-scaled investment plan to be drawn up.

Finally, barriers and external, as well as internal, relationships are specified. These may also include referring to the dynamics of the company's development, as well as succession.

References

Fiduccia, B. (2001) 'Whether you're selling your business', *Entrepreneurs Start-up Magazine*. December issue. Available at: http://www.biz-appraisals.com/Company%20Worth.pdf

Mason, C. and Stark, M. (2004) 'What do investors look for in a business plan? A comparison of the investment criteria of bankers, venture capitalists and business angels', *International Small Business Journal*, 22: 227–48.

Mellor, R. B. (2003) *Innovation Management*. Copenhagen: Globe.

Pricer, R. and Johnson, A. (1997) 'The accuracy of valuation methods in predicting the selling price of small firms', *Journal of Small Business Management*, 35: 24.

Further reading

Blackwell, E. (2004) *How to Prepare a Business Plan*. London: Kogan Page Ltd.

Covello, J. and Hazelgren, B. J. (2005) *Your First Business Plan*. Sourcebooks, Inc.

Mellor, R. B. (2003) *Innovation Management*. Copenhagen: Globe.

Web links

Business plan templates

I recommend you write your own business plan rather than use a standard template, but it can be useful if you need to write 4–5 simultaneously. You can get plenty from the web (Google returns over 23 million hits for 'business plan'), try the one on www.smallbusinessadvice.org.uk/busplan bpdownloads.asp

(Continued)

Business formation

Check out your proposed company name at

www.companieshouse.gov.uk/WebCHeck/fastrack/. You can download all the info you need to start your own firm from Companies House, or several specialist firms will help you for a modest fee, e.g. www.ukbf.com

Business support

Business Link for London, www.bl4london.com

The Business Link central website, www.businesslink.gov.uk

The National Federation of Enterprise Agencies, www.localbusinessadviser.co.uk

Enterprise Hub Networks, www.commercialise.org.uk

Other advice

www.listentotaxman.com

www.hmrc.gov.uk

www.telecomsadvice.org.uk

PROWESS, advocacy organisation for women in business, www.prowess.org.uk

Ethnic Minority Business Forum, representing ethnic minority businesses in England; www.minority4business.co.uk and www.neighbourhood.gov.uk/page.asp?id=695

Investor relations firms and associations

There are very many VC firms and business angels, the following is purely a small random selection and constitutes neither an endorsement nor recommendation of the authors or publishers.

London Business Angels, www.lbangels.co.uk

British Business Angels, www.bbaa.org.uk

British Venture Capitalists,www.bvca.co.uk

Compass Point Group, www.compasspointgroup.com

Pondel/Wilkinson Group, www.pondel.com

Sequoia Capital, www.sequoiacap.com

Suggestion for exercises

Start preparing your business plan.

Part III

Context

7 Intellectual Capital

Robert B. Mellor

Introduction

For a prospective or new venture, the question of survival involves identifying 'core competencies' – and the subject of this chapter is identifying what capital a company has and how to lever it.

With the dramatic decline of manufacturing in the West, there are two ways for a company to make progress: one is the efficient exploitation of existing ideas and processes (e.g. soap manufacturers make the same product cheaper), the other is innovation, for example, to branch out into making soap-on-a-rope. Clearly, one can try to do both (those interested in this topic should Google the terms 'backward vertical integration', 'forward vertical integration' and 'horizontal integration') and this is simply a matter of corporate strategy, and many companies have tried to introduce semi-formal programmes for inducing innovation – ideas copied abroad are called 'creative imitation'. All these approaches have one thing in common; they depend upon turning human thought into value. This is intellectual capital.

The three types of intellectual capital

Intellectual capital can be divided into three elements:

1 Organizational capital: patents, processes, databases, etc. owned by the company.
2 Human capital: the skills, capabilities and the sum of knowledge and knowledge potential in the employees.
3 Social capital: the quality of relationships with partners, customers and suppliers (this overlaps with 'goodwill').

Some of this organizational capital – mostly inventions – can be formalized into patents. In the case of possible legal protection, it cannot be emphasized enough that all possible protection matters should be discussed with an expert on a case-by-case basis.

Creativity often cannot be formalized, but may well be written into an employee's job description or contract, while diversity innovation is best promoted by what is generally described as 'good working conditions'. Generally speaking, rights to the exploitation of intellectual property fall by default to the employer. The employer will then have a 'right of first refusal' on whether to accept responsibility and to sponsor the patenting process. Thus while the individual(s) remain inventor(s), the patent and all rights of exploitation are the property of the employer. Should the employer declare in writing (a 'waiver') that they have no interest in the invention, then the employee responsible for the invention is free to apply for a patent in their own name(s).

Patenting and employers' rights

Jake and Bill both work at a company making radios. Both are part-time inventors, making things in their free time in their respective garden sheds. Jake invents a new type of radio, while Bill invents a new type of bicycle. Preliminary searches show no existing patents in the areas involved and preliminary marketing plans forecast large market demand for both products. Both Jake and Bill rush off to the Patent Office (based in Newport, Wales), the body responsible for intellectual property rights in the UK, to apply for patents. Who has the highest chance of being finally able to own a patent?

The answer – all other things being equal – is Bill. This is because Jake stands a strong chance that his right will be contested by their employer, who can claim ownership of the patent on the basis that making radios is part of Jake's job, and that he used knowledge gained at his place of employment to rush home and simply put the final touches on the new radio. However, the company would stand very little chance of success with this type of argument in Bill's case.

Patents and other formal IPR

Having Intellectual Property Rights (IPR), especially a patent (invention innovation), is often quoted as helping entrepreneurs on the road to success. In 1976, the number of patents granted to US universities was 264. Twenty years later this had doubled and the number is still exploding. However, if the proportion of patents making money is 5 per cent, then the number will have significantly increased. Some 'tread water' but it is the 5 per cent that typically account for 70–90 per cent of all revenues generated. That is one general reason why the possession of several patents is a marker of large companies and not of SMEs. So even when possessing a patent, it is still a rocky road, and all the more dangerous because in start-up companies the company normally has one product (i.e. patent, product and producer are synonymous), whereas larger companies can afford to have patents which turn out to be flops. Larger companies, furthermore, will often submit a series of complementary patents in the hope of deterring attackers, a strategy seldom open for small companies. For this reason, smaller companies try to encourage the 'smaller' forms of innovation, e.g. diversity innovation (see Chapter 2).

Types of company classification

Companies differ wildly in their size and aims and this underlines the need to classify companies into meaningful groups. These categories are somewhat fluid; clearly a hairdresser employing nine people would be a large company by hairdresser standards. Similarly a company with 240 employees would be considered small if it were a foundry or shipyard. Eurosat defines companies according to their number of employees (as below). However, there is little agreement on exact borders between the categories, e.g. in the UK, the British Bankers' Association defines small firms as having an annual turnover of under £1 million (i.e. not number of employees at all), while the Companies Act defines small firms as having an annual turnover of under £2.8 million. Current US definitions extend 'Medium sized' up to 500 employees.

Micro-organizations	1–9 employees
Small organizations	10–99 employees
Medium-sized organizations	100–249 employees
Large organizations	250+ employees

However, before encouraging innovation, it is reasonable to see how innovation spreads inside a company and between companies. Furthermore, understanding the spread of innovations in populations is needed in order to prepare a more realistic marketing plan for the finished product.

Large organizations typically will have significant amounts of invention innovation (patents, etc.) and try to achieve economies of scale in this area. The scale of this can be so large that multinational companies have had to set up 'regional innovation relays' to bring knowledge out from the centre (home country operations are usually the principal contributor of innovation for global transfer) to national subsidiaries (Asakawa and Lehrer, 2003). These 'travelling committees' make a portfolio of the company's inventions and travel from branch to branch of the same company to instil the knowledge that these inventions exist into the consciousness of regional managers. Clearly this can also be a two-way process, as national subsidiaries often possess better knowledge of local conditions. At this level there is a transition from organizational capital to human capital, which leads us on to discussing knowledge and knowledge potential in the employees in the context of innovation.

Innovation in organizations

As discussed in Chapter 2, innovation can be divided into three categories: invention innovation, creation innovation and diversity innovation. Innovation, in all these categories, contributes towards a company's intellectual capital (sometimes called 'human capital' or 'social capital'). Interestingly, it has been found that the most powerful influence on knowledge sharing is social, and that IT systems made little significant impact (Lagerström and Andersson, 2003). This may also explain why related efforts like Total Quality Management (TQM) – despite proven success – have fallen out of favour in recent years.

This lack of formal promotion of innovation activities in SMEs is alarming, since SMEs are well known as the drivers of employment. For example, Gregory (2003) reports that since 1983, SMEs have created more that 78 per cent of all net new jobs in Canada and that small businesses (fewer than 50 employees) alone account for 42.5 per cent (6.7 million jobs) of total Canadian employment. Increasingly their competitive advantage is driven by differentiation, their ability to provide unique and superior value in terms of quality, special features or after-sales service, etc. (Porter, 1990).

Simple size and structure considerations mean that SMEs are much better positioned to use diversity innovation, conversely, they rarely use formal invention innovation: 'Mice' SMEs rarely possess a patent, and 'gazelle' SMEs have often spent so much on their one or few patents, that it is doubtful as to whether they have sufficient financial muscle left to be able to successfully defend them against serious attack.

When considering possible barriers to the spread of innovation in SMEs, one should consider that the innovation process is tied to a process of adoption, normally (Rogers, 1983) defined as:

1 A difficulty is felt.
2 The difficulty is located and defined.
3 Possible solution suggested.
4 The consequences of the solutions are considered.
5 The solution is accepted.

However, the classical theory – 'diffusion of innovation' (DoI) theory (Rogers, 1983) cannot be applied to the spread of innovations in SMEs because the lack of free space means that unrestricted 'Brownian' intellectual movement between people, and between ideas and people, is not allowed in a containerized company environment. Traditionally, the major theory concerning innovation between constrained social groups is the trickle-down (TD) theory (Simmel, 1904). In its most basic form, TD theory states that two conflicting groups act as a motive force for innovation, where subordinate groups seek to establish parity by imitating the clothing, attitudes, etc. of the superordinate group. The superordinate group, in turn, abandons these status markers and must therefore invent new ones in order to preserve the difference in status. TD theory has been modified by McCracken (1988: 93–103), who noted first that the direction of diffusion is not 'down', but up, and who added complexity ('trickle across') by introducing groups of intermediate social standing (gender, age and ethnicity) into the equation.

Human capital, the life-blood of small companies

Trickle-down could be e.g. successful lines of innovation being started by social minorities seen as inferior, which, upon success, become more important, prestigious and expensive while being increasingly controlled by someone from the socially superior majority as the project ascends through the hierarchy. Evidence (see Table 7.1) for trickle-down mechanisms has been found among employees in companies in mature market situations, but much less in companies in immature (sometimes called 'emerging') market situations (Mellor, 2005). In the example in Table 7.1, in companies in mature markets, natives, who are more likely to be admitted into the consensus group than foreigners are, are those leading major projects, while foreigners – often seen as socially lower – have less project responsibility. Note that major projects have a high failure rate. Therefore the high failure rate of natives in mature market situations should not immediately be taken as a sign of incompetence (although that is always possible), but first that larger projects mostly inherently contain a disproportional higher risk.

Table 7.1   IT-related project accomplishment by foreigners

	Highly qualified foreigners	Natives of that country
Mature market	Low (and only minor projects)	High (but prone to failure)
Immature market	High	High

Source: Data adapted from Mellor (2005) and Mellor (2007)

A newer theory, Adaptation-Innovation (A-I) Theory (Kirton, 2003), characterizes mature markets and companies in them as 'adaptive' and immature markets (and companies in them) as 'innovative'; A-I Theory says that humans, being social creatures, form groups (Figure 7.1, overleaf). These groups are usually formed on the basis of common interests and common perceptions, i.e. a common cognitive style. Employees in companies in mature markets are likely to solve problems in a certain way, and this way is agreed upon by consensus within the ruling group. Such a ruling group obviously includes the leaders ('opinion leaders', in DoI parlance). In such environments, innovators, being outside the group, may be viewed warily, their ideas appearing risky, peripheral or even silly. Conversely, 'adaptive' employees, e.g. from the major consensus group in a mature market situation – if magically transferred to an immature market situation – may be ignored and treated as having ideas that are merely fine-tuning and hardly creative.

Since it is important to be able to access the knowledge needed by both the business and the people, these situations demand that forums for general thinking are created, as well as systems for sharing knowledge. It is important that 'information gatekeepers' are open and committed change aides. The general rules for getting information to circulate are:

- Secretive or biased persons should not be allowed positions as 'information gatekeepers'.
- Interface problems must be tackled by an impartial leader.
- Eliminate small problems before they become big problems.
- Involve all parties in projects from the very beginning.
- Open communication is an explicit responsibility for everyone.
- Break large projects into smaller projects.

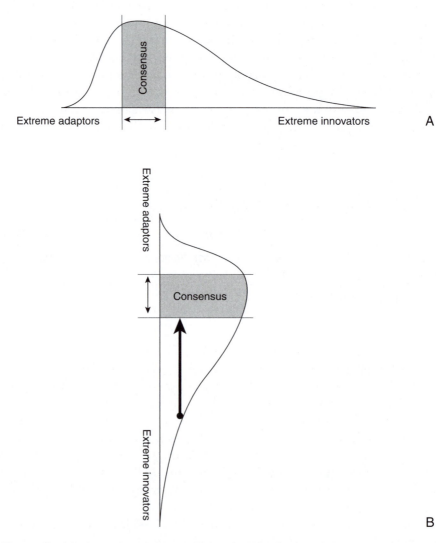

Figure 7.1   A-I Theory. Part A shows the number and numerical distribution of adapters and innovators in a human population, classified according to their innovative abilities (A-I Theory). Part B shows the same data, the bold line illustrating input from innovators outside the consensus group, a 'trickle down' challenge to the ruling group. Where the arrow meets the consensus group is often called 'the glass ceiling'

Source: Adapted from Kirton (2003: 230)

The literature is full of case studies demonstrating that ignoring such rules can be extremely expensive, both in terms of money and careers.

Who is especially innovative?

In particular, the role of multi-specialists (see Figure 1.1) has recently been the subject of much debate: Katz (2004) says, 'Research studies … indicate that the broader the range of skills and abilities … the more likely it is that that person will … become a more effective and successful contributing member of the organisation', and there is increasing evidence connecting multi-skilling and increased innovation. It is believed that multi-specialists, e.g. an engineer with an MBA, or a chemist with a degree in IT, are responsible for around 40 times more innovations (mostly incremental innovations), than people with a single specialization (Mellor, 2004). However, they often encounter resistance in the workplace because 'adaptive' administrators in companies operating in mature markets are wary of them.

Normally, education courses or degrees fall into one of the following categories:

Generalist	A little bit of a broad selection of disciplines.
Cross-disciplinary	A good grounding in a narrower selection of disciplines.
Specialist	A deep study of one discipline.

However, multi-specialists have taken a specialist education in one area, followed by a specialist education in a different area. Thus they represent a fourth type:

Multiple-specialist	A deep study of two (or more) disciplines.

Clearly workplace innovation (diversity innovation) is promoted by variety among work disciplines. This could be, e.g. the meeting between different people where they are specialists in different fields. The problem with such meetings is that the two (or more) types of expert have difficulty understanding each other. Therefore workplace innovation is at its most simple (and powerful) when communication problems do not exist, where the two or more specialists are literally embodied within the same person. Thus one person is able to look at a problem with the eyes of a, say, geologist and with 'MBA-eyes' simultaneously. To put it differently, the transaction costs for innovation can be very high (especially for diversity innovation, see Chapter 2), but multi-specialists represent a situation where the transaction costs for this cross-discipline communication are zero.

Mixing skills promotes innovation

The above effect is especially pronounced where the multi-specialist possesses 'hard' skills and also qualifications in 'soft' subjects. The interface between R&D and marketing is a typical problem area where participants cannot understand each other (or, in terms of A-I theory, do not want to understand each other). In SMEs, this could be e.g. the Internet, where misunderstandings between marketing people and the IT department are both common and crucial. Clearly a multi-skilled person straddling this gap is especially innovative and useful. Highly qualified multi-skilled trans-migrants are an especially notable group.

The international movement of labour and the role of foreigners are well established as an important positive factor in the historical establishment of European culture and economic systems (Cipolla, 1997) and indeed the role of trans-migrants and refugees has long been recognized in the development of European capitalism (Kamen, 1971). The role of trans-migrant foreigners has, however, recently undergone a new revival with studies on innovation with studies (e.g. Mellor, 2005) showing not only that persons who have a multi-skilled background are often innovation nuclei, but also that prominent among this group are highly qualified trans-migrants. Highly skilled trans-migrants have also previously been reported as exceptionally innovative (Kamen, 1971; McCracken, 1988; Cipolla, 1997) and research indicates that highly educated trans-migrants can, in the correct environment, be responsible for between 60 and 80 times more innovations (mostly incremental innovations) than native people with a single specialization, or around twice that of a multi-skilled native. However, they often encounter massive resistance in the workplace (often described in interviews as 'the glass ceiling'), especially if the workplace is in a mature market (i.e. 'adaptive').

How, then, do highly qualified trans-migrants manage to get a multi-specialized educational profile? The answer would appear to lie in the process of becoming a 'foreigner'. Today there is a floating population of people leading a nomadic existence, who are driven from country to country by curiosity, persecution or other grounds. During this process they need to adapt, be flexible, innovate and show self-responsibility and initiative. For some (not all), this initiative often results in a rich and varied experience and a wide variety of qualifications. Typically such people will have had a university education in their homeland. Then they could either be just plain curious and move to another country voluntarily, or they may be more inquisitive than their government allows, with the same end effect – albeit not voluntary. Other skills are needed in their new country; this often means starting from the beginning with a new education. Obviously, during this time their intelligence, innovative ability and flexibility will be tested to the limit. The result of this process is not only flexible people with a deep knowledge of many different areas (enabling innovative cross-fertilization to take place) but also, having endured the Darwinist rigours of internationalism, they are indeed expert and creative problem solvers.

Trickle-down rebound

As stated above, under 'adaptive' conditions (in companies operating under mature market situations), highly qualified foreigners/trans-migrants are very unlikely to have their ideas adopted. However, some highly persistent individuals can get small innovations accepted by going straight to the top leaders. In more extreme mature markets, even this direct approach no longer works or is even expressly forbidden (see e.g. Rose and Lawton, 1999: 292). In either case this is often a once-only option, as going directly to the company leaders will provoke negative reactions in middle management and flip change agents into resistance agents. This effect, known as 'trickle-down rebound' is suspected to occur in companies as small as 50 employees and is well documented at size 120+ employees (in companies in mature markets). Once 'trickle-down rebound' has happened, then especially non-natives will often fall prey to 'fundamental attribution error' (Burger, 1991), a common example being that speaking with an accent and using less sophisticated terms will bias the hearer to group the person, despite their high education, with lower-class, poorly educated natives. This often overlaps with the 'halo effect' (Murphy et al., 1993), inasmuch as once a negative impression is formed, then others tend to view what that person does, even things about which they have no knowledge, in unfavourable terms. Clearly this is a descending spiral, de-motivating potential innovators, perhaps driving them out of the company, which therefore is unable to use their innovative talents and thus achieve more optimal growth.

However, heterogeneous groups (those with wide diversity, e.g. having an ex-pat as boss and a high proportion of trans-migrants) are more difficult to recruit because it is not always apparent what selection criteria are. Furthermore, they are more difficult to manage, a factor that may take resources away from the groups' task – the actual problem solving. But trans-migrants are more comfortable with crossing boundaries, so in the right environment, they are more efficient over a wide range of problems. However, accommodating diversity costs extra effort and it is reasonable to examine cost against benefit.

Harvesting human capital

The situation of e.g. a multi-skilled trans-migrant outside the consensus group is that the innovation is bottom-up diversity innovation, but that the innovator is outside the consensus group and thus does not have access to sympathetic change agents, i.e. an innovation acceptance mechanism does not exist in most companies. This is important because it can lead to 'guileful behaviour' (Williamson, 1995), which in turn may lead to the negation of the basic assumptions of transaction cost theory, and can finally end up working diametrically against the organization's best interests – obviously one factor that must be taken into account when SMEs are deciding whether they should pursue a growth strategy or not, or when larger companies decide to pursue a rejuvenation strategy. Therefore, some established companies in mature markets consciously try to remain entrepreneurial by harvesting and using innovations and ideas from employees: intrapreneurship.

Intrapreneurship, or corporate entrepreneurship

This process is called either intrapreneurship or corporate entrepreneurship and a corporate entrepreneur is therefore a person who initiates innovative changes in mature companies. Increased openness to change after opening the consensus group has been known for over a decade (e.g. Fox, 1994).

Change agents (as defined by DoI Theory) are extremely important. Even where the intended change has its origins in the dominant group, a supporting executive must believe in the intrapreneurial idea and provide the resources needed. Chandler et al. (2000) report that mature companies actively supporting intrapreneurship may have an advantage in times of rapid market change, and thus the type of innovation involved may well be diversity innovation (or at least, not invention innovation). Lessem (1987) shows that in order for intrapreneurship to function, a strategic 'champion' (sometimes called an 'enabler') is needed to protect the new innovation, and that this protector must have well-schooled change agents in place if the innovation is to successfully be realized. In Lessem's argument, change agents are explicitly activated as a result of a top-down change and this could be seen as an extension of the behavioural focus as expostulated by Man and Chan (2002) 'person-to-person, group-to-group interactions based on co-operation, communication and trust'.

Technology transfer

After considering how innovation can spread within a company, the question can be raised about how innovation spreads between companies. Typically SMEs do not have resources to constantly monitor their competitors, so innovations spread by the rotation or replacement of staff within a branch or sector of industry, but are hindered by the general difficulty in imitating knowledge assets. Thus there is a period of temporary excess returns when the innovating SME may develop products and or business routines (knowledge assets) but competitors eventually imitate these (Meade, 1984).

Although low-level knowledge may well be spread by word-of-mouth, the rotation of personnel, etc., knowledge spread between companies may also be formalized. There are two normal routes: technology transfer and strategic alliances.

If invention innovation is protected by IPR, then it can be spread between originator and other companies by licensing agreements, 'technology transfer', which in turn may be exclusive or non-exclusive. This is obviously a sensitive area, with a good deal of input from the legal profession. The major pitfall is that the licensee may well buy rights to an invention, but will lack the know-how about how to build or operate it. It is therefore becoming more common to include knowledge transfer in the deal. This could take the form of 'secondment' of key personnel to the licensee for an appropriate period, or include a 'help desk' type arrangement based at the patentee's premises. This is becoming a more common ingredient of arrangements between universities and companies licensing newly developed technologies.

The ins and outs of strategic alliances

Strategic alliances are another example of useful mechanisms between like companies, or unlike companies. A simple example of unlike companies could be that one company is in the process of developing a 3-D computer mouse, and they work together with a company designing 3-D graphics. The graphics company get the prototypes free to experiment with, and the feedback duly flows back to the hardware company. An alliance is simply a business-to-business (B2B) collaboration. Another term that is frequently used is establishing a business network. Note that simply contracting out work is not normally regarded as an alliance or co-operation, even if B2B relationships tend to be long term and familiar, and where the services provided are highly customized, i.e. tailored to the contractor.

Alliances are formed for joint marketing, joint sales or distribution, joint production, design collaboration, technology licensing, and research and development (Figure 7.2). Relationships can be vertical between a vendor and a customer, or horizontal between vendors, local, or global. Learning alliances develop new technologies through collaborative research or transfer skills between partners. Many alliances exhibit combinations of these goals.

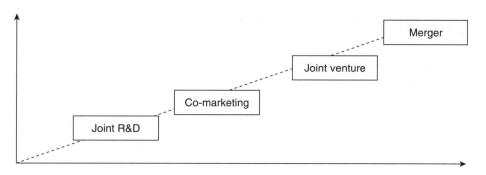

Figure 7.2   Illustration of the degree of integration involved in alliances, starting with co-operation and leading through co-marketing (see Chapter 5), through to a merger

As far as like companies (i.e. companies trying to innovate within a similar area) are concerned, the relationship between innovation and co-operation is not straightforward. Most companies still develop their new products, processes and services without alliances or other formal co-operation agreements. However, statistics show (Tether, 2002) that companies are much more likely to engage in alliances if they are aiming to introduce high-level innovations, i.e. 'new to market', rather than merely 'new to company'.

Alliances, by their very nature, are open-ended and ever changing. If all the terms of an exchange between two companies can be completely specified and agreed upon at the outset, they need not form an alliance; a simple purchase order or legal contract would do. An alliance is a way of sharing control over future decisions and governing future negotiations between the firms. It is a recognition that the initial agreement is in some sense incomplete. That is why success in alliances depends so much on their governance structures and on the ongoing relationship between the firms, including the personal relationships between managers. Many regional alliances of SMEs are being formed, specifically in order to achieve the amount of leverage that a large company has.

This tendency of alliances to change over time is often misinterpreted as a weakness. Managers complain about the high 'divorce rate' in alliances, and academics conduct statistical studies of the 'instability' of these structures. The attention to termination rates misses the central point, the survival of the alliance is not the goal, and only the success of the alliance strategy is. Sometimes, the strategy will call for using alliances as transitory mechanisms on the way to a full acquisition or full divestment. At other times, particularly when market or technological uncertainty is high, the strategy may involve launching several alliances at the same time, and determining over time which ones are worthy of further investment and which ones should be terminated (e.g. in January 2007 Yahoo announced the launch of a mobile Internet, involving 80 partners; it will be interesting to see how many partners are left at completion date) and such a strategy is no different from internal investment strategies that have companies hedging their bets or pursuing parallel projects to develop new products.

Mergers and acquisitions

An escalation of strategic alignment is mergers and acquisitions (M&A). M&A are often associated with market shakeouts, i.e. a defensive mechanism in a shrinking market. However, M&A can also be used aggressively in an expanding market, for example, some observers believe that the software market, in terms of applications, is expanding so rapidly that Microsoft will no longer be able to keep up if it depends purely on its own in-house development. Therefore, technology scouts are sent out in defined market areas to locate the best technology and buy the company (see Chapter 10). An example of this could be that Microsoft judged that Content Management Systems were the next logical step to build on their Internet Information Server, and thus bought N Compass Labs, rewrote some code and launched MS-CMS as their own product.

Chapter summary

Only a small proportion of an organization's intellectual capital is generated in a formalized way. What can be – invention innovation and creativity innovation – may be protected by patents and copyright or trade marking respectively.

However, the vast majority of an organization's intellectual property and capability comes from human capital – especially 'diversity innovation' (see Chapter 2) or a kind of mutual inspiration among its employees. Among the employees multi-specialists are responsible for many incremental innovations because the transaction costs for communication between specialists are reduced. Multi-skilled, highly educated trans-migrants are especially rich sources of innovations. In organizations working in immature markets, these innovations can be used rapidly, but in organizations in mature markets the major barrier to using these innovations is that the multi-specialists, especially the trans-migrant multi-specialists, are outside the consensus group. The trans-migrant multi-specialist groups thus tend either to be rapidly de-motivated, or pursue their ideas so aggressively that change agents become resistance agents and a negative rebound ('trickle-down rebound') occurs. This effect is often overlooked by middle management and Human Resources, but can have financial consequences at least as large as patenting.

If organizations need to innovate in order to survive and grow (Kotler and Trias de Bes, 2003) then indeed their most important intellectual capital is in the heads of their employees, and needs to be managed appropriately.

References

Asakawa, K. and Lehrer, M. (2003) 'Managing local knowledge assets globally, the role of regional innovation relays', *Journal of World Business*, 38: 31–42.

Burger, J. M. (1991) 'Changes in attribution errors over time, the ephemeral fundamental attribution error', *Social Cognition*, 9: 182–93.

Chandler, G. N., Keller, C. and Lyon, D. W. (2000) 'Unravelling the determinants and consequences of an innovation-supportive organisational culture', *Entrepreneurship Theory and Practice*, 24: 59–76.

Cipolla, C. M. (1997) *Before the Industrial Revolution: European Society and Economy, 1000–1700*. London: Routledge.

Fox, S. (1994) 'Empowerment as a catalyst for change: an example from the food industry', *Supply Chain Management*, 2: 29–33.

Gregory, M. (2003) 'SME job engine drives Canadian employment growth', *Small Business Research*, 3: 1–6.

Kamen, H. (1971) *The Iron Century: Social Change in Europe, 1550-1660*. London: Weidenfeld and Nicolson.

Katz, R. (2004) 'The motivation of professionals', in R. Katz (ed.), *The Human Side of Managing Technological Innovation*. Oxford: Oxford University Press.

Kirton, M. J. (2003) *Adaption-Innovation in the Context of Diversity and Change*. London: Routledge.

Kotler, P. and Trias de Bes, F. (2003) *Lateral Marketing*. Chichester: John Wiley and Sons, Ltd.

Lagerström, K. L. and Andersson, M. (2003) 'Creating and sharing knowledge within a transnational team: the development of a global business system', *Journal of World Business*, 38: 84–95.

Lessem, R. (1987) *Intrapreneurship*. Aldershot, Gower.

Man, T. and Chan, T. (2002) 'The competitiveness of small and medium enterprises: a conceptualisation with focus on entrepreneurial competencies', *Journal of Business Venturing*, 17: 123–42.

McCracken, G. (1988) *Culture and Consumption*. Bloomington, IN: Indiana University Press.

Meade, N. (1984) 'The use of growth curves in forecasting market development: a review and appraisal', *Journal of Forecasting*, 3: 429–51.

Mellor, R. B. (2004) *Sources and Spread of Innovation in Small e-commerce Companies*. Copenhagen: Globe.

Mellor, R. B. (2005) *Achieving Enterprise: Teaching Entrepreneurship and Innovation in Business and Academia*. FGF Entrepreneurship Research Monographs, 49, Cologne: Eul Verlag.

Mellor, R. B. (2007) 'Innovation nuclei in SMEs involved in Internet B2C e-commerce', KURIR-2007-T1: Kingston University Research and Innovation Reports. http://kurir.kingston.ac.uk/mellor2007.pdf

Moore, G. (1995) *Inside the Tornado*. New York: Harper Business.

Murphy, K. R., Jako, R. A. and Anhalt, R. L. (1993) 'Nature and consequences of halo error: a critical analysis', *Journal of Applied Psychology*, 78: 218–25.

Porter, M. E. (1990) *The Competitive Advantage of Nations*. London: Macmillan.

Rogers, E. M. (1983) *Diffusion of Innovators*. New York: Free Press.

Rose, A. and Lawton, A. (1999) *Public Services Management*. New Jersey: Prentice Hall.

Simmel, G. (1904) 'Fashion', *International Quarterly*, 10: 130–50.

Tether, B. S. (2002) 'Who cooperates for innovation and why? An empirical analysis', *Research Policy*, 31: 947–67.

Williamson, O. E. (1995) *The Economic Institutions of Capitalism*. New York: The Free Press.

Further reading

Bridge, S., O'Neill, K. and Cromie, S. (2003) *Understanding Enterprise*. Basingstoke: Palgrave Macmillan.

Burns, P. (2005) *Corporate Entrepreneurship*. Basingstoke: Palgrave Macmillan.

Teece, D. J. (2000) *Managing Intellectual Capital*. Oxford: Oxford University Press.

Web links

The state offices: www.ipo.gov.uk

Free databases for patent searches: www.freepatentsonline.com

European Patent Search: www.espacenet.com/index.en.htm

Trade Association for the UK high-tech industry: www.intellectuk.org

Patent agents and lawyers

There are many patent agents and lawyers, the most famous is probably Garching Innovation (www.max-planck-innovation.de), which has handled the majority of the intellectual property coming out of the Max Planck Institutes since 1970.

Briffa (www.briffa.com) specializes in all kinds of protection for clients which are small start-ups

J.A. Kemp & Co. (www.jakemp.com) are specialists in all kind of technology protection

The above is a purely random selection and constitutes neither an endorsement nor recommendation of the authors or publishers. Indeed there are probably hundreds of patent lawyers and advisors, e.g. a list of European Patent Attorneys is available at www.european-patent-office. org/reps/search.html and others at www.cipa.org.uk or www.itma.org.uk. A Google search will reveal many more.

Suggestions for exercises

1   Look up and comment on 'the diffusion of innovators' (Rogers, 1983) and explain how this compares with the 'innovation chasm' model of product development (Moore, 1995, see Chapter 11).
2   Compare 'fundamental attribution error' with the 'halo effect'.

8 Knowledge Management

Robert B. Mellor

Introduction

A century ago, Britain produced 50 per cent of the world demand for cloth and iron, and 70 per cent of the world demand for pottery and coal. Today Britain's exports have grown by 300 per cent, but manufacturing – in total – accounts for only 13 per cent of that. The huge increase has been in areas associated with knowledge. But what is the 'knowledge economy'? This is the topic of this chapter, because without knowledge of this, levering intellectual capital (Chapter 9) will be very difficult.

The knowledge economy

Observations, facts and ideas have been documented, collected and preserved for countless generations. These repositories were at first open, but eventually grew so large that they were organized on more formal lines, the forerunners of the modern libraries. The most wide-reaching method of organizing subject matter was invented by the American librarian, Melvil Dewey (1851–1931) in 1876, because already by this time, library collections had become so large that they were difficult to access by lay persons and indeed demanded the services of a 'knowledge go-between', the librarian. The more recent explosion in computerization of records has led to several overlapping terms being commonly used, e.g. data, information, knowledge and intelligence. Dictionaries define these as:

- *Data*: Factual information, especially information organized for analysis or used to reason or make decisions.
- *Information*: A collection of facts or data.
- *Knowledge*: Familiarity, awareness, or understanding gained through experience or study; the sum or range of what has been perceived, discovered, or learned.
- *Intelligence*: The capacity to acquire and apply knowledge, especially toward a purposeful goal.

If the data is '200 degrees', then information could be 'the fire is 200 degrees', and the knowledge could be; 'the fire is very hot, one should avoid putting one's fingers in it or one will get burnt'. Knowledge is related to the ability to understand truth or fact – and appraise the consequences of this – through reasoning and experience. Thus, knowledge consists of information + learning. Some authors divide knowledge into four types (personal, proprietary, public knowledge and common sense) and others into two (explicit knowledge and tacit knowledge). Unfortunately there are still uncertainties. Desisting from putting one's fingers into the fire may be tacit or public knowledge, or common sense, for us, but for a hypothetical mermaid who by virtue of living under water has no experience of fire, it is more likely to be unknown or explicit knowledge, proprietary to air-dwellers.

Thus knowledge has value. Obvious examples of this is could be in buying a house or speculating on the stock market, where those lacking specialized knowledge will not realize the promised gain, but rather will soon realize that they are failing; ranging from paying too much to losing everything. However, more and more products – also concrete products like mobile phones – consist more and more of knowledge. The knowledge that workers possess about how to manufacture products, to work machines, etc. is of primary financial status. This has led to many initiatives concerned with how to retain and pass on knowledge as a valuable commodity.

The value of knowledge

In her book *The Theory of the Growth of the Firm* (1959). Edith Penrose argued that markets send price signals that influence decisions about the allocation of resources in companies. Such decisions may typically involve how activities will be performed, what resources are required, which resources are allocated to different activities and, ultimately, how many resources are used. The implication is that growth, competitiveness and survival are dependent upon internal processes and insights ('social capital') rather than external market prices. Unfortunately decisions about internal processes inherently contain a certain degree of risk because decision-makers typically do not have access to the full knowledge required to act in an optimal way. This may be because either full information is unavailable or because the information is not widely distributed. Indeed, in the western knowledge-driven economies, companies are becoming more and more aware that individual and collective knowledge is a major factor of economic performance. The larger the company is and the stronger their connection with technology-intensive industries, the more likely they are to set up policies and systems to promote knowledge management. The term 'management' here is very important because it implies that simply owning resources is not necessarily going to provide any kind of advantage to the company or organization. Advantage, rather, is based upon the workers' skills and experiences, as well as their ability to absorb new knowledge. Therefore, while knowledge (especially e.g. Intellectual Property and any associated rights, see Chapter 7) is a resource in its own right, the way in which knowledge – true 'intellectual capital' – can be managed and applied will also have a great effect on the quality of services that can be leveraged from the resources owned by the organization. This places knowledge management in a central role within the organization.

There are very few concrete studies linking aspects of knowledge management and financial performance, however, Capon et al. (1992) did find that acquiring other companies as a way of accessing new knowledge did not significantly affect the ability of an organization to innovate. On the other hand, hiring scientists, spending money on applied R&D to develop new products and encouraging scientific discussions, did enhance the ability of a firm to innovate. Since innovation is widely thought to promote financial performance (see Chapter 2), this represents a link between the management and dissemination of knowledge, and financial performance.

Information and data management are important supports for knowledge management. Managing employees' files, sales performance reports and financial statements is information management and information management focuses on controlling and archiving the historical data, plans and activities that need to be performed to control an organization's records. The way in which this information is stored may furthermore be strictly governed by external sources, e.g. the Inland Revenue.

Information, knowledge and learning

Knowledge management, however, has come to encompass broader issues and, in particular, addresses the creation of processes and behaviours that allow people to transform information into human-understandable forms in order to fold that into the organization, create and share knowledge. Such systems deal mostly with converting tacit knowledge into explicit knowledge and this involves some similar processes, such as managing explicit knowledge, but it also involves some very different processes, such as the sharing of rules, operating procedures (formal and informal) and learning experiences.

Although both information management and knowledge management are similar insomuch as both require a high degree of human involvement, their objectives are often very different. The ultimate purpose of information management is to store and retrieve information, while the ultimate goal of knowledge management is more closely linked to organizational outcomes, e.g. an organization may state that their knowledge management target is to facilitate product innovation, or customer relations, or similar. Knowledge management involves several steps, starting with a discovery or generation step involving the creation of new ideas and new patterns. This knowledge needs to become abstract (i.e. codified), followed by knowledge transfer and then steps ensuring the exchange and dissemination or diffusion of knowledge between individuals, recipients and departments. These steps involve the identification of information needs, information acquisition, information organization and storage, information distribution, information use and, lastly, information retrieval and understanding (i.e. presenting it in context). Re-combination and learning experiences should, ideally, be added at any of these stages.

How can knowledge be captured?

If your line manager came to you and asked you to write everything you know into a database, do you think you could do it? Do you think you would want to do it, even if it were possible? Finally, how do you think it would affect the way the company values you?

The most basic knowledge management systems involve rapid aids to decision-making and at this level the Simon model (for review, see Davis and Olson, 1984) for decision process is probably the best-known model. Traditionally it consists of three main phases: Intelligence, Design, and Choice:

1 Intelligence involves searching or scanning the environment for conditions calling for decisions; data inputs are obtained, processed, and examined for clues that can help identify problems or opportunities.
2 Design involves inventing, developing, and analysing possible courses of action; this involves understanding the problem, generating solutions, and testing the feasibility of the solution.
3 Choice involves selecting an alternative or course of action from those available.

Under 'Choice', the various outcomes for alternatives may be:

- *Certainty* (involving the complete and accurate knowledge of outcome of each alternative; there is only one outcome for each alternative).
- *Risk* (multiple possible outcomes of each alternative can be identified, and a probability of occurrence attached to each of these).
- *Uncertainty* (multiple possible outcomes of each alternative can be identified, but there is no knowledge of the probability of occurrence).

Each of these three phases can call on support mechanisms and an information system is most effective if the results of a design are presented in a user-friendly form, preferably one which enables feedback to be given and used in future reassessments of that choice.

Human capital revisited: knowledge assets

There have been many extensions to Simon's rather mechanistic model and the main proponent of holistic management of knowledge assets is Max Boisot (1998). Boisot adds a further dimension to the intelligence-gathering phase by considering raising the data gathered to an abstract level so 'truths' and insight gained can be applied elsewhere. As an example, bored students may regularly look out of the window. Those bored students gathering intelligence may note that the grass is cut on a regular basis in summer, tending to start when the outside temperature exceeds 7°C, with the frequency falling off in autumn when the outside temperature falls to below 7°C. Thus a system based on Simon's model would enable the user to type in the temperature and a decision could be made as to whether to cut the grass or not. Boisot's model allows data to be raised to an abstract level; in this case 'grass only grows when the outside temperature exceeds 7°C'. This allows users to extend research to other areas, in this case perhaps other members of the graminaceae (the grass family) like wheat, corn and barley as well as bamboo, reeds and even sugar cane. For Boisot, knowledge follows a three-dimensional circular path called the 'social learning cycle' (SLC) in the 'I-Space' (information space). The I-Space can be visualized as the space enclosed by three axes (the X, the Y and the Z-axis) and where these different axes represent the degree to which knowledge is either tacit, or codified, concrete or abstract and diffused or undiffused (Figure 8.1).

The six phases of the SLC are:

1   Scanning ('scouting', i.e. similar to the Simon model).
2   Problem-solving (mulling it over).
3   Abstraction (is there a unifying principle or theory which makes the solution generic?).
4   Diffusion (e.g. publication).
5   Absorption (learning).
6   Impacting (a change in behaviour).

It is important to realize that each stage follows logically and inevitably from its predecessor. One further related and highly valuable concept is the recognition that different regions of the I-Space exist in different states of entropy. Entropy is at a minimum in ordered systems, i.e. that part of the I-Space where knowledge is not-diffuse, is well codified and abstract. Where entropy is high, then value is low, i.e. a book is 'ordered' and has low entropy and high value, but the individual pages, torn out and 'diffused' around the room, have higher entropy and correspondingly less value. A high entropy situation is the situation most often encountered in organizations; the workers around the organization each have scraps of useful information and knowledge management solutions, especially IT-driven knowledge management solutions, exist to bring order (i.e. lower entropy thus increasing value) to the system (although Lagerström and Andersson, 2003, report that the most powerful influence on knowledge spread is social, and that IT systems made little significant impact, see Chapter 7).

Unfortunately Boisot's theory states that short-cuts across the SLC are not allowed, therefore efforts should concentrate on increasing the speed of throughput, i.e. shortening the time taken to get from 1 to 6 without missing out the intervening stages. Often computer-aided learning (or 'e-learning') is used, simple examples of which include the 'help' files or 'office assistants' built in to many common office software packages.

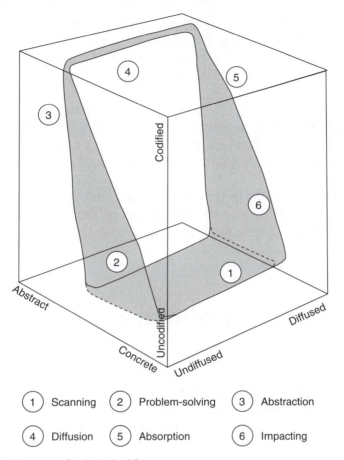

Figure 8.1   The Social Learning Cycle in the I-Space

Source: from Boisot (1998) *Knowledge Assets.* Reprinted by permission of Oxford University Press.

E-learning; an example showing that the benefits may not be where you expect them

Masters degree students learning programming at the IT University of Copenhagen took part in a series of experiments to see if e-learning could help them learn. All of the students attended regular classes but half of the students were given an e-learning

(Continued)

version of the course material as well. Quizzes were built in to the e-learning material at the beginning, mid-way and end points of the courses and quiz results showed generally that participants found the material useful and that participants had progressed in their learning. But when the exam results were published, the group that had used the e-learning material had a lower average grade than the control group!

Further investigations showed that, in the control group, good learners learned well but the poor learners became de-motivated and left the course. Conversely, in the group exposed to the e-learning material, there was a much lower dropout rate among poor performers and it was their (still poor) exam performance that lowered the group average.

Thus, although e-learning did help improve the performance of poor performers, the main effect of digitalizing the material and producing interactive e-learning material was to encourage poor learners and thus reduce costly drop-out rates.

Information systems software

IT-driven knowledge management systems mainly try to help the lowly user achieve the minimum acceptable performance; indeed, those with advanced knowledge may well find them trivial. This is also a valuable lesson for prototyping, which should be carried out using 'lowest common denominator' test subjects, not super-users. Solutions should furthermore repeat key information and allow users to make – and recover from – mistakes. Fortunately an average of only 35 per cent of material in e-learning courses is new for the user, repetition and reference materials making up the bulk of the solution (Mellor and Mellor, 2004). Finally it should always be remembered that IT-driven systems will probably increase motivation and retention, but may not improve average 'class performance'.

Knowledge management IT systems of varying sophistication are commercially available but often the support measures (a positive incentive to use the system, training and support on the use of the system) are thinly stretched and the consensus seems to be that big and expensive IT-driven knowledge management systems are not achieving their potential and even are seen as off-the-shelf products insensitive to the needs and character of the organization. Some say that the future includes bottom-up systems of 'blogs' and email and the place to start may well be with people's motivation (or not) to share, which in turn is based on group dynamics and the culture of the organization involved (see Chapter 7).

However, the emerging picture is that the adoption of knowledge management systems is dependent on size and sector. Big players, with earmarked budgets and dedicated IT departments, are very different from smaller organizations where perhaps only one person is responsible for technical decision-making. Firms with a high IT content in their core activities also think more strategically and indeed in some organizations informal learning has been made semi-official by the creation of volunteer 'champions' with expertise in particular areas.

That notwithstanding, significant barriers exist and these include:

- Usage: it is easier to ask a co-worker rather than look it up. This is especially prevalent in IT-related tasks.
- Content: employees are unable or reluctant to input their knowledge.
- Technical: recalling the stored content in a meaningful context.
- Spiralling costs: pedagogy and programming rarely work well together.

Therefore, IT-driven knowledge management systems do not normally progress beyond an intranet-like stage.

Chapter summary

In Chapter 2, it was demonstrated that 'diversity innovation' is the most widespread and – in terms of growing the small enterprise – most important type of innovation. However, not all employees can talk to all others and Chapter 2 showed that this becomes a barrier when there are over 50 employees. Facilitating such interactions with larger numbers of participants falls under the remit of knowledge management.

Knowledge management is an extension of data or information management but is qualitatively different because knowledge management expressly includes aspects of experience, learning and prognosticating consequences in a cultural context. Knowledge management also ventures into tacit knowledge, as opposed to facts and figures.

In dealing with knowledge management, the most useful theory is that of Boisot because it links type of knowledge to value and gives strong hints as to how to manage knowledge.

Despite this solid theoretical base, IT-driven knowledge management systems have not made a large impact and, indeed, where they function at all, they tend to be rather primitive low-cost solutions.

References

Boisot, M. H. (1998) *Knowledge Assets*. Oxford: Oxford University Press.

Capon, N., Farley, J. U., Lehmann, D. R. and Hulbert, J. M. (1992) 'Profiles of product innovators among large US manufacturers', *Management Science*, 38: 157–68.

Davis, G. B. and Olson, M. H. (1984) *Management Information Systems: Conceptual Foundations, Structure, and Development*. New York: McGraw-Hill.

Lagerström, K. L. and Andersson, M. (2003) 'Creating and sharing knowledge within a transnational team: the development of a global business system', *Journal of World Business*, 38: 84–95.
Mellor, R. B. and Mellor, N. (2004) *Applied E-learning*. Copenhagen: Globe.
Penrose, E. (1959) *The Theory of the Growth of the Firm*. Oxford: Oxford University Press.

Further reading

Boisot, M. H. (1998) *Knowledge Assets*. Oxford: Oxford University Press.
Bouthillier, F. and Shearer, K. (2002) 'Understanding knowledge management and information management: the need for an empirical perspective', *Information Research*, 8(1) Available at: http://informations.net/ir/8-1/paper141.html
Mellor, R. B. and Mellor, N. (2004) *Applied E-learning*. Copenhagen: Globe.

Web links

Introduction to systems thinking and knowledge management: www.systems-thinking.org

A continually updated set of links: www.kmresource.com/exp.htm

Local t-Gov, applying change in government: www.localegovnp.org

Suggestion for exercises

Google Boisot (1998) and explain why short-cuts across the Social Learning Cycle are not allowed.

9 Presentation Technique

Robert B. Mellor

Introduction

Chapters 3–5 detailed some of the factors to be put into the business plan (Chapter 6), but the business plan is a written document and is thus rather static. In order to impress potential investors and others that you are to be taken seriously, verbal and other associated personal presentation skills are important. This chapter illustrates this – that the point of presentations is to effectively communicate the ideas in one person's head to one or several other people in such a way that they understand the idea – and can respond positively – as near to totally as possible.

Getting the message across

Various forms of communication can be used to get the message across. These almost always involve verbal techniques, but not always (e.g. skywriting, etc.). Indeed, pure verbal channels, for instance, telephone interviews for jobs, are used only infrequently because the quality of a pure verbal (i.e. telephone) conversation is generally known to be quite inferior to that of a face-to-face conversation and it is widely believed that only 11 per cent of information comes in through the ears, 83 per cent of information comes in through the eyes and 6 per cent through other senses (smell, etc.). Presenting in person also introduces the audience to a whole extra set of factors, such as:

- You as a person (appearance, dress): statistics show that people judged to be physically beautiful (and, for males, tall) are more highly regarded, progress better in their careers and earn more.
- Gestures and body language, including friendly good humour, especially if you possess the ability to radiate the impression that you are at ease, are enjoying the occasion and respect the opportunity to communicate with the audience.
- Presentation aids, usually texts and graphics (a poster, etc.), although audio (sounds) can be added to make multimedia presentations.

> # First impressions are important
>
> The vast majority of a person's regard for another is formed in the first four minutes and is nearly impossible to eradicate afterwards. Visual cues from the person, dress (clothing, accessories, body decoration and modification) are regarded as highly important, but not as important as facial expression. Visual cues often focus on the face. In video experiments where the screen showed only the face, even a slight distortion introduced into the picture decreased the ability of a test audience to interpret facial data (detect emotions, etc.) significantly.

The perception of communication

Experiments show that the information given in presentations goes to the brain through a variety of routes. Pease and Pease (2004) report that:

- 55–65 per cent is non-verbal (body language and visual aids);
- 10–15 per cent is verbal (words only);
- 20–35 per cent is vocal (tone, inflection, etc.).

Thus, mechanically reading text on paper will result in very little of the message getting across. While being intimately acquainted with the content of the subject material is obviously central to a good presentation, the way in which it is delivered (tone, inflection and body language) is apparently more important! This includes using the physical space effectively; slow steps – not a run – help you 'own' the available area.

Public speaking

The inexperienced speaker, giving a public presentation for the first time, will almost certainly suffer from one or several of the following effects:

1 An increase in body temperature, as reflected in sweaty palms, getting 'hot around the collar', a dry mouth and perhaps even beads of perspiration on the forehead.
2 Shaky feeling – especially around the knees – as a result of raised adrenaline levels.
3 Increased respiration (breathing) rates as a result of stress.

Biologists know that these effects are part of the adrenaline-induced 'flight or fight' response and research has shown that they are not necessarily signs of fear but rather indicate that the organism is gearing up its metabolism to perform. Almost all entertainers, public speakers and competitive sports people report the same 'pre-performance' symptoms and while they are extremely nervous, uncomfortable and tongue-tied, they still go on to give immaculate performances – indeed, the evolutionary root of this metabolic gearing-up is precisely in order to give an excellent performance.

Recognizing these symptoms for what they are should enable you to better cope with them. The most commonly recommended remedy is to develop a regular breathing pattern. Effective breathing is a fundamental ingredient of a good presentation technique and a shallow and irregular breathing pattern will result in a tight or constrained voice – even a squeak!

An easy exercise to help you develop deeper and more relaxed breathing

1   Standing with your feet shoulder width apart, place your hands on your back – on the bottom of your ribcage.
2   Now inhale deeply; you should feel your ribcage move outwards as the air fills your lungs.
3   Try to exhale over an extended period of about 25 seconds.
4   Repeat.

Regular practice will help you develop a reflexive deep breathing pattern that will give you more volume and power plus help control your nervous stress.

A 'conversational roadblock' is the term sometimes given to 'filler phrases' like the aggravating 'err-err-err'. People are socially programmed not to interrupt others, which is why such sounds are emitted; to create the impression that one is still speaking and thus to avoid others jumping in. Put concisely, the meaning is 'I've have nothing meaningful to say, but I desperately want to stop you from interrupting.' After a time, this will lead to hostile boredom among the audience. Similarly other meaningless phrases and expressions like 'Do you see what I'm saying?' or 'Know what I mean?' will also cause your listener to wonder if you have thought things through or you are desperately fishing for an idea, or perhaps you are just catastrophically bad at expressing what you have to say. Worst of all, it may lead the audience to wonder if you have anything constructive to say at all.

Body language

Body language is often overlooked when we check our appearance, but a posture of confidence and ease can set the tone of any meeting, in particular, nervous habits like twitches and twiddles, hands in pockets or scratching parts of your face or body will divert the audience's attention and result in disinterest. If you are standing, check your stance. Crossing your arms over your chest conveys the message that you are not receptive, i.e. that you are on guard and creating a defensive distance between you and them, your mind is closed to what is being said to you. Professionals counter such tendencies by practising open yet explanatory hand gestures; carried out below chin level (some say that gestures above chin level are too similar to begging gestures). Eye contact is also of paramount importance: You have probably been told that direct eye contact is a sign of honesty (wide-eyes 'nothing to hide' expression). However, a steady scrutiny makes people feel that you are trying to search their souls or read their minds. When speaking to crowds, it is best to maintain broad eye contact, sweeping the room and making eye contact from individual to individual, briefly holding their gaze. In one-to-one situations, lean toward the person with whom you are conversing, conveying the idea that you really care about what is being said and you don't want to miss a single word of it. If there are questions asked, nod slowly and give the appearance of total attention. It will give the impression that you are rather intelligent. Nodding repeatedly is a positive yes … yes … yes signal.

Appearance and dress code

Appearance is a further easily remedied fault; you do not dress for tennis when going for a job interview. How a person dresses can reveal a good deal about their personality; shaking on that good old comfortable chocolate-coloured jacket in the morning and popping your presentation into your trusty briefcase – and why empty it, you may get chance to look at that stuff on the train – tells an experienced person-watcher, 'Old clothes are the sign of someone who doesn't get around much to different social situations, may well be introvert; brown (excrement colour) may mean low self-esteem and the stuffed briefcase means still working to long-overdue deadlines, this person is probably quite disorganized.' Try not to turn up with your papers in a plastic shopping bag. Go for a plain black or dark briefcase-type bag instead. And don't forget a good pen and a pad of paper.

Dress, for men, is classically a smart grey jacket, provided it comes with a lighter coloured shirt. Recruitment consultants report that candidates who come in a navy or dark grey suit look better, except when the dark suit is worn with a dark shirt, as this ruins the contrast with the suit. But the shirt doesn't have to be white. Pastel-coloured shirts can look quite sophisticated. Any colour tie is OK, as long as the overall effect is not overwhelming. Bright or funny ties, e.g. with cartoon figures on, are not recommended. Shoes should be clean and polished, remember to take the price ticket off the sole. Looking good and professional will make you feel good and professional.

Women have a wider choice of colours; females can wear black suits, brown suits, or dark green coloured suits – just nothing too bright! Light blue radiates serenity and trustworthiness. Matters such as skirt length and high- or low-heeled shoes, jewellery, etc. should be selected on the grounds of what makes the wearer appear professional, relaxed and confident.

Getting a feel for the audience

Obviously presentations can be viewed from two sides, the speaker and the audience, so the presenter should therefore not only know how to deliver a good presentation, but furthermore should know what danger signs to look for in the audience. In this respect, Jeffrey T. Frederick has published many insights as a result of his legal work on how to select a jury (Frederick, 1995). Some danger signs in the audience:

- supporting chin by hand/thumb (or fist);
- closed eyes or rapid blinking;
- combination of the above two (preparatory to sleeping?);
- tapping feet, also in the air, or tapping a pencil, etc.;
- the leaning-back European leg-cross (especially bad if with crossed arms), a sign of sceptical disbelief.

Audiences showing danger signs should never be forced into a decision because once they have verbalized a 'no', it is very hard to go back. Simple remedies to fatigued audiences involve action. This includes the speaker moving around the stage or presentation area, inviting them to examine something (brochure, samples, etc.) or to invite intellectual action by finishing sentences with 'wouldn't you?', 'isn't that true?', etc.

Audio-visual aids

Visual support for a presentation is very important and you must first of all be sure that the visual support actually works, so professionals don't put all their eggs in one basket and have normally prepared more than one delivery method, e.g. a PowerPoint presentation is taken on CD, as well as on a USB memory stick (you can also e-mail it to yourself), but print-outs and the slides on OHP transparencies are also taken as a back-up in case the computer or PC-projector fails. A sharp pencil laid on the transparency is also an excellent pointer. Those taking their own laptop – especially if it is a Mac – should remember to take a power supply and any adaptors. You should also have a board-marker in your pocket so you can use a whiteboard or flip chart as a last resort in case of complete power blackout – as well as it being potentially useful to help answer questions.

A slide is just a useful tool for your audience to look at while you talk about the topic more extensively, so you should say more than is listed on the slide (and never just read the slide to the audience – it is reasonable to assume the audience can read it for themselves). Thus, slides typically just list the facts or the information being talked about in the presentation. As a rule of thumb, one slide approximates to two minutes talk (i.e. around 30 slides for a 60-minute presentation). A typical mistake is to put too much information on one slide; one should rather break the material down so each slide has its own topic with its own title, and use bulleted lists rather than complete sentences.

Slides, printed, are the most common base for a handout. Handouts can be distributed before the presentation starts if the presentation is long (45 minutes to 1 hour) or very complex and the audience is very professional and interested. This helps the audience to keep track of where they are. However, for short presentations, it can be counter-productive to have the audience busily reading while you are trying to make a presentation. In such situations the handouts should be distributed at the end, when the presentation is over, perhaps with your business card attached.

Visual support should entail graphical illustrations; these should not be gothic and complex, but simple and hard-hitting. A picture can – as the saying goes – be worth a thousand words, but you should also ensure that each image used in a presentation serves a necessary purpose. Certainly if the image count rises above three on a single slide, then you must consider other ways to achieve the same effect without adding more visual stimulation. If the images serve only a decorative purpose, they should be appropriate to the tone and style of the piece; Clip Art should be avoided. When using photographs, etc., it is always best to use your own original work, so as to avoid any possibility of copyright infringements.

For a multimedia effect, sound can be applied either as a Slide Transition (which happens as one slide moves to the next) or as a Custom Animation (which is an effect applied to the words or images on a slide). Be aware that checking the 'Loop until next sound' box, combined with not applying any other sounds, means that this sound will play through the entire presentation. Too much sound or too many sounds is NOT a good presentation technique as it can be very distracting to your audience. Furthermore you are making the assumption that a loudspeaker system is present and that the sound file format can be played on the software installed on that PC (e.g. not all Windows PCs will play all Apple file formats). If, however, the sound file really relates to the topic of the presentation, sound can be very effective.

The structure of a presentation

The presentation itself should also follow a logical structure and there are four 'golden rules' for a logical presentation:

- Introduce yourself and the topic.
- Involve the audience.
- Keep to time.
- Round off and summarize.

The introduction communicates to the audience what will be presented, in which order and why. Explaining the structure at the beginning shows what you are going to do and makes it easier for everyone to follow. At this time one can point to the screen (without turning your back on the audience) and explain the meaning of what you want to talk about. A good presentation has an introduction, a middle and an end. The end is very important because it is at the end when you repeat and/or summarize the main points. This forms the basis of the 'take-home message', the very core of what you want the audience to retain.

The 10-minute pitch to investors

- Introduction (1 minute)
- Industry: target market and competition (2 minutes)
- Product/service: the problem/opportunity addressed, the solution and business model proposed (2 minutes)
- Management: who they are and track record (2 minutes)
- Financing: summary of needs versus expenditure, projected margins, expected breakeven point and Return on Investment (2 minutes)
- End: repeat the important points (1 minute)

You should present only highlights (not the entire business plan), convey commitment and competence and anticipate questions.

Obviously it is reasonable to keep to the allotted time. It is not always necessary to keep glancing the clock, or have a timer, but you should be aware that it is irritating for the audience if you over-run, and it implies a lack of respect. If you think you will over-run, explain briefly to the audience that you will skip the next slides (you can always come back to them later). Conversely, one can also have some additional information to talk about in case you under-run.

End on a good note

As always, it is a good idea to allow time for questions and indeed it is seldom that no questions are asked, because a good chairman, fearing this embarrassment, will always try to have one question 'just in case'. During question time it is reasonable to wait until the lights come on, as a well-lit space will enable the presenter to see the questioner and better evaluate their body language and facial expression. As preparation, write down your most dreaded question and practise answering it. Repeat with the second most dreaded, etc. During question time, listen carefully, give the appearance of total attention, adopt a secure and open body language (legs planted slightly apart, arms by side, palms open), gesture as appropriate and keep nodding (it's contagious).

Finally, before leaving the stage, it is polite to quickly thank the audience and the organizer.

Chapter summary

The point of presentations is to get others to understand a logical and orderly sequence of thoughts, fact, figures and other information. To do this, a dual strategy is normally adopted, involving both audible and visual elements. The audible involves the presenter speaking and can include other sounds ('multimedia'), while the visual both repeats the verbally delivered material as condensed texts, as well as introducing graphical dimensions.

A further important factor involves 'believability': this rests on intangibles, the most important of which are voice tone and inflection, body language and general appearance. Paying attention to these factors means the difference between audience antipathy and applause.

References

Frederick, J.T. (1995) *Mastering Voir Dire and Jury Selection: Gaining an Edge in Questioning and Selecting a Jury*. Chicago: ABA Press.

Pease, A. and Pease, B. (2004) *The Definitive Book of Body Language*. London: Orion.

Further reading

Goldman, E. (2004) *As Others See Us: Body Movement and the Art of Successful Communication*. London: Brunner-Routledge.

Hindle, T. (1990) *Essential Managers: Making Presentations*. London: Dorling Kindersley Publishers Ltd.

Nelson-Jones, R. (2007) *Life Coaching Skills*. London: Sage.

Web links

www.businessballs.com/presentation.htm
www.presentationhelper.co.uk

Suggestions for exercises

1 You turn up at an important presentation with your USB data-stick with your multimedia presentation on it. You intend to use the PC in the speaker's podium. List two or three embarrassing things that could happen.
2 Practise your elevator pitch at home with friends or a mirror.

Specialisms

10 Technical Innovation

Robert B. Mellor

Introduction

This chapter introduces some of the concepts surrounding technical entrepreneurship and is suitable for students of the computer/IT-related disciplines and engineering, especially electrical engineering.

The influence of globalization

One hotly discussed subject in technical markets is outsourcing. Assume that a company making 'Product X' in London may be gaining in market share, but is paying its workers low hourly wages, say, £1. The low wage makes the company competitive in selling 'Product X', but is not boosting the prosperity of London, which would like to have its residents on high wages. However, if this hypothetical company raised wages to £2 per hour, it would mean that a rival company, which pays £1.50 per hour, would take over the market, illustrating that for a company operating in a certain marketplace, its gain in market share (Snowdon and Stonehouse, 2006) is some other company's loss of market share. This leads to the expression that competition between rival companies, in macro-economic terms, is a 'zero-sum game'.

However, when competing across locations the situation is different; the UK is not in competition with Japan in the same way that Coke is in competition with Pepsi. It is the output per unit of labour and capital that is going to determine the prosperity of a nation. Thus, nations compete in providing a platform for operating at high levels of productivity and therefore attracting and retaining a superior investment in those activities that support high returns to capital and high wages, so, to put it a different way, trade between nations is a 'positive-sum game'. Thus, the difference between the competitiveness of a company and of a nation is that for a company it is return on invested capital, whereas in a nation it is productivity measured by value (as opposed to productivity in the narrower sense of volume).

The stages of competitive development for nations involve moving from being a factor-driven economy (typical factors include the size of the local market, military issues and political ties, democratization and stability) to becoming an investment-driven economy, and finally to becoming an innovation-driven economy. Therefore, the major challenge for any national economy is to upgrade the sophistication of its industrial clusters towards more advanced high-value activities, the redirection of company strategies towards an emphasis on innovation and the development and production of high-value goods and services. Some evidence indicates that in the UK, companies are not allocating sufficient resources to innovation and modern managerial practices and the UK now needs a new approach that will upgrade its competitiveness based on innovation; it is important to create the right structure and environment to facilitate innovative thinking. This has led Western governments to invest large sums in helping universities and industry become more innovative, including giving state subsidies to science parks, business incubators (see Glossary), etc.

Does globalization promote 'corner cutting'?

The situation is illustrated by figures from Accenture in summer 2006 showing that IT-related salaries are rising at 20 per cent a year in the UK and thus it is worthwhile for UK companies to outsource their IT. Indeed, Accenture is recruiting 1,000 people a month in India (summer 2006) but already reckons the competitive advantage of outsourcing to India will last a maximum of five years, after which they will move on to e.g. China.

Company size and industry structure

The rapid pace of technological development means that companies need to carefully but rapidly assess where they are strategically in order to develop and steer technologies in productive directions. As a consequence, much development has become a 'major-player game', however, as seen later, these major players constantly fear relatively tiny competitors that may stumble onto the killer applications before they do – indeed the 2006 *Sunday Times* Tech-Track number 1 performer was Gamesys, which had never previously featured in the Top 100, achieving an incredible over 300 per cent increase in sales annually! Against this background is the nature of strategically managing innovation itself; technology moves so fast that some companies like Motorola and Nokia are faced with the situation that the PLC (the product life cycle or the selling period) for a product is actually shorter than the development time required. Thus innovative companies rarely achieve a 'cash cow' situation (see Figure 4.3, the Boston Matrix) because they have to abandon their lead products – and indeed cannibalize them) immediately once a better alternative is found (indeed, who could sell a 16-bit computer operating system like Win 95 once a 64-bit one like Win 98 came out?). Another example was the long-awaited replacement for the diskette; as diskette capacity became too small, various replacements (Zip drives, etc.) were introduced but no competitor had the market muscle (as IBM did when it introduced the 3.5˝ HD 1.44 MB diskette in 1987) to establish an industry standard. However, in 1998, the unknown Israeli company M-Systems introduced the flash drive – also known as the USB Pen – which, by 2005, had swept the market worldwide.

Both older and emerging technologies find themselves in their own diffusion S-curves; however, the S-curve for the diffusion of a technology is not the same as the diffusion of use of a technology (for the Diffusion of Innovations Theory, see Rogers, 1983). For example, the speed of diffusion of using spreadsheets to organize office work is different from the speed at which Microsoft Excel is adopted. As Schilling (2005) also points out, the curve for a newer technology – if it is to be successful – can either be steeper than for an existing technology, or it can be higher (Figure 10.1).

Extremely successful technologies may, of course, both diffuse faster and contain added benefit (e.g. the replacement of the vacuum tube by the transistor). Although companies developing new technologies are aware that they 'sit' on an S-curve, it is extremely difficult to find out where they are. For example, IBM thought it had reached the performance limit of ferrous oxide disks and stopped manufacturing them, which opened the market to Fujitsu, who were able to increase the upper edge performance limit eight times before they reached the limit.

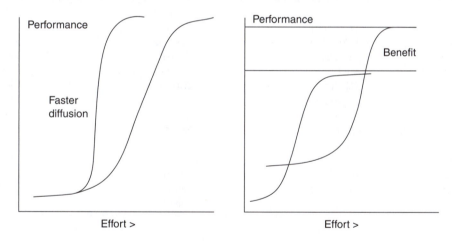

Figure 10.1   The diffusion rates for the use of new technologies can be steeper (faster spread) or higher (increased perceived benefit)

First mover advantage

How and when a technology is introduced is also dependent upon the nature of the technology and proprietary rights (e.g. intellectual property rights like patents). If a technology is hard to imitate (e.g. well protected by one or several patents), then the owner can choose when to enter the market. But when the technology is easy to imitate (which is most often the case), then there is a spread of possibilities. If there are few imitators, then one may often choose a fast race to market and try to harvest 'first mover advantages', but if there are many imitators, then it may be better to adopt a wait and see attitude and await a 'market shakeout'. Low barriers to entry exist in most IT application areas and even when not, barriers can be circumvented (e.g. Xerox thought it possessed total superiority on photocopying technology, but Canon eventually managed to produce superior and cheaper photocopying machines without infringing any of Xerox's patents). Indeed, first mover advantage is actually rather rare if the follower, the second mover, is still an early mover (windows of opportunity open and close rapidly. There is rarely a 'third mover' in major innovations; smaller opportunities for subsequent 'movers' only open as the innovation moves from more radical to more incremental – see Chapter 2) (Table 10.1).

Table 10.1   First movers, followers and winners for a series of high-tech products

Product	First Mover	Follower	Winner
8mm video	Kodak	Sony	Follower
Disposable diaper	Johnson & Johnson 'Chux'	Proctor & Gambol 'Pampers'	Follower
CAT-scanner	EMI	Siemens	Follower
Jet airliner	de Havilland	Boeing	Follower
Float Glass	Pilkington	Corning	First Mover
Instant camera	Polaroid	Kodak	First Mover
Microprocessors	Intel	AMD and Cyrix	First Mover
Safety razor	Gillette	Wilkinson	First Mover
Microwave	Raytheon	Samsung	Follower
PC	Altair (MITS)	IBM	Follower
PC operating systems	Digital Research	Microsoft	Follower
Spreadsheets	VisiCalc	Microsoft	Follower
Word processor	MicroPro	Microsoft	Follower
Web browser	Mosaic	Microsoft	Follower
Video games	Magnavox	Nintendo	Follower
Micropipette	Finnpipette	Gilson	Follower

The dominant design

This situation precipitated the realization that existing technology (the technology that the new product is trying to replace) does not exist alone. As well as switching costs, existing technology is augmented by complementary goods. As shown in Figure 10.2, the increase in technological benefit has to be huge before a new product becomes attractive:

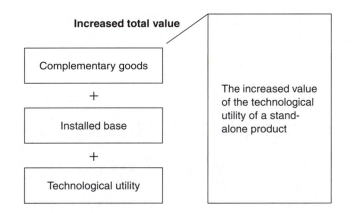

Figure 10.2   User benefits for existing technology consist of the actual technological utility, plus any benefits of an installed base (technological compatibility), plus benefits arising from complementary goods. Thus the technological utility of the new product (right) has to be enormous before it is perceived as having a higher overall benefit value

Thus, in order to become the 'dominant design', new technologies have to be backwards compatible (see Glossary) (in order to keep or increase the installed base) as well as being bundled with complementary goods. This means that new products can successfully be introduced, which have only a marginally increased technological utility (Figure 10.3).

Examples of this are that VHS won over the better technology (Betamax) because of the wide availability of pre-recorded films on VHS; in the early CD years, Philips (the inventors of the CD) was a large sponsor of music companies producing an incredibly wide range of

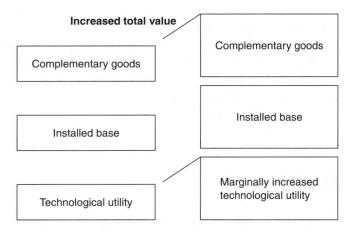

Figure 10.3   New products with only a marginally increased technological utility can be introduced if they match or increase the old contender's installed base and range of complementary goods

re-issues and 'rare' recordings on its CD format; Windows operating systems were successful because many programmers produced Win-compatible software. Even today Apple's iPod addresses these issues through iTunes.

An example of switching costs

To illustrate 'installed base' and 'switching costs', think about if the UK wanted to standardize motoring in line with the rest of the EU – driving on the right. The costs of switching the installed base (i.e. replacing every vehicle, every road junction and every traffic sign) would be astronomical.

Installed base (i.e. backward compatibility) is also an issue which is becoming more important as investments increase, and thus the switching costs increase in parallel. In 1991, both Sega and Nintendo published incredible exaggerations about their market share in the video games sector, hoping to convince customers to buy their products because their proprietary technology was the largest installed base and thus the *de facto* standard. But later Sony would dominate the market, due to the backward compatibility in its PlayStation. Similarly Apple/NeXT marketed a PC with 25MHz chip and 8MB RAM in 1988. Although being technically way ahead of IBM, it was not IBM compatible (the dominant standard since the introduction of the extremely popular IBM 5150 in 1981), so the technological utility was small. Even UNIX has fallen out of favour because there is no one body protecting the standards, so there are many incompatible versions of UNIX.

Thus large new products have enormously higher chances of becoming the dominant design if they have widespread technical compatibility and are propped up by the wide availability of attractive complementary goods. However, the dominant design is rarely 'leading edge', since it has to appeal to everyone, and furthermore the dominant design is only very rarely produced and marketed successfully by the inventor. The view that 'build a better mousetrap and the world will beat a path to your door' (a quote popularly attributed to Ralph Waldo Emerson) is undoubtedly not applicable to high technology innovation.

Digital innovation

Fortunately the IT and other high technology branches do not depend much on new product breakthroughs (refer back to the apex of the pyramid in Figure 2.4, Chapter 2), but mostly on providing 'enabling' services and products to very many branches of industry, including their own. They do this by creating new products and services that are cheaper, more convenient and better than previous products, but which are not expressly IT or high-tech products (e.g. CD-based car maintenance manuals). These are rich areas for entrepreneurs.

Two areas, which are still the domain of larger players, are:

- the convergence of telephony and computer technologies;
- the convergence of media (publishing, music and art production) and computer technologies.

Transmitting speech over the Internet was always a possibility, but lack of sufficient bandwidth was a problem for home users, and the low QoS ('Quality of Service', meaning low quality due to dropped IP packets) were problems. The Voice over Internet Protocol (VoIP) was introduced in 1995 and used commercially by such offerings as Media Ring Talk in 1998. However, these were largely ignored – partly because the Session Initiation Protocol (SIP) was revised in 2002. However, interest returned when Skype (founded 2003) was bought by e-Bay in 2005. Many other major players are now interested in the VoIP technology being developed by small IT companies: Google has announced Google Talk, which features voice chat, Yahoo bought the small start-up Dialpad, and Microsoft bought the small start-up Teleo.

The film *Jurassic Park* (Universal, 1993) was by no means the first to show computer generated graphics, but it was the first blockbuster to show Computer Generated Images (CGI) interacting with live action figures and landscapes in a way that made them seem real. With this, related sectors like IT-supported modelling (e.g. in architecture); 3D transformations; virtual reality, interactive graphics (computer games) and multimedia really started to take off. Computers are now central to art and creative design and IT has revolutionized both the music industry as well as the music industry's business model. Computer-mediated language independence is also a serious sector for those who wish to hear their favourite US pop star sing in Spanish (or German or whatever they choose) and indeed the technology can now be used for the deaf, with small computer-generated marionettes generating the sign language.

Discontinuities open up new avenues

As websites become more common and much cheaper, web bureaux have to radically cut down on expensive programmer time. Thus script libraries – the recycling of software – have become a significant part of Internet business. Building on the ashes

(Continued)

of Boo.com, which invested huge amounts in sophisticated programming, back end technology development and operations, as well as other award winning technology, Venda went on to recycle the Boo.com programming scripts to provide generic software needed to make on-line shops. Venda's founder, Dan Wagner, expects the company value to be £800 million by 2010.

Jan Smith started up End-O-Line, a recycling company offering to take unwanted equipment such as monitors, PCs, printers and photocopiers. She would do a complete audit of the items received and if any piece of equipment still had some value, she would pay the owner for it, if not, the owner would pay her a small fee to take it away. The equipment would then be either refurbished for resale or the parts stockpiled, less than 10 per cent goes into recycling. End-O-Line has 42 employees and turns over more than £3 million annually.

A major sector where small companies (which is most companies and also the point where almost all entrepreneurs start) operate is in enabling other small businesses (SMEs) to operate more profitably. These can be implementing text (SMS) services for taxis or pizzas or absolutely anything else at all. Even pure Internet shopping can still be profitable, although established 'Clicks and Mortar' players take most of the almost 100 million shoppers, figures like over 70 per cent of Internet shoppers shop from their place of work underlines the value of the 'convenience factor'.

Hosting systems is also an option offered by small IT firms. Given the widely held view that building IT systems is a costly and often time-consuming process, SMEs – where losing investments can be especially critical – are going over to Application Service Providers, externally hosted systems. For systems where high security is not mission critical and, since one web-server is basically as good as another, this is a reasonable solution for SMEs who want to keep a low 'IT footprint' in their own business. However, despite the resurgence of systems based on Open Source code, SMEs are increasingly wanting best-practice standard, like Microsoft Dynamics for hosting Customer Relations Management (CRM) systems, because of the added advantage that Microsoft systems are supposed to communicate with each other, lowering the risk of broken deadlines and overspend even further.

However, large numbers of small new companies are either acquired by large companies in convergence-driven mergers or take-overs, or enter into strategic alliances (e.g. Pixlar with Disney, or Ocado with Waitrose). The investment bank Regent Associates reported that in 2006 there were 3,295 purchases worth £221.6 billion in the technology sector, a 25 per cent increase since 2005, with 27 per cent of the M&As in the UK. Note that companies who time their market entry wrongly will be weak and thus become objects for disadvantageous take-overs (e.g. webvan, who timed their entry much earlier than e.g. Ocado).

Chapter summary

The management and implementation of high technology innovation are regarded as strategic goals at national level. However, building a new technological product that works better is rarely a recipe for success. The dominant design is rarely 'leading edge', since it has to appeal to everyone; it is only very rarely produced and marketed successfully by the inventor and it has to have both widespread technical compatibility (to minimize switching costs) and be supported by the wide availability of attractive complementary goods.

The result should be that the S-curve for the diffusion of the use of the new product is either steeper than that for an existing technology, or it can be higher, or both. If this is not the case, then the new product will not become (or remain) the dominant design and will fail.

However, it is difficult to judge where the product is on the S-curve and thus it may well be that even without this knowledge a company may, at very short notice, have to decide whether to abandon their leading products (and indeed actively cannibalize them) with alacrity once a better alternative is found or when they think the end of the S-curve has been reached. Either way, in a universe of extremely short product life cycles, companies involved in high technology innovation are finding it near impossible to reach the classic 'cash cow' (see Chapter 5) situation.

That notwithstanding, entrepreneurial opportunities abound for those interested in applying technological solutions to everyday situations – especially those concerned with increased convenience. Low barriers to entry favour small innovative firms and the simultaneous rapid expansion of the major players into unknown areas has left many gaps open. Small firms inhabiting these 'overlooked' areas are attractive take-over candidates.

References

Rogers, E. M. (1983) *Diffusion of Innovators*. New York: Free Press.

Schilling, M. A. (2005) *Strategic Management of Technological Innovation*. Maidenhead: McGraw-Hill.

Snowdon, B. and Stonehouse, G. (2006) 'Competitiveness in a globalised world: Michael Porter on the microeconomic foundations of the competitiveness of nations, regions, and firms', *Journal of International Business Studies*, 37: 163–75.

Further reading

Bouwman, H., Van Den Hoof, B., Wijngaert, Van De, L. and Van Dijk, V. (2005) *Information and Communication Technology in Organisations*. London: Sage.

Web links

Center for Strategic and International Studies (CSIS): www.csis.org

Council for Science and Technology: www.cst.gov.uk

Department for Business Enterprise & Regulatory Reform: http://www.berr.gov.uk/dius/innovation/index.html

'Intellect', the trade association for the UK hi-tech industry: www.intellectuk.org

Suggestions for exercises

1   Explain what is meant by 'Boo crashed and burnt' and what were the most significant factors in their downfall?
2   Google 'webvan' and compare their failure with the success of 'Ocado'.
3   Have you ever been put on eternal hold by a call centre? What is meant by 'customer backlash' with respect to outsourcing? Imagine how a company could profit from refusing to outsource to other countries.

11 The Biotechnology Revolution

Gary Coulton

Introduction

Common definitions of biotechnology range from very strict interpretations like: 'The use of micro-organisms, such as bacteria or yeasts, or biological substances, such as enzymes, to perform specific industrial or manufacturing processes' (OECD, 2005) to broader definitions such as the one published in 1999 by the journal *Nature Biotechnology* (http://biotech.nature.com):

> The broad definition of biotechnology is simply the industrial use of living organisms (or parts of living organisms) to produce foods, drugs, or other products. The oldest biotechnologies include fermentation and plant and animal hybridization. The newest biotechnologies range from protein separation technologies to genomics and combinational chemistry.

Some fields that fall under the 'broad umbrella' include: bacteriology, biochemical engineering, bioinformatics, bio-processing, cell biology, chromatography, computational and mathematical modelling, developmental and molecular genetics, DNA technologies, electrophoresis, embryology, immunology, materials science, microbiology, nucleic acid chemistry, protein engineering and virology. Furthermore, the Organization for Economic Co-operation and Development takes the view that 'Biotechnology cannot be considered as an industrial sector but rather as a set of technologies developed in the field of life sciences' (OECD, 2005).

As such, this chapter is aimed at students in what can broadly be called Life Sciences.

Biotech is unique in many aspects

Characteristics of the biotech area include that it is being driven by a seemingly unstoppable river of radical innovation and discovery arising from basic research, a constantly changing regulatory environment driven by national and international legislation in areas including safety and patent law, set against a background of paradigm change at both technical and societal levels. Another peculiarity of the biotech start-up industry is that it really makes sense to inhabit specialized incubators and science parks. The costs of e.g. waste disposal (biohazard, radioactive, etc.) and of safe storage of dangerous chemicals, means that start-ups cannot easily 'go it alone' but have to physically cluster and share common facilities. These costly facilities are another factor distinguishing biotech entrepreneurship from other – IT, etc. – types of start-up.

Opportunities for biotech entrepreneurs

The opportunity landscape for entrepreneurship in biotechnology is no different conceptually from any other area of high-investment technology like e.g. aerospace (see Figure 2.3). Delineating the opportunity depends upon several key factors that can be categorized into 'internal', 'organizational' or 'external' factors.

Internal factors

Many very talented individuals have failed as entrepreneurs (see Chapter 1) because they have misjudged what it takes to be successful. Thus, it does not matter how good the idea might be. If the fledgling entrepreneur is not the best person to drive it forward, the embryonic business will certainly die. Perhaps the most important element underpinning a successful biotech enterprise is the personal readiness of the people driving the project, thus the skill set, track record and attitudes of the individual entrepreneur are crucial, especially so because biotechnology by its nature springs from large organizations, where the potential entrepreneur (in these circumstances often called 'intrapreneur') must interact with a wide range of different individuals, e.g. the intrapreneur's bosses, to bring the project out of the organization. This is in addition to convincing venture capitalists (often several), regulatory authorities and – of course – customers, that the idea is worthy. Therefore, first-time entrepreneurs start from something with which they have an intimate knowledge, including not only how something is done, but also practical knowledge of the need of others (many others) to be able to do the same thing.

The expert entrepreneur: Alan Agar

After leaving the RAF as a squadron leader, Alan spent many years in fundamental research, studying all aspects of electron microscope design with the aim of improving resolution. After being Head of Laboratory and project manager for electron microscopes in the USA, his redundancy notice in 1972 triggered some urgent thought. In Alan's own words, 'It was perhaps not too difficult to try to start my own business; I was 52 when made redundant, so there was a very poor prospect of a new job elsewhere. I had plenty of technical knowledge in the field I eventually chose, and knew many of my prospective customers personally. On the negative side, I still had an outstanding mortgage on our home, and had one daughter at university, and two more at school; and had very little capital and no more mortgagable assets!'

Agar Aids started by providing a range of test and calibration specimens for electron microscopes (EM). These could be made by any operator, but were tedious to make, time-consuming, and the commercial sources were of poor quality – so he made a more extended range than was available elsewhere and of higher quality – controlled by EM observation. To supplement these items, he sold a range of good quality EM grids and other small items.

At first, Alan expected consultancy and training courses would be the principal source of income, but by month six, there was only a tiny income from this source. However, they had sold more consumables than expected and so decided to give away the advice for free in the hope that people would be further encouraged to buy consumables. A periodic newsletter was started as a marketing device, and in year 2 they published their first illustrated catalogue, at an initially frightening cost, but the expense of which was paid off in only three months.

Crucial elements are: Alan Agar used his extensive background as an expert user of EM to identify bottlenecks and thus introduce new items that were exactly what the market needed as new techniques appeared. Agar established and maintained a reputation for a complete and reliable service for EM, recognizing that a significant number of people needed a job done that was not satisfied by the currently available offerings. His innovations were of higher quality, saved the customer time and allowed them to concentrate on their science. Agar Scientific, as it became, still provides many hundreds of products to electron microscopists around the world.

As we have seen in earlier chapters in this book, a fundamental understanding of what an innovation comprises is crucial before embarking on an enterprise. Certainly the defining feature of any successful enterprise is that it has an element of innovation (novel service, piece of equipment, process, etc.), but it is a basic misunderstanding that simply moving a good idea from science research to the biotechnology arena is the recipe for commercial success. Most spinouts from universities are established on the basis that great research will convert into a successful company, yet unfortunately it is a maxim within the industry that most fail within around three years – usually because they cannot find a market for their products that is capable of sustaining the cost of delivering the technology.

Organizational factors

Because enterprise in biotechnology is inherently complex, costly and time-consuming, requiring the synergistic interaction of many multidisciplinary skill sets, the likelihood of a single individual bringing a breakthrough technology to market is extremely rare – the stages involved are simply beyond the scope of one person. It may be that new ideas arise from a single mind, but, as seen earlier (Chapters 2, 7 and 8), innovation is a direct consequence of the continuum of work that has been done in preceding years. Individuals sit within a multi-dimensional structure of direct and indirect colleagues (e.g. within a university department or a company) as well as all of the other people around the world engaged in related areas within a myriad of other organizations. Due to the complex framework involved, biotechnology is by definition a team sport and therefore the type, structure and mindset of the organization within which the entrepreneur works (see especially Chapter 8) are key elements influencing likely success.

Is a commercially successful company one that grows each year, delivers profits and, if owned publicly, returns significant dividends to its shareholders? Christensen and Raynor (2003) describe how most big companies are increasingly less able to develop truly innovative products as they grow and their products become more commoditized due to the almost inevitable development pipeline that companies go through as they grow and mature. Although a company arises from its ability to develop and introduce a technology that disrupts the status quo, as it matures, it needs to concentrate on maximizing its share of the emerging market, merging into the trend to cut costs by modularizing components and by outsourcing to cheaper sub-contractors (see Chapters 2, 8 and 16). Finally, the managerial structure is no longer conducive to entrepreneurial endeavour, meaning that bringing a new idea forward is extremely difficult for the entrepreneur/intrapreneur working within the mature organization. The opportunity for the entrepreneur is to find a disrupting technology and get in 'under the radar'. Truly disruptive innovations address latent needs, in other words it does a job that people wished that they could do, but for which there is no current technological answer. Disruptive technology has a good chance of securing a market, i.e. the aim is to look into the crystal ball and determine where the money will be in the future – rather than compete as a small player in an existing market. In biotechnology the biggest success story concerning disrupting technology (i.e. discontinuous in terms of techniques and understanding) was the design and development of the polymerase chain reaction (PCR) by Kary Mullis in 1984.

The organizational entrepreneur: Kary Mullis and PCR

The 1950 to the 1970s were seen as the age of protein biochemistry – the zenith being the discovery of monoclonal antibodies by Köhler and Milstein (1975). While the drive to pursue nucleic acid-based research had been building since the structure of DNA was proposed in 1953, advances in this area were hampered by the absence of robust and reproducible analysis methods. The principal problem was the extremely small amounts of DNA available from a cell or organism and it was not possible to expand short DNA sequences from genomic DNA reliably. By the early 1980s it had been established how DNA was replicated by DNA polymerase enzymes but only linear amplification was possible and many artefacts were introduced into the copied DNA. The exact order of inventive events is shrouded in mystery and controversy, but Mullis – working at the Cetus Corporation – is credited with realizing a theory of a way to start and stop a polymerase enzyme's action at specific points along a single strand of DNA using two small lengths of chemically synthesized DNA that are complementary to the beginning and ends of the sequence to be amplified using cycles of alterations in temperature to develop an exponential chain reaction (Saiki et al., 1985). Thus, at one temperature, double-stranded DNA was denatured into single strands, and was followed by a temperature reduction titrated so that the short oligos anneal preferentially to their complementary sequences. The next step was to add DNA polymerase and deoxynucleotide triphosphates to allow polymerization of the new DNA strands, resulting in two double-stranded DNA molecules from one original. The next stage was to repeat the denaturing step, and so on. Thus, after many repetitions the final result is a product greatly enriched in just the sequence between the two oligonucleotides. It took the efforts of other scientists at Cetus, as well as the separate discovery of thermostable DNA polymerases from bacteria living in deep ocean thermal vents, to make this into a practical technique.

With hindsight, polymerase chain reaction (PCR) was a classical disrupting technology developed within an entrepreneurial company. It was a method that met the needs of people who had a major job to do and who were frustrated by their inability to achieve this objective while not competing directly with any other existing technology. Moreover, it came to the market in a form that was enabling; scientists rapidly realized that it was the key to a massive number of new scientific possibilities. Mullis received the Nobel Prize for Chemistry in 1993.

From this small beginning a multitude of methods, technologies and companies have been spawned. The entire Human Genome Project and the discipline of 'Genomics' owe their progress to PCR. Modern personalized medicine will in time be based upon pharmacogenomics and microarray technologies – all using PCR at one stage or another. The production of many drugs including the newer peptide and protein drugs would not be possible without PCR nor would developments in GM crops that might in some eyes be the answer to the world's food crisis. Entering the term 'PCR' into PubMed returns 285,579 peer-reviewed scientific publications!

For Kary Mullis PCR was first and foremost a scientific conundrum, but, once solved, he realized its potential to address an unmet need and he went on to use his moral authority – based on his track record within Cetus – to mobilize the organization's capabilities to make it a reality. Cetus for their part had created and maintained an atmosphere of innovation (see Chapters 8 and 16) that allowed them to support such ventures. In fact, Mullis did not at that time hold a very elevated position in their organization and was not in a position to order its development.

Of course there are also examples of where what was imagined as a disrupting technology in fact turned out not to be – with the eventual demise of the company in part or whole.

Ciphergen's plan to disrupt the proteomics arena

Recently protein chemistry has re-emerged as 'Proteomics'. This is conceptually similar to genomics in that technologies based mainly on mass spectrometry have allowed the development of massively parallel assays of perhaps 25,000 proteins simultaneously. Bill Rich, the founder of Ciphergen, saw that the field was controlled by a relatively small group of mass spectrometry hardware manufacturers who had a long track record in the field. However, while there was no doubt that the technologies available were immensely powerful, the hardware was expensive to buy and run, requiring expert researchers and statisticians to run it. Ciphergen's business plan was to bring proteomics to researchers who had not previously had access to the technology, such as clinicians and small R&D teams. The technology was aimed fair and square at what is termed protein biomarker discovery with the aim of identifying significant alterations in the levels of proteins, for example, in the sera of patients with cancer as opposed to normal healthy individuals. Ciphergen patented novel technology based upon surface-enhanced laser desorption and ionization–time of flight mass spectrometry (SELDI-TOF). Essentially, this is a marriage of classical chromatography on a solid support (protein arrays) with standard matrix-associated laser desorption and ionization mass spectrometry (MALDI-TOF). The system is excellent at finding biomarkers, but its Achilles' heel is that the biomarkers are delineated as differences in the amplitude of peaks in mass spectra only – the mass resolution of the Ciphergen mass spectrometer was not sufficient to identify proteins based upon mass alone and the sensitivity of the first machines was poor relative to the high-end machines available from other manufacturers. Indeed, it was only some eight years later that methods were developed for the actual identification of these differentially expressed proteins. Thus, the technology was not acceptable to the cognoscenti who were already expert in mass spectrometry and consequently the development of methods for the identification of the Ciphergen biomarkers did not come in time to save the company from repetitive losses and Ciphergen sold its biotechnology division to Bio-Rad in 2006 (who, interestingly, did not have a mass spectrometer in their product offering).

So, why was Ciphergen technology not disrupting? It appeared to offer proteomics at a low cost and fulfil unmet needs for the job to be done; it was cheaper than its competitors and did not require deep expertise. Yet instead they were seen as competing head-on with established players by offering a mass spectrometer with relatively poor performance. If Ciphergen had started marketing complementary downstream identification protocols much earlier, they would have had an impact.

Ciphergen is an object lesson to the entrepreneur and exemplifies the 'entrepreneur's paradox'. On the one hand, the safest ground for your innovation is in the area in which you have expertise and a track record, but, on the other, this almost inevitably implies developing ideas that are in direct competition with existing powerful players. There is no easy answer and it depends on how disruptive you want to be.

Where do disrupting biotechnologies arise?

While research does not equal innovation, scientific innovation cannot occur without research. The number of researchers based in universities in the general area of biology/medicine and allied subjects dwarfs the number in all the world's companies put together by several orders of magnitude. Furthermore, university research is without boundaries – limited only by academic interest – whereas company research is constrained by the bottom line. Thus, university research output should be a rich feeding ground for the entrepreneur, either an academic who wants to engage in the knowledge transfer process into the industrial world, or an external entrepreneur wanting to in-licence intellectual property. Indeed, the atmosphere of the 1980s and early 1990s was highly supportive of the development of spin-outs from universities but did not last – the biotechnology bubble burst almost alongside the dotcom bubble. Reasons for the collapse include that, until very recently, UK university academics had a very poor training in the way that businesses run and, indeed, for many, their only contact with industry was with the sales representatives of the companies from which they bought reagents and equipment. Others may have acted as scientific consultants, but, again, in such a role they would have been excluded from the actual business decision-making process. Many mistakes were made, such as not being able to discern good money from bad; not knowing basic business procedures; not being able to constrain spending; and, finally, not knowing when to exit. It would be invidious to give a specific example of such a disaster.

However, there is massive evidence of successful transition from academe to industry e.g. a tour around modern Göttingen will show that most of the modern industry there owes its origins to academic start-ups: Hoyer & Schinder, Zeiss, Deltalaser (optics); Schleicher and Schull (ultrafiltration) and dozens more are all major employers and all of them owe their existence to the university. Other notable academic start-ups around the globe include Amersham & Pharmacia (now part of General Electric), Monsanto, Sandoz, Hoffmann-La Roche and Novo-Nordisk. Let's take a look at what appears so far to be an example of the best success story, Genentech.

The most successful university biotechnology spin-out so far?

In 1976, venture capitalist Robert A. Swanson met biochemist Dr Herbert W. Boyer and within three hours Genentech was born. Boyer (University of California, San Francisco) and geneticist Stanley Cohen pioneered a new scientific field called recombinant DNA technology.

Though Swanson and Boyer faced scepticism from both the academic and business communities, they forged ahead with their idea. Within a few short years, they had successfully demonstrated the viability of using recombinant DNA technology to develop products with practical applications and, in so doing, launched a whole new industry. Genentech scientists started making medicines by splicing genes into fast-growing bacteria that then produced therapeutic proteins. Today Genentech continues to use genetic engineering techniques to develop medicines that address significant unmet needs and provide clinical benefits to millions of patients worldwide. Well-known products include Herceptin for the treatment of breast cancer and Avastin for patients with metastatic carcinoma of the colon or rectum.

(*Source*: Paraphrased from Genentech's account: www.gene.com)

Today start-ups in biotechnology can be classified by what type of discovery or idea they are building upon. Clearly major projects like basic research and new drug discovery tend to be the products of large research labs headed by renowned professors and supported by hordes of post-docs, but this is not always the case and occasionally some excellent ideas originate from final year research projects. And sometimes students realize that they are not employees bound by employment law and hence own the intellectual property (IPR) generated from their research project (unless contracts have been exchanged stating otherwise)! However, the general rule still holds because students most often lack the financial resources or business acumen to capitalize upon such IPR, e.g. the new Federal Drugs Administration's critical path for novel drug development pipeline takes five and sometimes ten years (in the case of vaccines) to make it past regulatory approval and exposure to the market. Thus, this arena comprises exclusively of companies and consortia of investors with very deep pockets. Thus, with long lead times and the massive complexity and cost of clinical trials (up to 10,000 participants in multiple countries, each with different regulatory landscapes), the development of blockbuster drugs inhabits the heavy end of the venture capital market. The cost of bringing a new drug to market is around $50–100 million.

Opportunities in outsourcing

Paradoxically there are many opportunities opening as big companies find it cheaper to close their expensive research labs and follow a two-pronged strategy of outsourcing some research to universities (or highly specialized small companies), as well as moving routine screening to third-party commercial laboratories with lower overheads (particularly in the developing world – thus mirroring developments seen e.g. in the manufacture of PC components, etc.). In 2007, Pfizer closed its well-regarded Ann Arbor Research Center and two manufacturing sites – Brooklyn, NY, and Omaha, NE – stating that this would simplify its R&D organization and improve productivity. A senior executive (Pfizer, 2007) said, 'This will give us the "best of both worlds", the entrepreneurial spirit of a small company, aligned with the world-class technologies, platforms and capabilities that only a company of Pfizer's size can provide.' Since large companies seldom disrupt themselves and survive intact (Chapter 2), this may reflect concern about the very few new blockbuster drugs coming onto the market while most of the existing ones are coming to the end of their patent protection.

Entrepreneurship for the recent graduate

A small biotech with a defined offering in a defined therapeutic area may only require $2-5 million over a five-year period. Even so, such figures cannot be achieved by business angels, but only by groups of venture capitalists syndicating together (see Chapters 2 and 6). If the project is well advanced, it could also be an interesting investment for one of the smaller investment trusts run by established banks. There are many VCs specializing in biotech and life sciences (Business.com lists around 30 such firms) and opportunities for establishing start-ups are best in the small equipment sector or specialized tools/services/reagents sector. Indeed, the financial service 'value line' (www.valueline.com) predicts 13 per cent future growth in the biomedical devices industry (benchmarked on the industry leaders: Medtronic and Boston Scientific). This market is attractive because being upstream in the supply chain/value network (see Chapter 2 and Figure 11.1) means that potential customers are many – universities, large and small companies, and perhaps even end-users. But successful entry depends – as always – upon having a good eye either for a service that will cut costs for the big players, or providing something that satisfies a currently unmet need.

Small is beautiful

There are a growing number of small companies using standard techniques to offer DNA fingerprinting and expert witness services. Presently they are concentrated around human issues (paternity, etc.) but these could snowball. For instance, is the grass on the lawn really the expensive grass cultivar that was ordered? Or do customers want to determine if the food they buy from certain shops is genetically modified? Obviously, overheads incurred like regulatory burdens (e.g. acquiring expert witness status) may still be high, but legislation always has to be taken into account.

If enough people need a job done – and they want the results badly – then there is a commercial opportunity; it just has to be delivered at an acceptable cost and level of reliability.

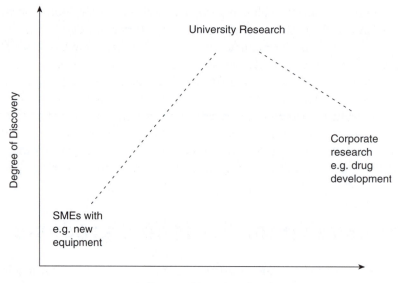

Figure 11.1   Illustration of three of the sub-sectors of the biotech industry and how they differ with regard to investment needs. Graduate entrepreneurship is mostly confined to the lower left-hand corner; note that from this position SMEs are well placed to supply other players with relatively high-value products

Indeed, many start-ups in biotechnology equipment have sprung from academics who saw a very specific need, for example, for professionally produced apparatus for protein and nucleic acid separation by electrophoresis (until the early 1980s this was done largely on 'homemade' equipment). Another example is a company that produced small chromatography columns, which fitted inside centrifuge tubes, for the gel or affinity filtration of very small volumes. However ingenious, it must be admitted that most people in the world do not want to de-salt 2 micro-litres of sterile solution, so such products were restricted to the innovators as referred to in the classic 'Diffusion of Innovation' theory (Rogers, 1983, see Chapter 2). The challenge for such companies to cross the 'innovation chasm' (Moore, 1995, see Chapter 5) is huge and depends upon the ability of the company to survive until the later adopters step in to buy the product. The irony is that with the advent of proteomics there is now an increasing demand – 20 years later – for the filtration and concentration of small volumes of solutions. However, the larger chromatography companies are now reaping the benefits after acquiring the IPR cheaply from the originating small companies. Nevertheless, it is an example of the entrepreneur identifying a need and developing a technology with which it can be satisfied.

Such small companies often come to equilibrium with less than 10 employees in a highly specialized niche market, but they are inherently unstable because their small size prevents them from establishing themselves in several niches simultaneously. This means that the more successful of these companies are soon bought up by the bigger firms (e.g. Biometra by Whatman), whereas others stumble along until they fail. Additionally, many small highly specialized companies actively erode their own customer base: the peculiarities of biotechnology include that some reagents such as DNA-based vectors are capable of bio-replication and companies selling bio-reproducing materials such as phages, plasmids, cloning vectors, etc. actually lose a customer every time they make a sale, as one sale could cover the customer's needs (theoretically) perpetually. This problem could be offset by setting up a pipeline of new vector development or acquisition from academics under licence, but this, in time, becomes merely a sustaining activity with low profit margins. Another option is to succumb to a merger or acquisition: academic start-up Amersham merged with Pharmacia and Nycomed in 1997 before being subsumed into General Electric. This underlines the importance of having an exit strategy (see Chapter 6).

One could be forgiven for thinking that first movers would have competitive advantage, after all, how many different designs are there for e.g. micropipettes? But the lesson in biotechnology – as it is for other industries – is that first movers rarely become dominant (see Chapter 10). The market innovator in adjustable micropipettes (Finnpipette) soon had to yield to imitators (Gilson as well as Eppendorf), despite there being very little obvious technical difference between these three companies' products (Gilson – another academic start-up – had an ejector mechanism for the disposable tip). In fact, many a new postgraduate student is told that they need to master how to use a 'Gilson' – the trade name now being synonymous with micropipette!

The customer mindset

The problem of over-specialization led a number of companies to diversify into the apparatus market that was complementary to their existing products, e.g. integrated kits including dedicated consumables, like Clontech's subtraction hybridization system. Although this may seem like 'save the customer time and allow them to concentrate on their science' (see the case of Alan Agar, p. 124), it is vital to really research the mind-set of potential clients. Assume a novel consumable (a tube) is envisaged that fits well into an automated process like high throughput cell-based assays (part of drug discovery pipelines). If the novel consumable is of unproven worth, the large company will not move its leviathan-like research decision-making system (nor its equally cumbersome purchasing system) to take advantage of the modest improvements that the new technology may bring. Similarly, the university small-scale research units will also not adopt, as they do not have the investment capability to invest in large-scale automation. So, not only is the instrumentation market treacherous without detailed market research (Chapter 5), but equally so the consumable market, which indeed has polarized between the high-prestige e.g. human research customer segment and the less centralized bioscience research sector. At the one end, large research organizations save money by squeezing supplier margins on indispensable disposables like latex gloves, while at the other end, it is normal to see researchers in small university labs save money by washing disposables for re-use and racking micropipette tips by hand prior to autoclaving.

Thus, companies who migrated to the disposables market soon found that having only a few very powerful customers (the customer mindset) made the market much less attractive (see Porter's analysis, Chapter 4) and have often been driven to move production to areas of the world with lower overheads, principally labour costs. Some have also tried a mixed strategy, e.g. giving the capital equipment away free of charge, knowing that the equipment needs a continuous supply of expensive disposables or reagents to run. However, this is a very high-risk strategy that is open to a new disrupting technology.

Paradigm shift – the world changes around you

In certain cases what starts out as a highly competitive arena can disappear. The rapid pace of development (paradigm shifts) in particular areas of biotechnology have also been a significant factor in determining the dominant design of new technology. For example, the company LKB produced an excellent flatbed apparatus for rocket immuno-electrophoresis, but uncertainty led them to try to develop this into a 'multi-kit' for a range of protein analysis techniques (SDS-PAGE, electrofocusing, etc.). LKB also ignored that in the 1990s (because of the Human Genome Project and others) the focus of research was moving rapidly away from protein analysis to nucleic acids. In brief, the limits of the design were soon reached – a kit only for proteins, not nucleic acids – that did nothing very well. Shortly afterwards, LKB was swallowed by Pharmacia. However, Pharmacia also failed to properly grasp the paradigm shift and nucleic acid instrumentation was transiently monopolized by more flexible firms like Bio-Rad, as well as new entrants like Hybaid and Invitrogen (Pharmacia being subsumed by General Electric). The irony again is that a new paradigm shift has occurred and the main bioscience interest is once again with proteins, but unfortunately LKB are no longer here to reap the rewards.

Paradigm shift among consumers

In the 1970s and 1980s, agronomists concentrated on studying the interaction between legume plants (pulses) and Rhizobial bacteria because the symbiosis between the two enabled the plant to fix atmospheric nitrogen and thus flourish without fertilizers, reducing e.g. the amount of nitrate in ground water. Twenty years of research on this system produced a lot of what we know about plant biochemistry today. For example, the first in vitro translation of plant mRNA was using soybean root nodule leghaemoglobin. Then, in the 1990s, research on nitrogen fixation collapsed due to public eating habits swinging dramatically away from pulses (peas, beans, etc.) to hard varieties of wheat (durum, etc). Even staples like potato (not to mention cabbage, turnip, etc.) were threatened in what EU experts called 'the spaghetti-eating revolution'. Today – another 20 years on – research on nitrogen fixation is still largely abandoned and the majority of the ancillary start-up companies (production of Rhizobial inoculants, etc.) went bankrupt – not to mention that artificial fertilizers are still applied to agricultural land and nitrate in ground water is still a health hazard.

Thus, the paradigm shift – the sudden popularity of pasta – which swept the food sector was completely outside the control of anyone in agroindustry, yet had far-reaching consequences for biotech entrepreneurs.

Bio-Rad fared better than the LKB example above and maintained their independence by expanding by acquiring a number of novel technologies over several years, currently covering a wide range of technologies from protein chemistry/proteomics to cutting-edge microscopy.

Further barriers: the legislative environment

Success in the biotech sector is to a great extent dependent upon public acceptance (e.g. the present debate on 'GM foods') and political legislation as much as the needs of the end user. Several works of legislation, including the European Union's drinking water Directive (91/676/EEC) and Directive 2002/96/EC on waste electrical equipment, have all failed to provide the promised entrepreneurial opportunities. Several companies invested heavily in water treatment research in anticipation of Directive 91/676/EEC and then flopped spectacularly.

What's happening right now: stem cell biology

Regenerative medicine promises to be the source of new treatments for a range of inherited and chronic diseases. There are two main divisions in stem cell biology: embryonic and tissue-derived.

Human embryonic stem cells derived from early fertilized human embryos can generate cell lines capable of differentiating into any cell type and the aim is to develop industrial-scale methods for the generation of cells for regenerative medicine (i.e. injecting them into individuals lacking normal function of that cell type due to inherited mutation, disease, etc.). In 2001, President Bush announced that federal funds may be awarded for research using human embryonic stem cells if certain criteria are met but this is complicated by State/Federal conflicts. As long as cloning is not performed,

(Continued)

private companies in the USA are free to work with and exploit human embryos, again under certain conditions. Conversely, in the UK, the legal landscape gives broader support for such efforts, however, the UK may not draw much competitive advantage because the patent 'space' around stem cells is unclear, as is the accessibility of a market for UK-produced stem cell products in the USA, which is by far the biggest potential market for regenerative medicine.

Meanwhile researchers in the USA are free to investigate tissue-derived (also called 'adult') stem cells for the same purpose. If these endeavours bear fruit, they will obviate the need for embryonic stem cells and destroy overnight the perceived advantage the UK has, as these cells are much easier to obtain. Indeed, the legal situation surrounding use of human embryonic stems cells is again under review at time of press. Thus one could imagine that a good strategy would be to develop a generic platform of technologies appropriate for both embryonic and adult stem cells.

This example underlines again that the successful entrepreneur should look to where the money is going to be and not where it is now – and that only lawyers build businesses on legislation.

Chapter summary

The degree of success of a new entrepreneurial venture depends upon appreciating and dealing successfully with a number of clashes that include:

1   Individual vs organizational objectives.
2   Ideas vs utility.
3   Utility vs consumer acceptability.

The high expense incurred means that biotechnology involves large organizations and thus innovations often occur by 'intrapreneurship', therefore, it is vital for the individual entrepreneur to have a deep and full understanding of the sector in which they wish to engage and a broad range of scientific, business and personal skills to achieve their aims.

The generation of novel research findings from the world's universities is almost immeasurable, but immensely chaotic. The majority of this output is useless to the entrepreneur as the IP is often poorly protected and its ownership is usually fragmented. Not only this, but much of it is not needs driven. In other words, the invention was not a consequence of a careful analysis of what jobs are needed to be done by people in the real world – yet the only basis for a viable business is supplying real tools for real jobs.

Success in the biotech sector is dependent upon public acceptance and political legislation as much as the needs of the end user. Equally, the sector is subject to paradigm shifts – often based on new discoveries in unforeseen areas of science – that sweep away the market and destroy the best-laid business plans. Long lead times mean that the development of biotech products is particularly sensitive to paradigm shifts.

A large part of the biotechnology sector demands extremely high investment and is almost certainly beyond the reach of the sole graduate entrepreneur; however, there are still very large portions of the supply chain – equipment, reagents, and services – which offer immense and lucrative opportunities.

Start-up companies should aim for 'good' sources of funding that underpin modest early growth but a short lead-time to profitability, followed by re-investment to support diversification into related areas.

References

Christensen, C. M. and Raynor, M. E. (2003) *The Innovator's Solution: Creating and Sustaining Successful Growth*. Boston: Harvard Business School Press.

Köhler, G. and Milstein, C. (1975) 'Continuous cultures of fused cells secreting antibody of predefined specificity', *Nature*, 256: 495–7.

Moore, G. (1995) *Inside the Tornado*. New York: Harper Business.

OECD (2005) Statistical definition of biotechnology. Available at: http://www.oecd.org/document/42/0,2340,en_2649_33703_1933994_1_1_1_1,00.html

Pfizer (2007) 'Pfizer announces priorities to drive improved performance, position company for future success and enhance total shareholder return', Pfizer press release. Available at: www.pfizer.com

Rogers, E. M. (1983) *Diffusion of Innovators*. New York: Free Press.

Saiki, R. K., Scharf, S., Faloona, F., Mullis, K. B., Horn, G. T., Erlich, H. A. and Arnheim, N. (1985) 'Enzymatic amplification of beta-globin genomic sequences and restriction site analysis for diagnosis of sickle cell anaemia', *Science*, 230: 1350–4.

Further reading

Christensen, C. M. and Raynor, M. E. (2003) *The Innovator's Solution: Creating and Sustaining Successful Growth*. Boston: Harvard Business School Press.

Gresshoff, P. M. (1996) *Technology Transfer of Plant Biotechnology*. New York: CRC Press Inc.

Web links

www.advisorybodies.doh.gov.uk/uksci/uksci-reportnov05.pdf

www.biotech.nature.com

www.business.com

www.guardian.co.uk/science/story/0,,2074597,00.html

www.gene.com

www.isscr.org/public/regions/index.cfm

www.pfizer.com

http://stemcells.nih.gov/policy/

www.valueline.com

www.ventureworthy.com/Biotech-venture-capital-fund.asp

www.versantventures.com

Suggestions for exercises

1 Comment on what is meant by 'disruptive technology' and 'paradigm change'.
2 Biotechnology developments often need long lead times. Why? How does this make biotechnology entrepreneurship different from other types of entrepreneurship?

12 Green Entrepreneurship

A sustainable development challenge

Anne Chick

Introduction

Entrepreneurship is widely acknowledged to be the engine of economic growth (see Chapter 2) and entrepreneurship and innovation thrive on discontinuities. There is general agreement that several major discontinuities, for example, global warming and associated cultural change, face us in the near future. This chapter explores this topic in more detail and is suitable for students studying most disciplines, including architecture and design or politics, human geography, sustainability, etc.

The imminent discontinuities

There is mounting evidence that, over the past few decades, traditional economic growth has caused ecological deprivation and social injustice: climate change, unacceptable pollution levels, loss of biodiversity and land degradation, as well as unfair trading and unjust employment practices. This suggests that major changes in the global and industrial systems are needed if the world is to achieve a sustainable state before the middle of this century (Volery, 2002). One major consequence is the rising pressure from consumers, governments and lobby-groups for the global business community to adopt environmentally and socially responsible practices. As seen in various chapters of this book, unmet customer needs are the drivers for entrepreneurs.

It would be foolish to claim that the private sector has totally embraced the need to become 'greener' (shorthand for moving towards environmental sustainability) although the topic is increasingly prominent in business decision-making, strategic planning and performance management. This has created environmental entrepreneurship opportunities both within and outside existing businesses. Of most relevance to this book is the growth in 'green-green' businesses – businesses that are founded on the principle of sustainability (Isaak, 1998). This chapter will focus on presenting the opportunities of 'green-green' start-ups and businesses in order to stimulate interest and inspire students and others who maybe interested in becoming 'ecopreneurs'.

Green entrepreneurship

As this book has already emphasized, entrepreneurs are catalysts for change and innovation in society. They should play a central role in shifting our economy from being based on exploiting natural resources – soil, water, biodiversity, climate (which, once lost, can never be replaced) to one that could lead to a future that preserves and conserves these resources. Never before has there been such an opportunity and imperative for innovation that meets the needs of consumers without damaging the planet's natural resource base.

The road to long-term sustainability will require more efficiency – a management strategy that promotes environmental and economic performance. The World Business Council for Sustainable Development (WBCSD) first coined the concept of eco-efficiency. They defined it as 'the delivery of competitively priced goods and services that satisfy human needs and bring quality of life, while progressively reducing ecological impacts and resource intensity throughout the life-cycle, to a level at least in line with the earth's estimating carrying capacity' (WBCSD, 1997: 3).

These worthy aspirations have had shaky advancements. *The Economist* (2002) argues that progress has been achieved, largely, due to three factors:

- more decision-making at local level;
- technological innovation;
- the rise of market forces in environmental matters.

Entrepreneurs play a central role in the last two factors as they can identify opportunities and bring new technologies and concepts into active commercial use (Shane and Vankataraman, 2000).

What is sustainable development?

The term sustainable development now generates a huge literature on meanings and interpretation. This chapter will not expand on this topic further apart from linking it to entrepreneurship. In the late 1980s, the World Commission on Environment and Development (WCED, 1987), led by Gro Brundtland, developed the concept of sustainable development in an attempt to reconcile economic growth with environmental and social issues. At the Rio Earth Summit in 1992, the agenda for sustainable development (as stated in Agenda 21) related two sets of issues. The resulting problems from the developed, industrialized nations' material consumption and production processes are in contrast to the problems of poverty which beset the people of poorer countries. As Volery (2002) clearly explains, 'Sustainable development seeks to resolve the environmental problems of affluence and the social problems of poverty within a transformed approach to the process of development.'

A concept often used is the triple bottom line (TBL) – the three pillars of sustainability: economic, environmental and social. TBL is the simultaneous pursuit of economic prosperity, environmental quality and social equity (Elkington, 1997).

One side effect of this increasing pressure on businesses is 'Greenwash', the habit of large corporates buying up small green companies regularly harvests complaints from lobbying organizations such as the Ethical Consumer (www.ethicalconsumer.org).

Defining ecopreneurship

Ecopreneurs identify environmental innovations and their market opportunity and successfully implement these innovations resulting in new products or services (Lober, 1998; Isaak, 2005; Schaltegger, 2005). Most authors do not restrict their definition of ecopreneurship to single factors such as founders of environmentally oriented organizations or environmental intrapreneurs who are operating within an existing organization. Instead, most definitions also consider ecopreneurial organizations, i.e. organizations that behave ecopreneurially and foster ecopreneurs and environmental intrapreneurs.

An ecopreneurial organization: Remarkable (Pencils) Ltd

Remarkable was established in 1996 by Edward Douglas Miller to explore the possibility of turning one everyday waste item into a new product. He began by experimenting with plastic cups with the aim of trying to turn one plastic cup into a pencil (Micklethwaite and Chick, 2005). Why? Because it had never been done before and it would prove to the world that you could take one everyday, throwaway item that would usually just go straight to landfill and, instead, turn it into a new product which was fun, functional and had a long second life (Remarkable, 2007).

(Continued)

In early 2003, the company was still a 'micro' enterprise with fewer than 10 full-time employees, dedicated to the manufacture of a range of stationery products from recycled plastics, rubber tyres, leather, and paper (Micklethwaite and Chick, 2005). It was a successful green niche product company but wanted to take recycled stationery into the mainstream and sell products via large supermarket outlets, but unfortunately their brand was largely unrecognized by consumers. The company realized that to break out of its niche market it needed to develop its marketing and its brand. Thus a new brand was launched in early 2004, following a branding research project with the Sustainable Design Research Centre at Kingston University, Dragon Brands and Will Harris (the marketer behind the Orange and O2 brands).

Remarkable's 'I used to be' range of stationery is now stocked in hundreds of Sainsbury's and Tesco stores as well as other retailers. In addition, Remarkable works with Habitat and Waterstones to develop bespoke recycled ranges for them.

In response to demand, Remarkable moved from its 9,000 sq. ft factory in south-west London to a 40,000 sq. ft factory in the West Midlands in 2005. The company continues to develop and expand. It is moving towards becoming a sustainable enterprise by focusing not only on using recycled materials but also by making its production more sustainable by promoting energy-saving activities and considering all aspects of the product's life cycle. In 2006, the factory was converted to run off recycled cooking oil (Remarkable, 2007).

Gerlach (2003) undertook a comprehensive review of the key conceptual approaches of ecopreneurship, social entrepreneurship and sustainability entrepreneurship. She emphasized that the terms 'ecopreneurship' and 'environmental entrepreneurship' are used synonymously and mean 'innovative behaviour of single actors or organisations operating in the private business sector which see environmental aspects as a core objective and competitive advantage'. More specifically, Isaak (2005) uses the expression 'ecopreneur' to mean individuals who create green-green businesses in order to radically transform the economic sector in which they operate. 'Ecopreneurs are counter-cultural or social entrepreneurs who want to make a social statements, not just money.' Taylor and Walley (2004) develop this theme, distinguishing ecopreneurs from other types of green entrepreneurs who pursue profit goals by means of ecological or socially orientated businesses. In the context of the need to move towards a truly sustainable society, Isaak and Taylor and Walley stress ecopreneurs are increasingly seen as crucial change agents, or champions, driving the sustainability transformation process. Thus it is clear that whatever the rationale for categorizing types of green entrepreneur (whether ethically-driven, opportunistically-driven or whatever), the unifying factor is that they all contribute to the move towards a sustainable society.

The development of the green market

The business case for sustainable development and the greening of industry is based on many different arguments but, as Schaper (2005) points out, the entrepreneurial perspective has until recently been overlooked. Academics are now seeking to analyse and explain the behaviour and world-view of ecopreneurs to pass on lessons and advice that may signal barriers and the required support that can help green entrepreneurship. As we have seen in earlier chapters, entrepreneurs are individuals who are able to identify new commercial ventures (Chapter 2). Authors stress this often involves a willingness to 'think outside the box' and examine issues in fundamentally different ways from more conventional approaches (Chapter 3). Then they incubate ideas and champion their adoption, assemble the resources needed to bring the idea to commercial reality (such as money, people and technologies) and, finally to launch (Chapter 6) and grow the business venture (Chapters 8, 9 and 16). By identifying an unresolved problem, or unmet need or want, which they then proceed to satisfy, they transform the existing status quo (Schaper, 2005). The adoption of environmentally responsible business practices can, conceivably, open up an additional range of opportunities for entrepreneurs. The examples cited in this chapter illustrate convincingly that there are a growing number of opportunities in green entrepreneurship.

Are environment and economics opposed?

The move towards addressing sustainable development in a business context provides numerous niches that enterprising individuals and firms can successfully identify and service. These can include (Schaper, 2005; Khare, 2003):

- development of new products and services;
- improvements in the efficiency of existing firms;
- new methods of marketing;
- reconfiguration of existing business models and practices.

Considering the apparent antagonism between environment and economics, Volery (2002) warns that there seems to be no painless pathway to sustainable growth and Walley and Whitehead (1994) remark in the same spirit that discussions on 'win-win' solutions are cheap, while environmental initiatives are not, because of four main factors:

1. 'Easy' environmental problems have been fixed.
2. As environmental challenges become more complex, costs are rising.
3. Costs are destined to increase even more, especially since the increase in regulations shows no signs of abating.
4. New policy instruments such as tradable permits, pollution taxes, and quotas require in-depth cost–benefit analysis and complicate the management's decision-making process.

Governments, pressure groups, the media, academics and advisers nevertheless agree that there will be an increasing number of green entrepreneurial opportunities in the future because of several factors:

- Entrepreneurs will always find opportunities to make profits and these have been growing in number since environmental concerns have become pressing.
- The 'push' factors: regulations, costs of waste disposal, and scarcity of natural resources.
- The 'pull' factors: consumer demand and green partnerships.

These latter two are worth looking at in greater detail.

The 'push' factors

Environmental regulations and increasing environmental costs, such as for waste disposal, force companies to innovate improved or new products and services. At the same time, some natural resources have become scarcer and more expensive. Hence business strategies built on a radically more productive use of natural resources can solve many environmental problems at a profit (Lovins et al., 1999).

The 'pull' factors

Another source of opportunities for environmentally and socially/ethically conscious goods and services comes from the marketplace. Recently there has been a lot of media coverage of environmental and ethical consumer issues, especially relating to the climate change debate. It is predicted that this will bring an increase in green consumer awareness, markets, goods and business management. There is evidence this has already happened in a number of markets such as the travel and confectionery sectors. For example, a general drive towards conscience-led eating has resulted in the confectionery market scrambling to keep up with ethical consumers, particularly chocolate products where customers are becoming increasingly aware of the ethical and environmental concerns surrounding cocoa production. According to the Pesticide Action Network (www.pan-uk.org), cocoa is second only to cotton in its high use of pesticides, however, organic production of the beans entails natural methods of pest control and has been praised for its contribution to sustainable farming (Pesticide Action Network North America, 2007).

Green and Black's

In May 2005, Cadbury Schweppes acquired the organic brand Green and Black's, which is now the UK's leading supplier of organic chocolate. This company is a testament to the fact that consumers are willing to pay more for certain ethical products, in this case, organic fair trade chocolate, and are attracted to green companies.

Their sales rose from £10m (€14.8m) to £50m (€73.8m) between the years 2003 to 2006 (Boal, 2006).

Green and Black's was founded in 1991 by the journalist Josephine Fairley and her partner Craig Sams, an organic foods specialist, who were inspired by the taste of the cocoa they savoured on a holiday in Belize. Fairley was a chocoholic who had repeatedly returned from assignments abroad to complain that the dark chocolate she found in other countries was not readily available in the UK. After deciding to make their own chocolate, the couple chose the name Green to represent the organic nature of the product and Black for the 70 per cent cocoa solids it would contain (Green and Black's, 2007). Green and Black's strategic decision was that rather than dominate the organic chocolate market (of which it already had about 95 per cent share), they would compete as a chocolate in their own right, using organic as one of the things that sets them apart. (Burrell, 2006).

The rise of the Green and Black's brand has not been entirely smooth. Its reputation has had to cope with disquiet among their customer base due to them now being owned by a giant food conglomerate. Indeed, William Kendall, the chief executive, felt obliged to post a notice on the company website to appease malcontents. Kendall argues that Cadbury was checked out 'pretty thoroughly' and scores highly on ethical issues. 'We do not have time for prejudice at Green and Black's and this includes a prejudice that all big companies and the people who work for them are bad,' he says (Burrell, 2006; Siegle, 2005).

Characteristics of the green marketplace

The two major characteristics of the green marketplace are:

1   The more people believe that they as an individual (or many working in concert) can 'make a difference', the greater the likelihood that they will buy greener products and services (Ottman, 2004).
2   But although public opinion polls consistently show that consumers would prefer to choose a green product and service over one that is less friendly to the environment, these good intentions are not always transferred into action (Micklethwaite, 2004; Ottman, 2004) because consumers are unlikely to compromise on traditional product attributes, such as convenience, availability, price, quality and performance (Meyer, 2001).

Thus Ginsberg and Bloom (2004) emphasize that there is no single green marketing strategy that is right for every company. Indeed, one further complication is that there is rising confusion about transparency; how green is the product?

Transparency in the 'responsible travel market'

Awareness of ethical travel issues is already strong among British travellers, in that around a fifth of the population is prepared to pay to offset carbon emissions from flights (only 2 per cent of UK consumers' carbon is currently offset) and indeed Britain has a budding green travel market with over a million responsible holidays, worth a total of £409m in 2006 and forecast to grow to 25 per cent of the travel market.

Obstacles to a greater take-up of ethical travel products include public scepticism over corporate practices and consumers' saturation with ethical concerns. An independent study found that an overwhelming 63 per cent of consumers believe that companies are 'just using green and ethical issues for PR purposes' and that greater transparency and consistency among carbon offsetting businesses would increase consumer confidence.

(Adapted from: Katz, 2007)

External market influences can range from the 'push factors' such as regulation, economic incentives to 'softer' socio-cultural influences such as personal networks and education (Taylor and Walley, 2004). Figure 12.1 shows Taylor and Walley's proposed range of influences in the external environment of the potential green entrepreneur. In some ways it resembles Porter's Five Forces (see Chapter 4), but this model includes some 'question marks' because it is not clear at this stage, what specific influences might be identified by individual entrepreneurs. Taylor and Walley (2004) explain:

> The black inner circle illustrates the view, as reflected in the entrepreneurial literature, that the influence of the external environment is mediated by the individual characteristics of the entrepreneur – such as his/her personality and competence. These will all impact on the nature of the green business that emerges.

Fostering ecopreneurial behaviour

Although the body of literature on the topic of ecopreneurship is small, it is growing and this interest is spilling out into the broader entrepreneurship texts and teaching. Initiatives designed to specifically foster and promote ecopreneurship are mushrooming, as evidenced not only by the business schools introducing modules and units in environmental entrepreneurship in higher education institutions.

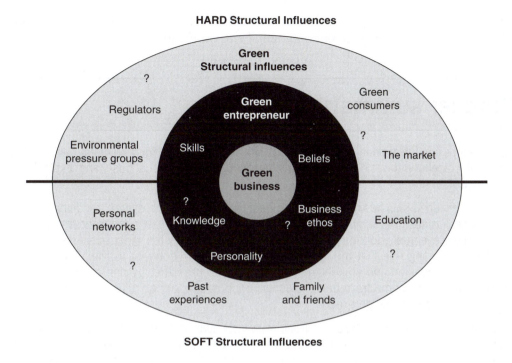

Figure 12.1   Influences on the green entrepreneur
Source: Taylor and Walley (2004) reprinted with permission from the authors.

Furthermore, for eco-start-ups and practising ecopreneurs in business, specialist business support and training now exist, as well as micro-finance and business funding schemes. Investment banks are now launching serious environmental initiatives. In late 2005, Goldman Sachs announced, to worldwide commentary, its aim to be the leading American developer of wind energy through its subsidiary Horizon Wind Energy by investing $1 billion in renewable energy and energy-efficiency projects (CNNMoney.com, 2005). Commentators stated that Goldman Sachs is ground-breaking for its comprehensiveness, its outright acknowledgement of global climate change and for recognizing its responsibility as gatekeepers of the capital markets and its calling to ensure that environmental externalities are properly priced in the marketplace.

There are now also specialist business incubator centres for new firms with a sustainability orientation and schemes to make entrepreneur advisory services greener; one of the more advanced programmes being the non-profit World Resources Institute. However, there is still much more that needs to be understood about ecopreneurship, to establish 'ground rules' both from the research and practical perspectives. Legislation, government regulation and industry support agencies all have a role to play in shaping the way business – including eco-business – conducts its activities. Other stakeholders, such as lobby groups, non-governmental organizations (NGOs), venture capitalists, industry associations and local communities can also influence the context in which ecopreneurs operate. These bodies are beginning to develop activities that encourage environmental entrepreneurs.

Chapter summary

Never before has there been such an opportunity and imperative for innovation that meets the needs of citizens without damaging the planet's natural resource base and exploiting the world's poor.

Green entrepreneurship has the potential to be a major force in the overall transition to a more sustainable business paradigm. In a market-based economy green entrepreneurs play a critical role in the eventual adoption of green business practices by the wider business community through the leading role that they provide to other firms. In contrast to the 'push' factors of government regulation and stakeholder or lobby group pressure, by demonstrating the economic benefits that come from being greener, ecopreneurs act as a 'pull' factor that entices other firms to proactively go green.

This is an exciting area of entrepreneurship with individuals developing business solutions that help to move enterprise from a 'smokestack' model to more sustainable solutions while addressing some of our most pressing issues. There are still numerous unknown areas in developing ecopreneurship theory and academics and consultants are increasingly focusing upon understanding them.

References

Boal, C. (2006) 'Green consumers push for organic cocoa', 13 Sept. www.confectionerynews.com.

Burrell, I. (2006) 'Marketing Green and Black's: organic plus luxury adds up to the taste of success', *The Independent*, 17 April.

CNNMoney.com (2005) 'Report: Goldman Sachs goes green. Investment banking firm boosts environmental practices, encourages clients to be eco-friendly', 22 November. Viewed on 14 March 2006: http://money.cnn.com.

The Economist (2002) 'The Great Race: a survey of the global environment', *The Economist*, 6 July, pp. 3–5.

Elkington, J. (1997) *Cannibals with Forks: The Triple Bottom Line of 21st Century Business*. Oxford: Capstone.

Gerlach, A. (2003) 'Sustainable entrepreneurship and innovation', paper presented at the 2003 Corporate Social Responsibility and Environmental Management Conference. 30 June–1 July 2003, University of Leeds, pp. 101–10 (online).

Ginsberg, J. M. and Bloom, P. N. (2004) 'Choosing the right green-marketing strategy', *MIT Sloan Management Review*, 46(1): 79–88.

Green and Black's website: www.greenandblacks.com (Viewed: 18 March 2007).

Isaak, R. (1998) *Green Logic: Ecopreneurship, Theory and Ethics*. Sheffield: Greenleaf.

Isaak R. (2005) 'The making of the ecopreneur', in Schaper, M. (ed.) *Making Ecopreneurs: Developing Sustainable Entrepreneurship*. Aldershot: Ashgate, pp. 13–26.

Katz, L. (2007) 'Green travel market "set to grow 25 per cent a year"', Guardian Unlimited, 12 February.

Khare, A. (2003) 'Ecopreneurs: the changing role of entrepreneurs', paper at 18th Manufacturing Systems Engineering Salon conference, Ryukoku University, Kyoto, Japan, 13 November.

Lober, D. J. (1998) Pollution prevention as corporate entrepreneurship,' *Journal of Organizational Change Management*, 11(1): 26–37.

Lovins, A. B., Lovins, L. Y. and Hawken, P. (1999) 'A road map for natural captalism', *Harvard Business Review*, May–June: 145–58.

Meyer, A. (2001) 'What's in it for customers: successfully marketing green clothes', *Business Strategy and the Environment*, 10(5): 317–30.

Micklethwaite, P. (2004) 'The "recycled consumer": evidence and design implications', in Bhamra, T. and Hon, B. (eds), *Design and Manufacture for Sustainable Development*. Bury St Edmunds: Professional Engineering Publishers.

Micklethwaite, P. and Chick, A. (2005) 'Remarkable Pencils Ltd: breaking out of the green niche', *Design Management Review*, Summer: 24–9.

Ottman, J. A. (2004) 'Removing the barriers', *In Business*, 26(1): 31.

Pesticide Action Network North America website: www.panna.org (viewed on 18 March 2007).

Remarkable (2007) Background and philosophy [http://www.remarkable.co.uk/background.html. Viewed 30 March 2007].

Schaltegger, S. (2005) '*A framework and typology of ecopreneurship: leading bioneers and environmental managers to ecopreneurship*', in M. Schaper (ed.), *Making Ecopreneurs: Developing Sustainable Entrepreneurship*. Aldershot: Ashgate, pp. 27–42.

Schaper, M. (2005) 'Introduction', in Schaper, M. (ed.) *Making Ecopreneurs: Developing Sustainable Entrepreneurship*. Aldershot: Ashgate.

Shane, S. and Vankataraman, S. (2000) 'The promise of entrepreneurship as a field of research', *Academy of Management Review*, 25(1): 217–26.

Siegle, L. (2005) 'Chocolate tears', *The Observer*, 5 June.

Taylor, D. and Walley, E. (2004) 'The green entrepreneur: opportunist, maverick or visionary?, *International Journal of Entrepreneurship and Small Businesses*, 01(1–2): 56–69.

Volery (2002) 'Ecopreneurship: rationale, current issues and future challenges', in Radical change in the world – will SMEs soar or crash? Rencontres de St-Gall 2002, www.kmu.unisg.ch/rencontres/band2002/F_11_volery.pdf

Walley, N. and Whitehead, B. (1994) 'It's not easy being green', *Harvard Business Review*, May–June: 46–52.

World Business Council for Sustainable Development (1997) *Cleaner Production and Eco-Efficiency: Complementary Approaches to Sustainable Development*. Geneva: WBCSD.

World Commission on Environment and Development (1987) *Our Common Future* (The Brundtland Report). Oxford: Oxford University Press.

Further reading

Allen, P. (2007) 'Your ethical business: how to plan, start and succeed in a company with a conscience', ngo.media

Article 13 (2006). 'CRS best practice: Patagonia'. www.article13.com. Viewed on 18 March 2007.

Green Management International Themed Issue (2002) on Environmental Entrepreneurship. 38 (Summer). Greenleaf Publishing.

Ottman, J. A. (1998) *Green Marketing: Opportunity for Innovation*. Booksurge.

Schaper, M. (ed.) (2005) *Making Ecopreneurs: Developing Sustainable Entrepreneurship*. Aldershot: Ashgate.

Web links

1 % For the Planet Business Alliance: www.onepercentfortheplanet.org

Business for Social Responsibility: http://bsr.org

Ecostructure Financial: http://info.ecostructure.us

Green and Black's: www.greenandblacks.com

WBCSD: www.wbcsd.org

World Resources Institute: www.wri.org/wri/sep/index.html

Suggestions for exercises

1   Comment on what is meant by 'greenwashing'. How to avoid it? How can you measure how 'green' your product is?
2   Compare the approaches used by Greenergy (producers of low-carbon fuels that feature a blend of bio-fuels, such as bio-diesel or bio-ethanol, and mineral fuel, see www.greenergy.com) and Ecotricity, which 'is unique among power companies in that it ploughs all profit into building new renewable energy sources' (www.ecotricity.co.uk).

13 Enterprise in Health and Social Care

Antonia Bifulco

Introduction

While Chapter 11 looked at entrepreneurship in the life sciences, this chapter concentrates on health and other care downstream of drug discovery and related issues. The topics covered here relate to the spectrum of areas between the organization of primary health care right down to social and other care charities. As such, this chapter is aimed at health-care professionals, nurses, therapists and all those in work related to social care, including those (e.g. midwives) who are often self-employed.

Social desire and reward

Most people who are trained in, or work within the health or social care field, are motivated by a desire to help people deal with illness and disability, to promote well-being and health and to aid those who are disadvantaged in coping with adversity and improving their life skills. There is therefore at times an erroneous belief that these fields are foreign to entrepreneurship since they are either state-funded (through the NHS and local authority services) or occur through voluntary or charitable organizations. But modern configurations and the high costs of such services, coupled with the demands for health, well-being and fulfilling lifestyles in an increasing and ageing population, combine to offer greater opportunity perhaps more than ever before for entrepreneurial activity (which, of course, can also encompass social enterprise). This chapter discusses the specialist application of entrepreneurship in the health and social care sectors, concentrating how this might be applied in terms of opportunities and demand.

Entrepreneurial motivation

Why become an entrepreneur in health and social care fields, given the existence of a large publicly funded sector? Certainly in motivational terms there is some overlap between the ethical enterprises and social entrepreneurship, and the factors regarding green 'ecopreneurs' (Chapter 12) inasmuch as individuals feel the urge to contribute in areas where they feel the state doesn't (or not sufficiently). More specifically, there are a number of personal reasons why individuals choose to develop their skills and contributions to the field in entrepreneurial ways, including the desire for creativity and autonomy, but also more externally focused reasons, such as better provision of products and services than can be offered in large state-funded facilities (for example, swifter, more efficient, with more diversity and choice) for patients/clients and consumers. Individuals may also want to produce a broader range of services and products than is currently captured in state-funded provision, for example, offering well-being, preventative care, complementary/alternative approaches to treatment and lifestyle issues. In addition, individuals who no longer work in the publicly funded sector (for reasons of redundancy, burn-out, glass ceiling phenomenon, etc.) may still wish to use their skills and experience in innovative and entrepreneurial ways.

Finding the right niche

Tony Chancellor spent 25 years as a psychiatric nurse working for the NHS. In 1999, he founded a chain of private psychiatric hospitals, the Norfolk-based 'Chancellor Care'. Quickly raising equity by selling 49 per cent of the company's shares, he finally sold out to Lloyds TSB in early 2006, netting himself a total of £17 million.

Dr Charles Levinson founded Doctorcall in 1987 offering an out-of-hours GP service and for much of its life, Doctorcall employed few staff while Levinson concentrated upon his own GP practice. It was not until 2002 that Levinson re-applied himself to the company and expanded into occupational health, providing a wide range of services, e.g. health screenings, sickness reviews, etc. to corporate customers, as well as flu vaccinations in the supermarket chain Asda. In 2005, Doctorcall turned over around £3.4 million.

Pinnacle Health Group was founded by Michael Broxterman and John Couvillon in 1994 and is now one of the largest physician recruiting firms in the USA.

Market demand is increasing

What is the demand for entrepreneurship in health and social care? There is a large demand for the additional provision of services and products in these fields. First, there is a large market volume due to high expectations of health and well-being in the population, the increased demand for preventative treatments, demand for new treatments and solutions (e.g. those not pharmaceutically based) and for self-help (the 'expert patients'). Second, there is also demand for products and services to be more accessible and available more rapidly than is often the case with state-funded provision. Existing entrepreneurial activities range from large to small. Large companies include the pharmaceutical industry, national enterprises (for example, in eye-care provision or chemist shops), high street enterprises such as health food outlets and small enterprises such as single private practitioners in complementary therapies.

There is an increasing acceptance of, and positive attitude towards, entrepreneurship in health and social care. Both patients/clients and practitioners/providers can benefit from innovation and the input of entrepreneurial activity. With private–public partnership it is recognized that public services can work together with private companies both large and small, and the 'patchwork' NHS provision is viewed by many as increasing the quality and range of service to consumers. Market trends evolve in response to external factors, and some of the most powerful include:

- *Ageing demographics*: An ageing population with implications for the long-term treatment of chronic conditions, disability, residential care and aids for mobility, functioning and help for carers.
- *Prevention and lifestyle*: An emphasis on public health, preventative treatment and lifestyle issues to aid in early detection (or aversion) of common physical illnesses and other social problems. Thus, the proportion of the population that would not normally come within health or social care services (i.e. are not clinically ill) is now increasingly being targeted regarding managing personal health and lifestyle to avoid future problems.
- *Increased use of IT solutions for information storage and sharing*: IT solutions for the storage, retrieval and sharing of information on patients and clients are increasingly required as professional working becomes increasingly inter-agency and inter-specialism. This involves the collection of information and assessments in a manner suited to computerization, and that those computer systems are becoming sufficiently user-friendly for less experienced staff to access and use.
- *Increased knowledge exchange*: Greater expert knowledge is required in both health and social care services – and by the general public – in order to keep up-to-date with the latest research, methods and information concerning illness and illness prevention.
- *Workforce skills*: A large proportion of the workforce is employed in health and social care provision. Workers are required to improve their skills and knowledge base of disorder/social risks, their identification, assessment, treatment and monitoring. This requires constant continued professional development of the workforce involving increased training opportunities. It also has implications for staff recruitment and recruitment agencies.
- *Wider range of outlets*: There are increasingly new outlets for health and social care services and products. These have evolved from being the hospital and surgery to now include the workplace (as health issues become part of health and safety and sick leave becomes a major burden on businesses) and the high street (including e.g. increasing outlets for hearing aids to parallel increases in eye services or complementary medicine outlets, etc).

The product can be many things

Health and social care together cover a very broad spectrum of services, products, settings and practitioner skills (Figure 13.1). Thus, not only is there a dimension from well-being to illness, which encompasses sub-clinical conditions, early signs and symptoms or genetic markers for incipient disorder, etc., but at the illness end this includes physical and mental disorders, acute and chronic, disability as well as disorder and serious versus minor illness. At the well-being end it includes being symptom-free, well-functioning, health-knowledgeable and aware and active illness-prevention action. Entrepreneurial activity may choose to focus on any one of these degrees of illness or health.

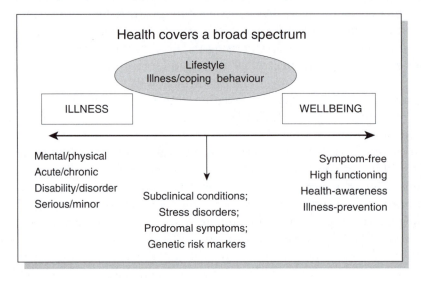

Figure 13.1   Illustrating the spectrum of health activities

Similarly, services and settings are varied and range from hospital or residential care, outpatient or intermittent service, GP or social care to visiting or other complementary treatments which may be high-street based. Well-being may include products on public information, health food shops, exercise facilities, de-stressing services (at work, health clubs and leisure or even beauty facilities) (Figure 13.2). Entrepreneurial activity may enter at any of these points.

The various customers

The potential customers for services cover more than patient/client and practitioner – although these are large markets. It also includes the patient/client's family members, carers and supporters, employers; needs for monitoring and aftercare; other treatment facilities, support/nursing staff and multi-agency involvement. Both patients and practitioners have growing needs and expectations, for example, for quick diagnosis, full information, flexible and

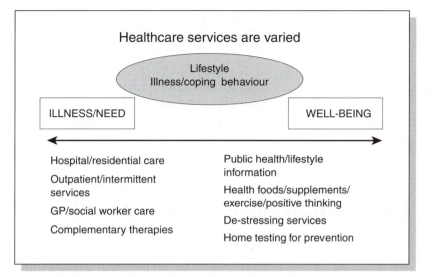

Figure 13.2   Illustrating the spectrum of service response

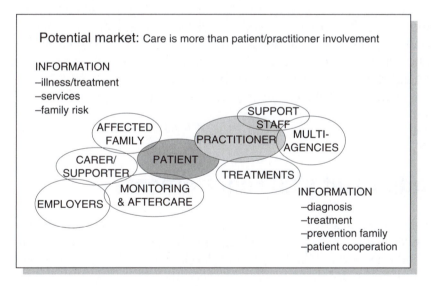

Figure 13.3   Representation of several market groups

acceptable treatments, easy service access, trust in practitioner and lack of stigma regarding service use. Practitioners in turn need easy and early access to patients, aids to diagnosis/assessment, easy delivery of treatment, access to evidence-knowledge-base, preventative and monitoring strategies, trust in patients to undertake treatment and update of skills and knowledge (Figure 13.3). Thus there are clearly many opportunities in these combinations for entrepreneurial activity, ranging from just-in-time learning to hiring staff or re-packaging disposables (see Chapter 11 for a discussion of entrepreneurship in biomedical equipment).

In order to identify new entrepreneurial opportunities in the value chain/value system (see Chapter 2), it is necessary to be able to spot where improvements can be made in current products or services, or in more cost-effective or efficient delivery or improvising customer satisfaction with better access/prevention/self-help or developing new health care domains such as well-being or information dispersal.

Example of new outlets: workforce applications

Among the new arenas for delivering aspects of health care and social care are those in a workforce context. In this case it is motivated by employer requirements for staff satisfaction, worker well-being in terms of productivity and cutting down on sick leave, as well as complying with health and safety legislation (which includes stress and mental health issues) and complying with anti-discrimination legislation and avoiding litigation over work-induced health problems. Potentially this can lead to a number of on-site services being offered at the workplace including paramedic health testing (e.g. blood pressure, diabetes), on-site counselling services around stress and mental health issues, as well as more general information and awareness services.

Knowledge and skill requirements

In order to choose an area in which to develop their interests, the entrepreneur will clearly need to consider his/her skills and knowledge and interests to see whether partnerships are required to build necessary skills for product development and marketing (see Chapter 1). Some typical skills needed include specific specialized knowledge in an area of disease/disorder/treatment/assessment-diagnosis, etc. as well as an understanding of how to apply this knowledge from 'bench to bedside' and to make treatments or services user- and practitioner-friendly. Clearly, service-based entrepreneurial activity may demand further person skills with both practitioners and patients/clients. Furthermore, it would be prudent to possess an understanding of the health and social care knowledge base, how to exploit new findings and an understanding of the social and political contexts of health and social care delivery, as well as funding sources.

Example of needs of ageing population: residential care staff

Of the 21,000 care homes for adults in England, around 63 per cent are provided by the independent sector. The size of the social care workforce working with older people in England is estimated to be 609,000, of which 390,000 are employed in independently owned care homes. This particular workforce is overwhelmingly (up to 95 per cent) female. It is also ethnically diverse, with representation from black and ethnic minority communities higher than the average across other health and social care professions; many of these workers may be first generation immigrants for whom English is a second language. Estimates suggest that 80 per cent of care staff in England have no qualification for their work and pay levels are extremely low. Thus, needs within the sector include staff recruitment and training. There is a high staff turnover (rates of 50–75 per cent per year) leading to a lack of continuity and stability in care and miscommunication resulting in patient safety issues, worker injuries, poor morale and other quality of care issues. This has a major impact on costs in the care home sector. Although UK figures are not easily available, a US study estimated the turnover of nursing assistants to be $4 billion per year. One goal is to increase retention by improving the working environment for care staff. This can involve training and remuneration but also requires attending to staff stress levels and well-being. Opportunities for stress reduction interventions are, therefore, significant and are potentially of benefit to workers and managers in, as well as owners of, care homes, and ultimately the older people in their care. This can include information or stress therapies that could be financed by the care homes to ensure greater stability of staffing.

(*Source*: Skills Research and Intelligence, 2nd Annual Report, April 2005; TOPSS England Workforce Intelligence Unit. Available at: www.skillsforcare-yh.org.uk/files/SSA%20Summary%20doc%201%20webv2.pdf)

For those with expert knowledge in health and social care, the opportunities for knowledge exchange are now greater than ever before, with the need to update knowledge and urgent up-skill of the workforce becoming apparent. Thus, expertise, often in the form of independent consultants and/or university-based experts, is required to interact with services and practitioners, aiming at continued professional development. This includes training in new methods developed for practitioners, deriving products or new treatments arising from the latest research.

An example of knowledge exchange

Research in Practice (RiP) is an example of a knowledge exchange business emerging from a university and charity. It is an organization aiming to identify effective methods of understanding and using research by providing services to a collaborative network of committed agencies. RiP is a department of the Darting Hall Trust (Devon) run in collaboration with the University of Sheffield, the Association of Directors of Social Services and their network of over 100 participating agencies in England and Wales. They also have strong links with ConfED and NfER. RiP offers a six-strand programme for link officers/organizations including learning events; networking; publications; change projects and Research in Practice services. Its income is derived from an annual membership fee. Clients presently include statutory and voluntary services and organisations.

(*Source*: Research in Practice: www.rip.org.uk)

What you need to know

Potential entrepreneurs in this area need to familiarize themselves with government policy and initiatives on health and social care with updates from government departments such as UK Department of Health and NHS websites (including DfES for children's services). They need to understand the structure of statutory services, an area that is in constant change and flux. In particular, new graduates – who will probably be occupied in what used to be known as 'ancillary services', must understand the basis for private–public partnerships and for social enterprise, as well as the role of private practice, the self-employed and companies in provision of services and products (Table 13.1). This will involve researching the particular area of interest in terms of web-based, journal-based and commercial information. Having personal contacts and networks in the given area (including 'experience surveys' – interviewing known experts – see the Marketing Plan detailed in Chapter 5) is a quick way of becoming familiar with opportunities and obstacles. In all circumstances, knowledge of relevant ethical standards and governance is required, as well as registers of practitioners and professional bodies, large commercial companies and influential voluntary organizations.

Obstacles

Barriers to entry in this sector are mostly seen as 'medium'; resources are initially gathered by bootstrapping, networking, making critical alliances and using other people's resources, but unlike high-potential ventures (e.g. biotech, see Chapter 11) there is often no initial lump sum

Table 13.1   Examples of services/products

Patients/clients	Practitioners/workforce
Services	Services
Hip operations provided privately	New assessment tools
Complementary therapies provided	New techniques and systems
	Training for practitioners
Products	Products
Hearing tests and devices provided in high street shops or home services	New treatments, medications, techniques
Home blood pressure testing kits provided in high street chemists	
Knowledge exchange	Knowledge exchange
Information websites with updated research advertising products	Access to research information services
Information help-lines	Information sharing IT systems

or structured investment of capital from a venture capitalist to support the new venture; bank loans may well suffice. The obstacles to getting services and products developed can include ethics and governance/indemnity issues (charity law, etc.) and indeed, some areas are highly regulated to protect patients/clients and permissions include a high level of bureaucracy and delay. Insurance may also be a major issue.

The health field in particular is very competitive with some very large players in terms of multinational companies and therefore a small new player with a niche product may find it difficult to enter the market. A degree of specialist knowledge will often be needed, and the health field is one where there is a hierarchy of expertise in the medical system which may create barriers to others entering. There is also some resistance to the commercialization of health and social care from those who consider it should solely be a publicly provided service with no inequality based on income or class. It is also the case that many needy patients and clients will not be able to pay for services. In this latter instance entrepreneurs may want to consider social (not for profit) enterprises.

An example from the USA: social care and treatment facility

The Oregon Social Learning Model and associated developments is one of the most successful university-developed treatment programmes which has led to commercial and social enterprise activity in the USA. The commercial product of 'Multidimensional Treatment Foster Care' (MTFC) has a theoretical and university research basis

(Continued)

(University of Oregon), from which the developed intervention package was delivered from an independent centre (Oregon Social Learning Center). This was supported financially by federal research funds and grants from private individuals and foundations and remained a non-profit-making entity. It was only years later when the evidence base was established that a different business structure was formed with all MTFC service activities being transferred from the research center to Oregon Social Learning Center Community Programs, which has now become the organization dedicated to the delivery of evidence-based outpatient and MTFC services. The commercial and profit-making arm Treatment Foster Care Consultants Inc (founded 2002) then started to provide implementation services, consultation and technical assistance for sites that want to implement the treatment – MTFC. This works across the USA but also internationally in Europe and elsewhere. Thus a complex structure emerges of interlinked university, not-for-profit and profit-making activities which can capitalize on various funding from research councils, charities, social agencies and private donations.

(*Source*: Oregon Social Learning Center: www.oslc.org/about/overview/html)

Social enterprise

In the area of social care, there is a strong tradition for charitable, not-for-profit or social enterprise businesses to help tackle social inequality and adversity. Examples include Oxfam, Christian Aid, the National Trust and the Red Cross. Social and religious voluntary organizations have a strong history of being major providers in both the health and education sectors, indeed, the Peter F. Drucker Foundation (www.pfdf.org) reckons that the value of social entrepreneurship outweighs that of commercial entrepreneurship.

Between charities and commercial enterprises exist the community interest companies, a form of incorporation introduced in the UK in 2005. Companies inhabiting this mid-way position include Malagasy (socially acceptable production of gourmet ingredients in Madagascar sold to UK supermarkets) and Ealing Community Transport (founded 1979), offering transport for elderly people and now a £50 million group competing on the open market and ploughing profits back into the community. Innocent Smoothies give 10 per cent of their profits each year to charities in the countries where the fruit comes from (www.innocent drinks.co.uk). One Water is bottled water in recycling bottles produced by Global Ethics (www.we-are-one.org.uk) which uses their profits to install water pumps in Africa. However, the example of a similar company – Ethos Water – sold to Starbuck's in 2005 has given rise to concern to 'ethical whitewashing' (compare 'greenwashing', Chapter 12) where large companies simply buy an ethical façade.

Clearly the spectrum of ethical/social activity stretches from commercial organizations donating portions of their profits to social organizations under the banner of 'corporate responsibility', through not-for-profit organizations, to dedicated ethical non-profit models, finally ending in outright charities working in a non-commercial (i.e. perpetual loss-making, seen from a strictly accounting point of view) environment, which often rely on voluntary unpaid workers.

Social enterprise – definitions and scope

- A social enterprise is a business with primarily social objectives whose surpluses are principally reinvested for that purpose in the business or in the community, rather than being driven by the need to maximize profit for shareholders and owners (Social Enterprise London).
- The social enterprise sector is incredibly diverse, encompassing cooperatives, development trusts, community enterprises, housing associations, football supporters trusts, social firms, leisure trusts, etc. (Social Enterprise Coalition).
- Social enterprises tackle a wide range of social and environmental issues and operate in all parts of the economy. By using business solutions to achieve public good, the government believes that social enterprises have a distinct and valuable role to play in helping create a strong, sustainable and socially inclusive economy (Social Enterprise Unit: http:www.cabinetoffice.gov.uk/third_sector/social_enterprise.aspx).
- It is this essential social sector, in collaboration with its partners in the private and public sectors, that changes lives and builds a society of healthy children, strong families, decent housing, good schools and work that dignifies, all embraced by the diverse, inclusive, cohesive community that cares about all of its people (Peter F. Drucker Foundation: www.pfdf.org).

Accordind to Simon Caulkins:

The unsung story is that the not-for-profit, third, or social sector, as it is variously known, is rapidly catching up on corporations in productivity and sometimes surpassing them in creativity. It is seeing explosive growth. A Johns Hopkins University study of the economies of 26 countries in 2003 found that in the mid-1990s the non-profit sector accounted for $1.2 trillion in expenditures worldwide, employed 31 million full-time equivalent workers (nearly 7 per cent of the non-agricultural workforce) and was growing fast – throughout the 1990s non-profits were taking on staff at more than twice the rate of the economy as a whole.

(*Source*: *The Observer*, 12 February 2006: http://observer.guardian.co.uk/business/story/0,,1707636,00.html)

Not-for-profit organizations

There are fundamental differences between non/not-for-profit and commercial organizations. Both types intend to create some form of 'value' of their product or activity, but for the commercial venture there is a market test for value created using quantitative measures such as revenue growth and profitability, i.e. what customers pay for the good or service determines the economic reward (the primary goal of commercial ventures). In contrast to this simple equation, the central purpose of social ventures is to provide social benefit or do good works. This means that, for such organizations, economic self-sufficiency is often unattainable due to the inability of customers to pay a full cost price for the goods and services provided. Thus, in order to provide benefits, the not-for-profit venture depends upon a variety of 'subsidies', including the donation of funds, volunteer labour, and staff who are willing to accept wage rates that are below market average (perhaps below minimum, i.e. unpaid).

Put bluntly, the commercial entrepreneur looks to investors to help attain financial sufficiency whereas social entrepreneurs are – often constantly – trying to attract donors, gifts and sponsors. Very few social entrepreneurs (e.g. those with large independent charitable trust funds) achieve financial sufficiency, so constantly improving donation streams is a characteristic of social entrepreneurship.

Other areas requiring the attention of the social entrepreneur in addition to issues relating to funding (e.g. providing an operating cash flow – income being often donations, gifts and sponsorship) are human resource management (i.e., attracting, motivating and retaining staff); and performance evaluation (i.e., measuring success). While of these activities donation management would appear to be the most important, it is important that all three form a 'virtuous circle', i.e. that concrete measures of success (e.g. achieved by skilful HRM) provide good grounds for further donations.

Voluntary organizations: social entrepreneurship

Voluntary organizations have a long history and by the second half of the twentieth century they were a major force in filling gaps left by state provision. In a speech to the National Council of Voluntary Organizations in 1999, the UK Prime Minister Blair stated, 'Government cannot achieve the nation's goals without an active and thriving voluntary sector.' Social enterprises often aim to improve on, or complement, statutory services with a view to providing wider choice for clients/consumers and in a less bureaucratic and more efficient service. Such organizations can apply for government funding and also collect donations from the general public and from commercial enterprises as a part of their 'corporate responsibilities'. The number of charities in the UK has increased from 98,000 to 170,000 and includes 1.5 million employees and 6 million volunteers.

There is a debate as to what extent voluntary organizations should be allowed to pursue public service contracts – voluntary organizations wanting what they see as fairer and more equal government contracts that would enable them to compete with private organizations. Since social and religious voluntary organizations have a strong history of being major providers in e.g. the health sector before the area became 'professionalized' in the latter half of the last century, some see this as a course correction, swinging back to a mixed model.

Chapter summary

There is large and increasing opportunity for entrepreneurship in health and social care. This is due to a number of factors, but includes the increasing privatization of previously public services and a reliance on social entrepreneurship (the voluntary sector), increased demand for a range of well-being services and products, as well as health treatments, greater demands from an ageing population and increased needs for workforce development and knowledge transfer. Such entrepreneurship can be large- or small-scale and work through patients/clients, the workplace, or through the general population and high street sales.

Social enterprises are increasing in importance but they achieve capital flow not by profit but rather by tapping funds from governments, business corporate responsibility missions and public donations.

It is important to capitalize on skills and expert knowledge in the area, and to be aware of formal barriers (such as the law, ethical governance and indemnity) as well as opportunities (to increase customer satisfaction, and offer an improved service and more choice).

A major growth area is in ethical businesses, which return part or all of their profit to upstream suppliers or relevant charities (i.e. well-developed corporate responsibility).

References

Bornstein, D. (2004) *How to Change the World: Social Entrepreneurs and the Power of New Ideas*. New York: Oxford University Press.

De Leeuw, E. (1999) 'Perspective. Health cities: Urban social entrepreneurship for health', *Health Promotion International*, 14(3).

Grazier, K. L and Metzler, B. (2005) 'Health care entrepreneurship: financing innovation', *Journal of Health and Human Services Administration*, 28(3/4): 485–503.

Further reading

Drayton, W., Brown C. and Hillhouse, K. (2006) 'Integrating social entrepreneurs into the "health for all" formula', www.who.int/bulletin/volumes/84/8/06-033928.pdf

Nunns, A. (2006) 'NHS privatisation – the evidence', available at: www.labournet.net/ukunion/0610/nhspriv1.html

Cabinet Office (2007) *Third Sector Review Interim Report and 2nd consultation deadline February 2007.* HM Treasury and Cabinet Office. London: The Stationery Office.

Sexton, S. (2001) 'Trading healthcare away? GATS, public services and privatisation', Available at: http://www.thecornerhouse.org.uk.item.shtml?x=51985

Wainwright, S., Clark, J., Griffith, M., Jochum, V. and Wilding, K. (2006) *The Voluntary Agency Directory 2006.* London: NCVO.

Web links

ashoka.org

CORE – corporate responsibility: www.corporate-responsibility.org

Dept of Health social enterprise site: www.dh.gov.uk/en/Policyandguidance/Organisationpolicy/Commissioning/Socialenterprise/index.htm

The Institute for Complementary Medicine: www.i-c-m.org.uk

www.kimseyfoundation.org

National Council for Voluntary Organisations NCVO: www.ncvo-vol.org.uk

nonprofits.org

skollfoundation.org

Social enterprise alliance: www.se-alliance.org/about_us.cfm

Social enterprise coalition: www.socialenterprise.org.uk/page.aspx?SP=1345

Stress at work: www.hse.gov.uk/stress/standards

Unltd (pronounced 'unlimited') is a charity helping social entrepreneurs to set up their own social charities and enterprises. www.unltd.org.uk

The Voice of Complementary Medicine: www.bcma.co.uk

Workforce: www.skillsforcare.org.uk.

The Young Foundation: http://www.youngfoundation.org/about

Government links

www.dfes.gov.uk/(Dept for Children, Schools and Families)

www.dh.gov.uk (Dept of Health)

www.dwp.gov.uk (Dept for Work and Pensions)

www.homeoffice.gov.uk (Home Office)

www.nhs.uk (National Health Service)

www.nice.org.uk (National Institute for Health and Clinical Excellence)

www.communities.gov.uk (Department of Communities and Local Government)

www.scie.org.uk (Social Care Institute for Excellence)

Suggestion for exercises

Comment on why there is resistance to entrepreneurship in health and social care areas and what are the benefits. Use, if possible, a historical context.

14 Journalism and Media Entrepreneurs

Noha Mellor

Introduction

This chapter discusses entrepreneurship in media, a term used to refer particularly to journalism and news production. Journalism and media are part of what is known as 'the cultural industries'. However, as opposed to e.g. the music industry (see Chapter 15), journalists and other mediators are particularly responsible for the creation of meanings. As such, this chapter is particularly aimed at those studying communication, social science, media, culture and the various branches of journalism (broadcasting, etc.).

The first section of this chapter discusses the huge significance of the cultural industries to today's Western economies and helps distinguish between these and other, traditional, industries. Great emphasis is placed on freelancing, as this is the route to becoming well known and commanding the best positions and prices, with many aiming at becoming a 'venture' to be personally branded and marketed within a registered company framework. This is a viable alternative to sub-contracting (e.g. making CBeebies series) as sub-contracting demands an extraordinarily high degree of specialization. Technology also plays a key role in shaping journalism and news production and thus the following sections discuss the role and impact of technology on innovation in this sector. As shown below, technology has brought about threats to media entrepreneurs (e.g. the disappearance of the traditional printing industry) but also a wide range of new opportunities as well, including providing new platforms (satellite channels, Internet, etc.) for entrepreneurial newcomers to show off their skills.

Journalism as part of the cultural industries

Journalism belongs to the cultural or creative industries, a term that has provoked some controversy for its blurring of the traditionally distinct boundaries between 'art and commerce' (Negus and Pickering, 2004). Commerce was traditionally thought to either corrupt art or to serve as the incentive that fuels creativity, but as Negus and Pickering (ibid.: 46ff) remind us, art and cultural industries have always influenced and been influenced by commerce. Journalism, however, tends to be placed away from the entertainment end of the creative spectrum (see Chapter 15).

In general, the cultural industries are characterized by the co-existence of large cultural corporations alongside small and medium-sized corporations. These industries create, produce and distribute intangible/cultural content (goods or services), which are usually protected by copyright, thus it is knowledge- and labour-intensive (see Chapter 8). More specifically, Hesmondhalgh (2002: 3 and 11) defines these industries as those 'involved in the making and circulating of products … that have an influence on our understanding of the world' or those involved in the 'production of social meaning'. Hesmondhalgh has also narrowed his definition to those industries where the aesthetic and artistic outweigh the functionality of the product, therefore excluding industries such as fashion and car manufacturing, while including TV, publishing, software games, advertising, performing art, design, video, and architecture, although here we do not consider all of these but rather adhere to the definition by UNESCO (2007) that defines the cultural industries as those industries that 'combine the creation, production and commercialisation of contents, which are intangible and cultural in nature'. Media, in particular, have been assigned a significant role in Western societies, because media 'deals in ideas, information, and culture. They inform and entrain us, influencing how we understand ourselves and our world, as well as how we spend out leisure time' (Croteau and Hoynes, 2006: 1). Media and culture, therefore, are crucial to reproduce meanings – and a symbol in our lifestyle – in contemporary societies as well as being a source of pleasure.

Culture in post-industrial times

Several factors help promote the cultural industries and make them an apt substitute for traditional industries such as manufacturing. First, the growing disposable income of people in Western countries has resulted in a need to cater for new segments of consumers. Also, the expanding literacy and education rates, along with the increasing leisure time, have forced companies to think of new ways to service and even entertain their consumers. Finally, the triumph of consumerism in capitalist societies has forced creativity to find new ways to attract the attention of the customers (Hesmondhalgh, 2002). On the other hand, the diminished role of the state in regulating the cultural and media sectors gives space to the market forces of supply and demand as the main regulator.

Cavet (2000) distinguishes between cultural industries and other 'humdrum' industries highlighting several properties of the former. One central characteristic of the creative industries is that it is based on uncertain demand, thus it is not easy to predict the consumer's response to a creative service or product. Another characteristic is the enthusiasm of workers in the creative industries for originality, rather than stable work hours, wages or other work conditions. Moreover, working in the creative industries demands a multi-skilled labour force (see Chapter 7), whose skills can be differentiated. Also, the products of the creative industries are characterized by their durability, and hence workers can claim royalty fees for their work.

Why culture is important

Cultural industries are now central to the Western countries' economies, for example, cultural products constitute the largest share of the US export, e.g. TV programmes, films, music, publishing and software (UNESCO, 2007). In fact, the USA and the UK, Germany and France are the major four traders of cultural exports and imports. Thus, the cultural products not only sell in local markets but can indeed boost the export record of local companies in global markets. According to UNESCO, the international trade of goods has grown remarkably over the past two decades, from US$95 million in 1980 to US$287 million in 1998.

In the UK, the cultural industries generate more than £100 billion annually and employ more than one million people. It contributes with 6 per cent (rising to 8.5 per cent by 2010) of the GDP (Leadbeater and Oakley, 1999: 13). The UK government has allocated huge resources and attention to these industries, partly because they are likely to promote local economic growth, and partly because they are likely to promote city regeneration. Indeed, the Creative Economy Programme (www.cep.culture.gov.uk) was launched in 2005 as a reflection of the UK government's desire to make the UK the world's creative hub (although a host of similar initiatives exist e.g. the British Council's www.creativeconomy.org.uk). Cultural companies live on the trade between each another, thus enhancing local and regional jobs. Culture has also been one key factor in 'branding' cities, particularly those that witnessed the decline of its traditional industries. Glasgow, for instance, suffered the loss of jobs in traditional industries such as manufacturing, which forced the local and regional authorities to re-brand the city as the City of Culture, thereby creating more jobs in the service sectors, particularly media, design and financial services (ibid.: 51ff.). Some countries even justify the public spending on promoting the cultural industries by seeing culture as a new inclusive arena that encompasses the work of all citizens across different classes, gender and ethnicities.

Some developments and figures pertaining to the UK

The past century has seen a diversification away from rather monolithic establishment or state-supported structures, such as publishing, mainly news. These have been replaced with an explosion towards specialization (e.g. publications concerned with cars, cookery, etc.) combined with and/or regionalization (e.g. Guardian North, BBC London). The Publishers Association (www.publishingmedia.org.uk) calculates that the publishing industry (newspapers and magazines) is twice the size of the pharmaceutical industry and turned over in excess of £18 billion in 2000, employing 164,000 people. The telecommunications sector is estimated to be twice that size.

There are currently ten daily papers in the UK and 11 Sunday papers, with an average of 80 to 90 million copies sold per week. The best-selling paper in Britain is the tabloid the *Sun*. National British newspapers are controlled by large conglomerates, the largest of which is News International which controls ca. 35 per cent of the market of newspapers, including the *Sun, The Times, Sunday Times* and *News of the World*.

There are now approx. 8,500 magazine titles circulating in Britain, with two-thirds of them business-to-business and one-third consumer magazines. However, demand is highly volatile, and in common with other forms of cultural goods (see Chapter 15), in the publishing world only 20 per cent of the publications are 'cash cows' (see Chapter 4) that generate income to cover the other 80 per cent, indeed only 25 per cent of UK magazines actually make any kind of profit (Hesmondhalgh, 2002: 18).

(*Source*: The Guardian's Media Directory, 2006)

Moreover, the shift in the 1980s from the so-called Fordist economy to the post-Fordist sectors (see Chapter 2) has forced governments and corporations to prioritize the service and cultural sectors. Several other factors have also made it difficult for the Fordist business dogma to persist: the rise of education opportunities has created a large pool of highly skilled labour, in which individuals typically reject monotonous work and have sought more challenging and creative tasks. Likewise, in hyper-fragmented markets, consumer demand is no longer predictable, as the consumers opt for differentiated rather than standardized products and services. Thus, in the period from the 1980s onwards, corporations have been forced to move towards servicing many diverse and fragmented niche markets to match the needs of segmented consumers, and technology has played a key role (see below) in facilitating this move, in as much as it has been utilized as a means to rationalize production. Consequently, the employment rates in many traditional industries such as manufacturing and agriculture have been rapidly outstripped by the boom in the demand of personal and producer services. The consequences of this radical change include a dramatic rise in opportunities for independent media entrepreneurs.

Commercialization versus public service

In 2005, there were more than 15 million British households with access to multi-channels and digital TV, through satellite and digital terrestrial. The UK government aims at achieving digital switchover by 2012, a plan that caused great controversy

(Continued)

around the cost of the switchover particularly for vulnerable groups of society (see Guardian's Media Directory, 2006).

In fact, the commercialized media landscape in Britain plus the availability of free-to-view channels following the digital switchover will force a redefinition of the long-held 'public service broadcasting'. The traditional conception of public broadcasting as offering television programming for everyone is widely regarded as no longer being sustainable in the current competitive environment. According to the BBC Director of Television, Mark Thompson, the future is in 'genre or thematic TV channels' providing specialized contents, e.g. gardening, food, children, documentary, sports, news, etc. as niche channels are the only plausible strategy to maintain, not even increase, the market share of TV channels (Hutton, 2000).

Media and Porter's five forces

Porter's sixth force (Chapter 10) has today assumed enormous proportions as a barrier for various industries, e.g. car manufacturers should beware of environmental groups as a sixth force, but in journalism and media this can be reversed and pressure groups can become a rich and constant source to be tapped – environmental media, producing 'green' messages, etc. – and the same goes for pet owners or the RSPCA as a force, gun owners (e.g. the National Rifle Association in the USA) and by extension any owners of anything etc. This is truly a case where the tail wags the dog.

The rewards can be significant

Working as a media entrepreneur is a phenomenon that emerged in the twentieth century. Hesmondhalgh (2002: Chapter 2) provides a rough summary of the phases through which the cultural workers have moved. The first phase was the phase of 'patronage' and it extended from the Middle Ages to the nineteenth century, when artists were sponsored by aristocrats rather than being free entrepreneurs. The second phase, during the nineteenth century, saw the emergence of the cultural worker as 'market professional, where art was offered for sale in the market, thereby acquiring an exchange value'. This introduced the role of 'cultural intermediaries' into the new industrialized economy, allowing these agents to gain more professional and financial autonomy. In the third and final stage, extending from the twentieth century onwards, the cultural worker has turned into a 'corporate professional', benefiting from the expansion of the cultural industries and the need for a creative labour force.

In modern times, work has become 'an important source for self-actualisation, even freedom and independence' (McRobbie, 2002: 518). Thus, the cultural worker offers their services in an expanding and competitive market, not so much to make a profit as to prove themselves in a profession of their choice. We shall come to this point later in this chapter, when discussing the increasing market for freelancing.

The emergence of print and increasing literacy have been accompanied by recognition of the intellectual property of the media professional. National and international copyright laws define what makes a cultural work and protect such works from illegal copying, an important point since the rise of digitalization has made copying easier and more widespread than ever.

The rise of an independent breed of media entrepreneurs has been accompanied by increasing personal and professional pressures to cope with this demanding and risky media business. This independent breed has been forced to adopt a 'self-enterprise' stance, psychologically regarding themselves as a 'venture' to be marketed and promoted among media corporations, implying if an entrepreneur fails in securing new contracts, the failure is justified as a business strategy failure rather than a personal failure (Storey et al., 2005). In addition, the technological advances in this field have forced the labour force, whether on permanent or freelance contract, to enhance their skills in order to perform on multimedia platforms, although the small-scale and limited resources of the majority of companies in the creative industries mean that they often do not have an adequate technology strategy in place and the cost of accessing the hardware and software used on digital platforms is often prohibitively high for many small creative businesses.

The media convergence revolution

Technological advance is perhaps the most significant catalyst for changes in cultural industries in general and journalism in particular; indeed, this paradigm shift is a key change on the media landscape, resulting in structural changes in most media organizations as well as individual changes among journalists and producers. Convergence 'refers to some combination of technologies, products, staffs and geography among the previously distinct provinces of print, television and online media' (Singer, 2004: 3). Some oppose this convergence on the grounds that it promotes superficial familiarity with several jobs rather than allowing an in-depth knowledge of one job, e.g. photography or editing. Others see it as a chance to boost their career, and to enhance their portfolio.

Recent trends include horizontal mergers of media companies, with newspapers buying into television stations and online operations or even radio stations (Huang et al., 2006: 83). This has resulted in a massive skills convergence in the workplace, e.g. the journalist who is now required to deliver web-content, print feature, video casting, and TV reporting all at once. Huang et al. (ibid.: 95, n.5) showed that both news professionals as well as editors valued multimedia production as a new essential skill. Moreover, editors valued 'critical thinking', i.e. the ability to understand the legal and ethical aspects in news judgement and how to 'report with insight'. Huang et al. give example of such convergence and its impact on the journalists:

> At the online version of *The Chicago Tribune*, for instance, staff are supposed to cover stories, take pictures, operate video camera and create digital pages. The editors, too, need a wider variety of skills than the traditional paper editors … a new breed of journalists – digital or multi-media journalists – is expected. (ibid.: 86).

Organizational structure must also change to adapt to convergence and Boczkowski and Ferris (2005: 45) showed how the organizational structure of one European company changed over the span of 10 years from one single newsroom 'to a separate digital newsroom producing content for all the traditional media, to a single newsroom for each information division producing content for multiple media'.

In sum, big corporations are moving towards the production of multi-platform content, distributed across diverse media, or what Bustamante (2004: 806) and Croteau and Hoynes (2006: 5) call 'anycasting'. Technological advances have accelerated the number of media products available (e.g. satellite radio, like Sirius and MX) while decreasing 'distinct media industries', such as television (indeed, some, like Movietone News, which produced cinema newsreels 1928–63, are well extinct). In particular, the move to the online platform has resulted in a radical redistribution of advertising revenues among media platforms, as more and more companies move towards advertising on the Internet and recent figures show that the British online advertising is eating up print and broadcasting advertising, reaching half of what is spent on TV (Wray, 2006): £2 billion in 2006.

Innovation and journalism

Journalism is one key media industry that has adjusted to technological innovation at a rate perhaps even more rapid than other cultural industries. News media have embraced technological innovation and integrated it into daily practices; thus, reporters use Internet-based sources to gather news (Garrison, 2001, showed that several US newspapers have increased their dependence on online sources from 57 per cent in 1994 to 92 per cent in 1999) and also disseminate news – in 1999, more than 89 per cent of newspapers had their own websites.

Deloitte and Touche (2006) showed that British publishers acknowledge the need to understand and cater for customers using new digital media. Customers themselves are 'blogging, downloading, pod casting and watching mobisodes' (Deloitte and Touche, 2006) and most publishers see the customers' blogs and the so-called user-generated content (UGC) not as a threat but more as an opportunity to integrate this content in their products – hence it has become imperative for media corporations to provide their services across multi-platforms although such content has been claimed to compete directly with the publishers' core business (see e.g. www.technocrati.com, which specializes in tracking webblogs and other forms of independent, user-generated content).

The power of the blog

With rising access to the Internet, more and more individuals as well as corporations use webblogs as a means of communication in the virtual communities. The number of blogs in 2005 was estimated to be more than 60 million. As blogs can be launched by any individual and not necessarily a professional journalist, some media institutions expressed concern over the credibility governing such blogs. Yet, blogs can be a means to shake the authority of mainstream media. For instance, in 2005, the known anchor of the American CBS News, Dan Rather, resigned from his position after pressure by conservative bloggers who revealed that the CBS questioning of President Bush's military service was based on forged documents. Likewise, the CNN's news executive resigned after his off-the-record remarks on the US targeting journalists in Iraq were circulated by bloggers online.

Blogging then is both a popular source for news stories as well as being a new marketing tool for established media outlets. Jenkins (2004: 36) provides one example of a commercial media site (*Salon*, an online news magazine) that hosts the blogs of renowned writers and politicians. Thus, the Internet can be used as a means to express one's opinions as well as a means to increase one's portfolio.

Radio journalism has also witnessed harsh competition thanks to the technological advance of 'podcasting'. A podcast is a radio programme-style which can be downloaded from the Internet and transferred to an MP3 player. Listeners, particularly young people, appear to be abandoning radio, preferring to download favourite programmes and music tracks from the web and listen to them on MP3 players. Yet paradoxically, radio stations see podcasting as a new means to reach new audiences and Virgin Radio showed that 18 per cent of their listeners heard their shows on a medium other than radio (Twist, 2005).

For journalists and media professionals, the web is not only a place to find thousands of different podcasts for download, but also, more importantly, a new place to market their work. More and more media corporations acknowledge the popularity of podcasting and some companies even search among the thousands podcasts for new talent and the head of BBC Radio Interactive said: 'It won't be too long before this [podcasting] becomes the normal route to discover new talents' (ibid.). For consumers, however, podcasting is a means to control what they want to listen to when they want to, not to mention that they can skip parts of the programmes, e.g. the advertising, as they wish. In sum, media convergence has, for better or worse, resulted in new ways of consuming media, with new consumers becoming active contributors with little or no fixed loyalty (Jenkins, 2004: 37). Furthermore, the rise of the breed of independent freelancers illustrates the widened scope of opportunities available for media entrepreneurs to profile themselves and demonstrate their skills.

Freelancing, the fastest route to fame

There have been significant organizational changes in the media sector during the past two decades and the commercialization of the media markets in the UK has forced even the state-supported public service into harsh competition. One outcome has been the reduction of full-time contracts for journalists and the trend to independent contractors, or freelancers (Ursell, 2000). ITV ended up cutting 44 per cent of its staff and BBC around 33 per cent from 1987 to 1996, while the number of media freelancers rose from 30 to 60 per cent of staff from 1989 to 1996 (ibid.: 807). Freelancing tasks can vary and may include, *inter alia*, photographic assignments, sound recording, voice-over, web design, or substituting for permanent staff. Freelancers are regarded by media companies as a valuable addition to their resources and their professional services are seen as being equal to those provided by permanent staff, but in an attempt to rationalize their budget, media companies may use the supply and demand situation to impose reduced budgets on their independent producers and freelancers; for instance, one TV producer reported how he accepted a contract in 1998 to make a 43-part series with a budget similar to what he had received in 1995 for a 6-part series (ibid.: 814).

New approaches to self-entrepreneurship force independent media professionals to market themselves as an independent enterprise, e.g. developing their own marketing strategy, branding themselves, refining their understanding of the market and the competition, their USP, etc. (Storey et al., 2005). However freelancing is seen to entail a great financial risk, e.g. there is no redundancy pay or help in covering training costs, and freelancers usually do not have pension contributions. Some freelancers even accept work for which they were not qualified in order to secure regular short-term contracts. What is more, the rates of pay may vary according to the supply and demand in the market: the superabundance of media studies courses has, on one hand, secured a large, highly educated and well-trained creative labour pool, while, on the other hand, it has resulted in a surge of new recruits, university students seeking work placements and other aspirants, particularly among new graduates (ibid.) – in the UK ca. 30,000 people have graduated in media since the mid-1990s (Ursell, 2000: 814).

The importance of networking

Although the freelancing market, in principle, is open to anyone who possesses the basic skills and qualifications needed for such jobs, informal networks provide the safest route to secure freelance contracts, so those without a large network often lack knowledge of the opportunities available. To save advertising or agency fees, media companies often prefer to ask employees to recommend former colleagues for the freelance jobs. As one freelancer put it, 'people are selected for membership of the work team because they are known to turn in sound work, are easy to get on with, are reliable, and are, in any event, "the wife's brother" (Ursell, 2000: 812). In this environment, freelancers usually fear turning down a client, accepting any and every job to keep in touch with the same client. Although networking is a sociable route to find contracts, it is also a hindrance to enforcing strong collegial relationships among freelancers: some freelancers complain that if they refuse an assignment and recommend a colleague instead, they will lose their client to this colleague. As one freelancer put it:

> I got X an intro to one of the independents when they asked me to come in with them on a project and I couldn't. I sent her along instead of me. Now they use her all the time. I don't begrudge her the work, she's good worker. But so am I and the way I see it, she's taken my job now. (cited in Ursell, 2000: 812)

Nonetheless, the study by Storey et al. (2005) showed that freelancers indeed see the benefits of freelancing; flexibility in the working hours, even if it means occasionally working seven long days a week and working with a diverse set of assignments (ibid.: 1048). Additionally, Ursell (2000: 819) confirms that freelancers appreciate the ability to choose what they want while gaining social and professional recognition.

Freelancing can also be a route for ethnic media professionals, who are largely underrepresented in media outlets both in the USA and the UK; Ainley (1998), for instance, showed that in mid-1990s, only 1.8 per cent of the members of British journalists union were non-white, and only 15 per cent out of 8,000 journalists on local papers are black. Indeed, some permanent staff prefer freelancing contracts to avoid intimidation at the workplace; in London, for instance, several ethnic press journalists resorted to freelancing as a means to avoid racism in the workplace (The Commission for Racial Equality, 2005). Freelancing has thus been utilized as a means for ethnic media entrepreneurs to enter the creative market.

Q News

Fuad Nahdi, a native Kenyan with a degree in journalism, established the monthly magazine *Q News* in the UK in 1992. It has 20,000 subscribers, reaching up to 60,000. With the rising debate in the UK about Islam and British-Muslim identity, Nahdi thought the time was ripe to launch a magazine that contributed to the debate. Nahdi wanted to write in the language of the youth in the street, creating a magazine that is 'funny and witty' and yet deals with sober and provocative issues such as polygamy and fatwas. Thanks to the IT technology that has revolutionized the magazine industry, Nahdi and his collaborators could do the production at home and distribute copy in front of mosques and among friends 'by word of mouth', he said, targeting the second- and third-generation Muslims in Britain.

The letter Q was chosen not only because it appealed to the minimalist design prevalent at the time but also

> We knew the financial survival of the publication would have to depend on advertising, and the main source for advertising we targeted was the equal opportunity

(Continued)

advertising for local authorities and central governments. If we use Muslim names, people would see it defensive, so we thought Q News was neutral ... Q was nothing, it was just a sexy letter we deigned ... we've written articles about what Q means ... it meant nothing at the time, it could mean anything, Quran, Queer, Question.

Nahdi defines three aims behind *Q News*: (1) to provide a training context for young people – particularly women – who want to become journalists; (2) to serve as a mirror for outsiders as to what the issues are that concern Muslims; and (3) to reflect the real issues that should concern Muslims. What contributed to the success of *Q News* was the demand to get news stories about Muslims in the UK. In fact, more than 40 per cent of *Q News* subscribers are not Muslims, according to Nahdi; they are people who write about or work with Muslims such as British media institutions, central governments and local authorities. Now, *Q News* has a fast growing readership in the USA, yet there is no plan to move the magazine outside London, 'For London', said Nahdi, 'still remains the new centre for the Muslim world, if you want to give a message to the Muslim world, come to London ... this is because of historical reasons ... this country ruled most of the Muslim world, even the major Arab broadsheets have headquarters here in London.'

Q News has had to depend on the young ethnic talents to generate stories. However, at the time of launching the magazine in the beginning of the 1990s, most students in several British ethnic minorities were heading towards professional education in engineering or medicine, the two most prestigious professions among ethnic minorities at the time, while few fancied a career in journalism. According to Nahdi, 'Every country has an elitist profession, in the UK, this profession is media and journalism ... it is about which school you went to and who you now.' It was therefore *Q News* that took the initiative to organize regular workshops inviting young people to generate ideas to write about in the magazine. Since its inception in 1992, *Q News* has organized 177 workshops to generate ideas, which, according to Nahdi, is the backbone for the magazine's survival.

Today, *Q News* annually receives hundreds of applications from young people seeking training and apprenticeship at *Q News*. 'There are a lot more people studying journalism now', commented Nahdi, 'young British are now more educated and affluent and they are on the look-out for more cultural products.'

Working in media entrepreneurship, however, is not always financially rewarding work. Nahdi recalled that he has 'never been paid a salary by *Q News*' and that he had to do two to three other freelancing jobs to pay his bills. Yet, Nahdi and his staff of freelancers continue to do this job because they 'believe in the principles of the magazine'. 'Freelancing is a difficult way of surviving', said Nahdi, and it depends on two things: contacts and time.

The most vital criterion for success, according to Nahdi, is to know the target market: 'You must produce not what you want but what people need ... In *Q News*, we allowed the market to lead us ... not us to lead it'. For instance, the magazine introduced matrimonial ads so young people can use it to get contacts, and the magazine is written in a witty rather than aloof style. 'We invented the new way of talking about Islam', said Nahdi, 'we made Islam more humane ... we put cartoons in and made fun of ourselves and of others.'

(*Source*: Fuad Nahdi, personal communication 1 February 2007)

Entrepreneurial strategies and success factors

As mentioned above, the media sector is characterized by its economic risk both for employers and employees due to the volatile demands of the market. Media entrepreneurs are also under continuous pressure to enhance their skills to match their clients' need to work across diverse platforms, and the technological advances discussed briefly above have offered an opportunity to newcomers to present their work on multimedia platforms, while sharpening the competition among well-established professionals. Entrepreneurs have also used the Internet as a means to market their portfolio to a wider segment of clients than before, and yet the abundance of material on the Internet means harsher competition – not to mention the risk of having one's work illegally copied. The various risks and opportunities for media entrepreneurs can be summarized as shown in Table 14.1.

As in all industries, a clear strategy of one's aims and a clear business plan (see Chapter 6) of how to fulfil these goals are needed. A healthy plan will be based on market research (see Chapter 5) so it is vital for entrepreneurs to study the market, know their customers and keep abreast of new technological advances in their field. There should also be a sound learning strategy included, involving continuously seeking to learn new skills, as new skills also mean new opportunities. One means of enhancing one's entrepreneurial profile is

Table 14.1   Risks and opportunities for independent media entrepreneurship

Factor	Threat	Opportunity
Distribution	Risk of illegal copying on the Internet	Global reach
Market condition	Harsh competition	Open market
Economic benefit	Volatile	Occasional high rewards and royalties
Professional development	Pressure of multi-skilling	Chance to build a stronger portfolio across various platforms
Networking	Impediment to get to new customers beyond the network	A chance to enter the field

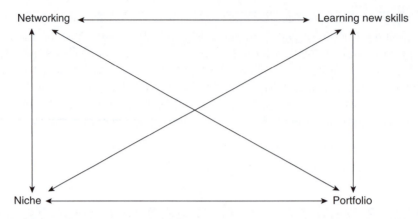

Figure 14.1   The relationships governing entrepreneurial niche

to find a speciality or a niche that matches one's interests while serving as a distinct property that uniquely distinguishes one's work from others'. Finally, contacts and networking play a decisive role in maintaining short-term contracts. This can be roughly shown in Figure 14.1.

A media entrepreneur then acquires two kinds of knowledge:

1   professional knowledge about their niche and the new techniques;
2   business knowledge about their audience and the possible market challenges.

A recent report (Department of Culture, Media and Sport, 2006) points out that the challenge lies in the second type of knowledge – career advice centres in higher education institutions are not geared to the particular needs of the creative sector. Thus, prospective media professionals are usually urged to take the initiative and obtain this type of knowledge themselves, e.g. by seeking professional advice from veterans. Several Western governments plan therefore to establish specialized career advice centres as well as councils (such as Cultural Industries Development Agencies, UK) to promote networking among media professionals and to ensure the constant benchmarking of good practices in the creative sector.

Chapter summary

The shift to the so-called post-Fordist economy has been accompanied by a series of changes on the media scene, e.g. fragmentation of producers and consumers and the rise of niche markets. Mainstream media has become very volatile as evidenced by e.g. the over-production of loss-making titles, but niches can be attractive assuming mastery of technological innovation and adoption of new technology in daily practices.

Journalism belongs to the 'creative industries' and shares the risks characterizing these industries such as unpredictable consumer demand. However, in common with all other branches of industry, the successful entrepreneur is able to generate cost-effective surprises. Another shared trait is that journalists, as a creative labour force, show enthusiasm for originality rather than seeking stable work hours, wages or other work conditions. Moreover, the independent breed of media entrepreneurs is under constant and increasing personal and professional pressure to cope with this risky media business while maintaining the self-image that constitutes the backbone of a professional's marketing strategy.

Thus, there is more than ever a need for 'a clear strategy', knowledge of the target audience/market and adjusting the services provided accordingly. This is often fulfilled by refining one's profile by specializing in a niche market, such as appealing to a certain ethnic group, gender, etc (e.g. www.asianwomanmag.com) or socio-economic group (e.g. *The Big Issue*).

References

Ainley, B. (1998) *Black Journalists, White Media*. Stoke-on-Trent: Trentham Books.

Beulah, Ainley (1998) *Black Journalists, White Media*. London: Trenton Books.

Boczkowski, P. J. and Ferris, J. (2005) 'Multiple media, convergence processes, and divergent products: organizational innovation in digital media production at a European firm', *The Annals of the American Academy of Political and Social Science*, 597: 32–47.

Bustamante, E. (2004) 'Cultural industries in the digital age: some provisional conclusions', *Media, Culture and Society*, 26: 803–20.

Cavet, R. E. (2000) *Creative Industries: Contacts between Art and Commerce*. Cambridge, MA: Harvard University Press.

Commission for Racial Equality (2005) *Why Ethnic Minority Workers Leave London's Print Journalism Sector*. London: CRE.

Croteau, D. R. and Hoynes, W. (2006) *The Business of Media*, 2nd edn. London: Sage.

Deloitte and Touche (2006) 'The net benefit of digital publishing', Available at: http://www.deloitte.com/dtt/article/0,1002,sid%253D2854%2526cid%253D123826,00.html.

Department of Culture, Media and Sport (2006) 'Developing entrepreneurship for the creative industries: the role of higher and further education', Available at www.culture.gov.uk

Garrison, B. (2001) 'Diffusion of online information technologies in newspaper newsrooms' *Journalism* 2: 221–39.

Hesmondhalgh, D. (2002) *Cultural Industries*, First edition. London: Sage.

Huang, E., Davison, K., Shreve, S., Davis, T., Bettendorf, E. and Nair, A. (2006) 'Facing the challenges of convergence', *Convergence: The International Journal of Research into New Media Technologies*, 12: 83–98.

Hutton, W. (2000) 'Switch channel or pull the plug', *The Observer*, 25 June. http://www.guardian.co.uk/BBC/Story/0,,336264,00.html

Jenkins, H. (2004) 'The cultural logic of media convergence', *International Journal of Cultural Studies*, 7: 33–43.

Leadbeater, C. and Oakley, K. (1999) *The Independents: Britain's New Cultural Entrepreneurs*. London: Demos.

McRobbie, A. (2002) 'Clubs to companies: notes on the decline of political culture in speeded up creative worlds', *Cultural Studies*, 16: 516–31.

Negus, K. and Pickering, M. (2004) *Creativity, Communication and Cultural Value*. London: Sage.

Ofcom (2006) 'The future of radio', Available at: www.ofcom.org.uk

Singer, J. (2004) 'Strange bedfellows? The diffusion of convergence in four news organizations', *Journalism Studies*, 5: 3–18.

Storey, J., Salaman, G. and Platman, K. (2005) 'Living with enterprise in an enterprise economy: freelance and contract workers in the media', *Human Relations*, 58: 1033–54.

Twist, J. (2005) 'Radio has its eye on podcasters'. Available at: http://news.bbc.co.uk/2/hi/technology/4267690.stm

Ursell, G. (2000) 'Television production: issues of exploitation, commodification and subjectivity in UK television labour markets', *Media, Culture and Society*, 22: 805–25.

UNESCO (2007) 'Cultural industries: a focal point for culture in the future'. Available at: http://portal.unesco.org/culture/en/ev.php-URL_ID=34603&URL_DO=DO_TOPIC&URL_SECTION=201.html

Wray, R. (2006) 'ITV drags rivals down a dead end street as advertisers switch to net', *Guardian*. http://business.guardian.co.uk/print/0,,329610654-108725,00.html

Further reading

Beck, A. (ed.) (2002) *Cultural Work: Understanding the Cultural Industries*. London: Routledge.

Hartley, J. (ed.) (2005) *Creative Industries*. Oxford: Blackwell.

Smith, C. (1998) *Creative Britain*. London: Faber and Faber.

Web links

www.cida.co.uk

www.creativeclass.org

www.creativeconomy.org.uk

www.culture.gov.uk

www.innovationjournlaism.org

www.publishingmedia.org.uk

Suggestions for exercises

1 What do you understand by the term 'cultural intermediaries'?
2 What are the advantages of being a freelancer over being a 'corporate professional'?
3 Name 4–6 well-known media freelancers of which two are so successful that the large national networks buy their products 'en bloc'.

15 General Characteristics of the Creative Arts

Alan Fisher

Introduction

The entertainment industry sector is one of the largest net exporters in the UK economy and this chapter deals with entrepreneurship in the creative, recreational or entertainment industries, focusing first on film (moving image), then on music. This chapter is of especial interest to those studying entertainment and the creative arts, including design, fashion, music, film and popular culture.

Characteristics of the creative arts industry generally

Psychologically, many individuals involved in the creative industries are by nature risk-takers, driven by a desire to be viewed as creators operating within a commercial environment, while maintaining their ownership of artefacts or performances. Given this major driver, many opportunities historically have arisen for a raft of entrepreneurs who effectively plug into the process of artistic creation, as in the musician and the promoter (see Chapter 1). Historically, the model has been for the artistic creators to rely upon other enterprising individuals to curate and nurture their output, maximizing the commercial opportunities while providing natural synergies with other creative industries, e.g. music and moving image. This model, however, is likely to change in the future as the creators themselves adopt new models of operation and entrepreneurial opportunities.

Numerous examples exist of individuals operating in quite distinct areas of practice, forming novel brands and essentially re-inventing the format of delivery and production. The ever-more rapacious appetite of the general public for these new modes of entertainment has expanded the possibilities for creative thinkers, while challenging old models of copyright control and intellectual capital. Without doubt this is the main battlefield for the future consumption and reward mechanisms for the creators of product.

Scope and challenges of entertainment

Every year, in America alone, people spend 120 billion hours of their available time and more than 200 billion dollars of family income on consuming legal forms of entertainment. Incredibly this vast figure also discounts the huge amount of illegal P2P (peer-to-peer) service in visual and aural material occurring globally. While there are over 1,200 record companies in the US alone, and over 2,600 labels (Vogel, 2007), 'the best-selling CD in the world is a blank, recordable one' (Kusek and Leonhard, 2005).

Many creators also follow the model of being natural early adopters of technological change, and as a consequence are increasingly becoming the stakeholders in all aspects of the production, manufacturing, and distribution chain (Figure 15.1). This degree of control is extremely attractive for artists as it opens up possibilities for maximizing profit, while retaining total artistic control; however, many challenges await in the ever-expanding, leisure-rich digital age. Many creative processes strain against the economic resources available for a given task, and have to satisfy the curators (gatekeepers) of their intrinsic commercial value or worth. Teams producing complex creative goods can be stable and long-lasting in some areas of practice (TV and orchestras, for example) while highly transient in others. In complex creative industries much information flows within and among companies, with a complex courting arrangement for embryonic projects being undertaken. Pitching a project between competitors is a natural part of the art of the entrepreneur in this sector of industry, as well as creating a buzz around a particular artist or project. This is illustrated by the relationship between the artist Damien Hirst and his approval by cultural gatekeeper Charles Saatchi, whose initial purchase vindicated the artist's worth, and thereby benchmarked the sale prices for subsequent works. These innovative initial breakthroughs can commonly be seen as spawning a particular movement (in this case the Young British Artist movement, 'Britart') and thus many artists and entrepreneurs will immediately align themselves to capitalize on an upsurge of interest in related commodities. This finger-on-the-pulse skill is vital for many entrepreneurs operating in the creative industries, and those most in-tune can effectively maintain longevity in a particular sector, constantly redefining their output and allegiances.

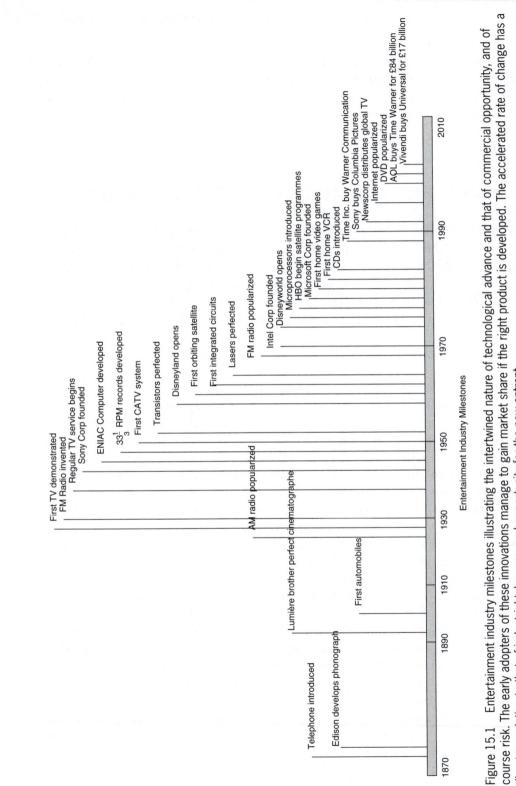

Figure 15.1   Entertainment industry milestones illustrating the intertwined nature of technological advance and that of commercial opportunity, and of course risk. The early adopters of these innovations manage to gain market share if the right product is developed. The accelerated rate of change has a direct correlation to that of industrial take-over, and opportunity for the new entrant

Source: Taken from Vogel (2007)

State support

For the entrepreneur, government agencies and grant aid for projects are another vital part of a package of seed-corn funding for projects, and, although competition is fierce, can provide a vital injection of capital. These gatekeepers of cultural endeavour constantly shift both emphasis and funding targets and thus it is vital the entrepreneur keep abreast of all initiatives. This highlights the extreme need for intense networking in the relevant circles.

Entertainment market analysis

Probably very little of the artistic activity the public sees is fashioned through *ars gratia artis* (usually rendered in English as 'Art for art's sake'), rather it is driven by the capitalist stimulus of profit motive. The post-artisan market has been massively expanded with economies of scale, mass manufacture and establishment of individual wealth in the developed countries of the world. One major factor today is the balance between the lowering costs of manufacture and delivery, on one hand, versus the threat of piracy and DRM (digital rights management), on the other. DRM is an expanding field and indeed one's own facial image carries copyright; in the ever-increasing world of computer-generated images, virtual actors will, in the future, need to carve out a career for themselves – a brave new world indeed!

Table 15.1 indicates how the consumption of creative output is shaped in the USA. As shown in Table 15.1, more than a third of an adult's day is associated with consuming some form of stimulus from a raft of creative industry output. This represents a massive potential for an entrepreneur to tap into, assuming one can gain an economic return for one's endeavours.

Who buys what?

The long-term growth in the creative industries is intrinsically linked to the rate of technological development through the economy; aggregate spending on entertainment is concentrated in the middle-aged groups where personal economic earnings peak. Conversely this occurs when free time for the middle-aged individual is scarce. As in many areas (fashion, etc.), consumption – especially in music – is rife in the teens and tweens (for notes on segmentation by generation, see Chapter 5), but there is a definite trend for parents to finance children's personal consumption over a broader range of products (film, etc.), and indeed an increasing percentage of the family's disposable income is jointly utilized in this area.

Barriers for the entrepreneur

Despite massive consumption (Table 15.1), the entrepreneur faces several additional hurdles presented to new entrants into established markets; these come from government regulations

Table 15.1   Relative consumption of creative content by vehicle, excluding 50 hours of Internet usage per week in 2000

	Hours per person per year	
Leisure activity	1970	2000
Television	1226	1603
Network affiliates	667	
Independent stations		189
Basic cable stations		661
Pay cable		86
Radio	872	1065
Home (None specific)		394
Out of home (None specific)		671
Newspapers	218	151
Recorded music	68	317
Magazines	170	80
Leisure books	65	93
Cinema	10	12
Home video		57
Spectator sports	3	15
Video games arcade		7
Home		69
Cultural events	3	7
Total	2635	3476
Hours per adult per week	50.7	66.8
Hours per adult per day	7.2	9.5

Source: From CBS Office of Economic Analysis by Wilkofsky Gruen Associates Inc. Figures for the UK market are similar, but with slightly fewer visits to the cinema and less time on the Internet, but these are compensated for by increased consumption of television programmes.

pertaining to broadcasting licences, and cable provision/digital broadband. This could look bleak for the entrepreneur; however, a balance has been struck with deregulation of broadcasting practices and an increasing trend towards the use of external content providers (see Chapter 14). This has led to large broadcast corporations acting increasingly as commissioning editors only. This deregulation leaves a wide entry point for content creators (as discussed in Chapter 14).

Most creative products are representative of one-of-a-kind talent: Coldplay, Oasis, David Bowie or brand name services, for example, MTV, Nickelodeon, Endemol, etc. Initial costs are usually risked without much knowledge of how many units will be consumed; this could potentially range from zero to practically infinite values. As such, the entrepreneur accepts far higher risk factors than probably any other industry. It is quite common, for instance, to see film productions fail in theatre ticket sales, but this loss can be ameliorated by creative marketing and alternative consumption formats such as viral marketing, DVD sales, TV licensing, and rentals.

Music industry profits models are increasingly shifting towards capitalization of performance, merchandizing and image rights, with little profit margins in the more traditional aspect of mass manufacture of single artefacts. The music industry is currently viewed as being in turmoil (e.g. video games have more influence on music than radio stations) with technology bringing powerful and disruptive changes to the established multinational companies (see below), and this shifting industrial reality is about to be unleashed on the moving image industry.

Several industry structures exist, including the near-monopolistic competition model characterized by few overlapping competitors in the same market offering somewhat differentiated products, resulting in only slightly diverse pricing and competition. Examples of this are books, magazines and the performing arts. Another common market structure is one of an oligopoly where only a few but clearly different sellers of close substitutes exist, and pricing structures are extremely sensitive to moves from one player. Examples of this type of operation include films, or recorded music network TV channels. The two types have differentials in the sensitivity to individual companies, e.g. striking an extreme pricing policy for however short a period as with the recent Virgin Media/Sky BSB pricing war. The old oligopolies are increasingly under threat by the new entrepreneurial sector, backed by the digital revolution and the ability to globally collect micro-payment for downloads.

Digital opportunities

- YouTube, founded in March 2005, was valued at US$1.5 billion in 2006 by its shareholders. Based in San Mateo, YouTube is a small privately funded company with 60 employees. Chad Hurley, one of its co-founders, serves as the CEO with its other two co-founders, Steven Chen, CTO, and Jawed Karim. Their tagline is 'Broadcast Yourself' and this largely represents their goal. Ever since it began, the company has had the goal to build a community rather than to make a lot of money. However, this growing phenomenon (with more than 65,000 uploads and 100 million videos being watched daily) meant they had to review their business plan in order to sustain their growth. In March 2007, Viacom launched a lawsuit against YouTube, based on infringement of copyright.
- Napster was developed in 1990, enabling connected computers to search for songs on a peer-to-peer basis. This was followed by Grokster and Morpheus, both of whom survived legal challenges under copyright law in 2003.
- The 'download threat' is becoming applicable to movies from software such as DeCSS, which allows copying of digitally encoded full-length feature programmes.

Various value measures are levelled at the creative industries, the prime one being the value placed on intellectual property and the potential for future exploitation, for example, the use of old musical recordings or film archives, either as samples or complete works being given new synchronization licences with visual works such as advertising or new releases. This is difficult to measure in guaranteed economic return because there is an element of decreasing revenue over time, counterbalanced by a sudden revival of interest in a work. The valuation of assets can also be subject to externalities that make a media object or property particularly valuable to a specific buyer, for example, when the buyer is interested in the community contacts as much as the content itself like the recent sale of YouTube, which made its founders instant millionaires. Value for the entrepreneur can furthermore be measured in a range of intangibles that are not closely associated with 'big business models', perhaps the closest parallel being the concept of goodwill in company sales. YouTube's young founders may have been the biggest beneficiaries of YouTube's sale in a $1.65 billion deal with Google, but they have some unexpected bed-fellows – old-style media companies that had been considered YouTube's biggest legal threat.

Three of the four major music companies – Vivendi's Universal Music Group, Sony and Bertelsmann's jointly owned Sony BMG Music Entertainment, and the Warner Music Group – each quietly negotiated to take small stakes in YouTube as part of video- and music-licensing deals they struck shortly before the sale, indicating a shift to a far more pragmatic viewpoint. These music companies collectively stand to receive as much as $50 million from the arrangements, because a significant portion of the videos posted to YouTube contain copyrighted songs or video material, and indeed the website had been considered a litigation landmine. Doug Morris, Chief Executive of Universal Music, called YouTube and MySpace 'copyright infringers' and said the sites 'owe us tens of millions of dollars'.

Universal also filed lawsuits against Bolt and Grouper, two smaller video-sharing sites, for allowing users to post hundreds of pirated music videos of its artists, including Mariah Carey, 50 Cent and the Black Eyed Peas. The deals that the music companies struck for stakes in YouTube should help to shield Google from copyright-infringement lawsuits, an issue that concerned some Google investors when the YouTube deal was first announced. Despite this, other copyright holders, including the Hollywood and television studios, could pursue legal action if their content appears on YouTube.

The film industry

Although all regions produce and distribute movies and television programmes, the dominant exporter remains the USA with a net trade balance of approximately $3 billion a year. One of the major drivers for this success is the fact that the language is English; English is the second most used language after Mandarin Chinese, and the majority of speakers reside in the wealthiest countries. Figure 15.2 demonstrates the massive increase in mergers and acquisitions in the post-war period, fuelled by the ability to cross-market product via different media outlets. Film and record companies now form virtuous publishing circles, marketed by print and media release publicity vehicles.

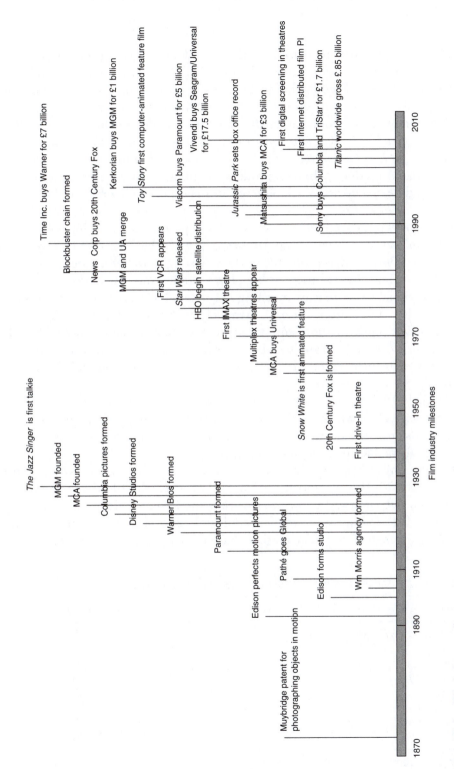

Figure 15.2   Film industry milestones

Source: From Vogel (2007)

Movie making is truly entrepreneurial, a triumph of hope over reality, and sometimes salvaged by crazed ingenuity, as with Terry Gilliam's failed 'Lost in La Mancha' project which went from being a feature film production to a successful documentary about a project locked in a downward spiral of unfortunate events. For the budding entrepreneur, this industry sector has a staggering potential for profit but, as discussed earlier, also for massive loss: *Star Wars* returned profits of over US $150 million on an initial investment of $11 million and more recently the returns on *The Lord of the Rings* trilogy have dwarfed this figure (if one includes the range of associated products). Indeed product bundling is an essential feature: think of where Disney would be if they had stuck only to films and not made branded dolls and other products.

A range of fiscal laws in each country affect changes in production planning, location shooting, etc. and thus influence manufacturing overheads immensely. A ratio of three in ten films could realistically be considered as profitable in their own right, therefore the success ratio for spread investments such as that afforded by 'big player' studios and distributors is considerably better than for individual entrepreneurs investing in single projects. Nevertheless, certain individuals can buck this trend, but one must be extremely cautious in this particular segment of the creative industries. Some of these entrepreneurs have had sustained success based upon establishing an initial core business and thus being seen as creators of a particular product, such as Merchant Ivory with their period productions, and George Harrison with his Handmade Films enterprise.

As shown in Table 15.2, the main film industry players are custodians of a massive amount of intellectual property, all of which have a variable market value depending upon a wide range of influences, for instance, the death of a film icon allowing a retrospective season to be promoted, or the digital enhancement of an original print.

Industries that require these large capital sums can usually be seen as evolving into oligopolistic forms, as with the automotive industry. However, the film industry views each project as a unique output, and this has meant that the larger-scale aspects of the industry still rely upon interfacing with small-scale highly specialized entrepreneurial companies. Also the existence of ancillary markets has enabled many entrepreneurs to finance

Table 15.2   The approximate number of major film titles up to 2004

Studio	No. of titles
Sony Columbia TriStar	2,500
Disney	700
Paramount	1,100
20th Century Fox	2,100
MGM	4,500
Universal	4,100
Warner Bros/New Line	4,500
Total	19,500

Source: From Vogel (2007)

their own films through presale of rights, with the maker assuming a majority financial risk. Risk is cushioned – but not directly limited – by this approach; producers require interim but relatively costly loans during the period of production, and often all the way up to theatre release. For the most part, this has engendered a climate of hedge-betting and cross-collaborative projects, allowing new entry entrepreneurs to gain a foothold as producers.

Production starts are sensitive to interest environments and the availability of credit, although there are some notable examples of young entrepreneurs bucking this industry model; for example, *The Blair Witch Project* showed that small-scale entrepreneurial endeavour can result in huge profit margins and have run-away success. More commonly, production starts lag behind by at least six quarters compared to financial conditions at the outset of a project and must be carefully considered by the entrepreneur while risking capital investments.

Most recently film fans are actually contributing, via new media, script re-writes and share purchases of new projects. This has given rise to a true democratization of the process, and is certainly one way for entrepreneurs to get initial ideas off the drawing board. The churn of assets can be seen in Table 15.3 (overleaf) where post 1980 we saw a rapid increase in investor competition, partly driven by new media conglomerates but also interestingly companies wishing to expand their portfolio of investments such as Matsushita and Coca-Cola.

Goodell (1998) reports that the financial foundations for the development of content include:

- industry sources;
- studio development;
- in-house productions;
- independent distributors;
- talent agencies;
- end users;
- actors;
- banks;
- insurance companies;
- distributors;
- public and private funders.

Entrepreneurs must take advantage of film completion bonds when investing in productions, as this allows a producer to take control of the film and take it through to completion (or alternatively abandon and repay financiers). This security is usually a prerequisite by investors and is vital in protecting one's investment in an enterprise, but comes at a considerable premium. Upon completion, films are usually distributed to the market that generates the largest marginal revenue first, and then handed sequentially downwards through the return chain, each of which should be carefully considered by the entrepreneur, with some films suiting particular release dates and distribution channels (Figure 15.3).

Table 15.3   Selected film library transfers

Year	Assets transferred	Sold by	Bought by	Approximate price ($)
1957	700 Warner Bros features, shorts, cartoons	Associated Artists	United Artists	30 million
1958	750 pre-1948 features	Paramount	MCA	50 million
1979	500 features	AIP	Filmways	25 million
1981	2,200 features, shorts, studio, and distribution	Transamerica	MGM	380 million
1981	1,400 features, Aspen skiing, Coke bottling, Deluxe film labs, five TV stations, International theatre chain, studio real estate	20th Century Fox	Marvin Davis Entrepreneur	722 million
1982	1,800 features, studio property, TV stations, arcade game manufacturing	Columbia Pictures	Coca-Cola	750 million
1982	500 features	Filmways	Orion Pictures	26 million
1985	4,600 features, 800 cartoons, shorts, Metrocolor lab, studio property	MGM/UA	Turner Broadcasting	1.5 billion
1985	950 features, distribution system, rights to MGM library	Turner Broadcasting	United Artists	480 million
1989	2,400 features, and 20,000 TV episodes, distribution system, 800 screens	Columbia Pictures and Coca-Cola	Sony Corp	4.8 billion
1990	3,100 features, 14,000 TV episodes	MCA Inc	Matsushita Electric	6.1 billion
1993	200 features	New Line	Turner Broadcasting	500 million
1994	900 features, 4,000 TV episodes, half USA network, teams, TV stations, publishing	Paramount	Viacom	9.6 billion
1995	3,200 features, 14,000 TV episodes.	Matsushita	Seagram	5.7 billion
1996	1,500 features, 4,100 TV episodes	Credit Lyonnais	Kerkorian	1.3 billion
1997	2,000 features	Orion/Samuel Goldwyn	MGM	573 million
2003	7,000 features	Artisan	Lions Gate	210 million

Source: From Vogel (2007)

The importance of distribution cannot be overestimated. The William Morris Agency in the USA can expect to earn between $21,000 and $100,000 per episode on a network distributed show and *The Cosby Show* returns a staggering $50 million in re-runs alone.

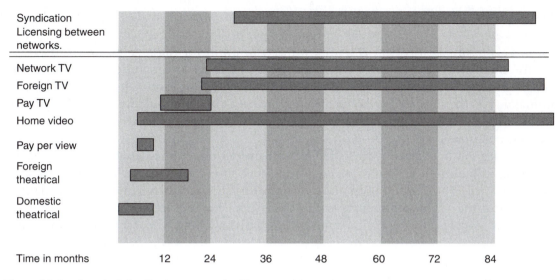

Figure 15.3   A typical distribution pattern for films
Source: Vogel (2007)

Standard contracts

Contracts between distributors and exhibitors usually take the form of a sliding scale on the gross less the house 'nut' (rents, mortgages, telephone, electricity and insurance, etc.):

- Week 1: 70 per cent of first week's takings after subtraction of overheads (the 'house nut').
- Every two weeks afterwards the scale of profit split moves in the following fashion; 60/40, 50/50 and so forth in the exhibitor's favour. I.e. the distributor loses over time, therefore a long-run film works to the advantage of the cinema owner; e.g. *The Sound of Music* on its first release.
- Holdover clauses are utilized should revenues unexpectedly remain at an exceptionally high level. These clauses address such anomalies in audience reaction and are usually a contentious aspect of contract negotiation.

It is increasingly difficult for new entrants into this particular segment of the industry, as many cartels have long been established with a downward pressure on available margins, although there continue to be some possibilities for new entrants into the independent operating chain if given a certain bespoke environmental treatment. Large multiplex chains capitalize on the vast majority of releases in the UK and US markets.

DVD distribution channels remain highly volatile, given increased use of 'TV on demand' and the associated ease of access and convenience; early entrepreneurial operators in this area such as Blockbuster are under increasing pressure to change their service model with on-line ordering and home delivery becoming necessary to compete for and retain customers. Store profits come from fast turnover in the first six months of release, with a typical break-even figure of 30 rentals of a video release; typical rentals run at a figure of 50 per title before resale. This results in a typical 20 rental window of profit for the retailer. In TV, deals are usually structured in a three-part staged payment of fees with a good deal to a production company being 5 per cent (per episode licence fee for life of the show), 5 per cent (tied to profitability of the show, only recoupable once net profit has been achieved), and 10 per cent (tied to back-end syndication revenues). Profits in the last segment can be significant for the strong negotiator.

Diversification over many projects reduces the overall risk to the entrepreneur; they must be willing to look to a variety of markets and move investments to tax-efficient havens of operation. Increasingly syndication and spin-off deals such as video games and toy markets are providing the active entrepreneur with massive opportunities to maximize profit with little to no risk involved (because all manufacturing and marketing costs are taken on by a third party).

Technology in the film industry

Internet-based technologies provide viewers with unprecedented control over what and when they watch, but marketing costs, however, remain high. Increasingly the control, storage and distribution of intellectual property are being compromised by copyright infringement by the general public and this has real threats to the entrepreneur seeking to capitalize on investments over the long term, and this model of consistent revenue streams may need to be closely re-examined in the future. The early history of the film industry features a succession of patent applications and consequent legal wranglings during the rapidly developing technological advance starting around the early 1890s. This process is ongoing and opportunities are still present for the technological inventor, given a move to advanced digital projection and production methodologies. Early entrepreneurs built the foundations of massive global organizations that now encompass most media formats, such as Carl Laemmle (credited with founding Universal Studios), and Marcus Loew (MGM). Milestone factors that have shaped the film industry thus far include:

- Technological advances in manufacture, distribution and storage.
- Development of sound synchronization.
- Democratization of the studio system.
- Appearance of independent film producers and independence of film theatres.
- The need for ever-larger pools of investment capital.
- The 1948 consent decree separating distribution from exhibition; the 1948 'Paramount consent decree case', the US Supreme Court ruled that for producers and distributors also to own cinema chains amounted to 'price-fixing conspiracies'. Distribution companies therefore had to dispose of their exhibition interests. This also had the effect of killing off any idea of the Hollywood majors controlling or buying into television.
- The emergence of large multiplex chains.

- Evolution of independent production and service organizations.
- Emerging digital delivery systems and immersive environments such as surround and IMAX cinema.

The music industry

Music pervades all aspects of society and is consumed in an almost transparent way by everyone, endlessly re-inventing its form and influences, thereby constantly allowing access to the new-entrant entrepreneur. As shown in Figure 15.4, mass marketing and sales-derived profits have only had a 50-year window of opportunity post rock and roll, before the introduction of new models of consumption and democratization presented massive challenges and opportunities to the entrepreneur. Larger-scale businesses have had to radically review their sales and marketing model.

Increased portability and personalization, combined with community-based websites and mechanisms for discovery and sharing, make music as popular and socially relevant as it has ever been. Yet the capacity of the music industry to capture economic value from these new exploitation models may not be commensurate with the opportunity. In one year, approximately 6,500 albums (LPs) are released in the most profitable market – America; of these only 112 sell more than 500,000 units. With a large percentage achieving only break-even sales, the majority rely on as little as 10 per cent of new material to make a profit, given the massive scale of sales for major hits and artists, this offsets losses elsewhere in a label's portfolio. Break-even artists are now no longer given time to develop their material and fan base; the need to buy success immediately with a fixed-cost base has become the major driver for the major record company. This has resulted in a major turnover of new artists with established figures such as Elton John, who has personally benefited from an earlier nurturing culture, providing the profitability of major companies.

Contrast these figures with the 25 per cent of printed publications making a profit (Chapter 14) and it can be seen that – in common with the press – the backbone of the major label strategy is to place far more material into the marketplace than can possibly succeed, but in the case of the music industry this is much more extreme.

The previous statement can be understandable with sales figures in the range of:

Michael Jackson, *Thriller* – 24 million,
Fleetwood Mac, *Rumours* – 17 million,
Led Zeppelin, *Led Zeppelin* IV – 16 million.

- Average break-even sales are in the region of 500,000 units for a major release.
- Average break-even sales for an independent release are only 100,000 copies, given the much smaller overheads involved.
- Average break-even sales via the Internet and in-house productions can be as little as 3,000 downloads.

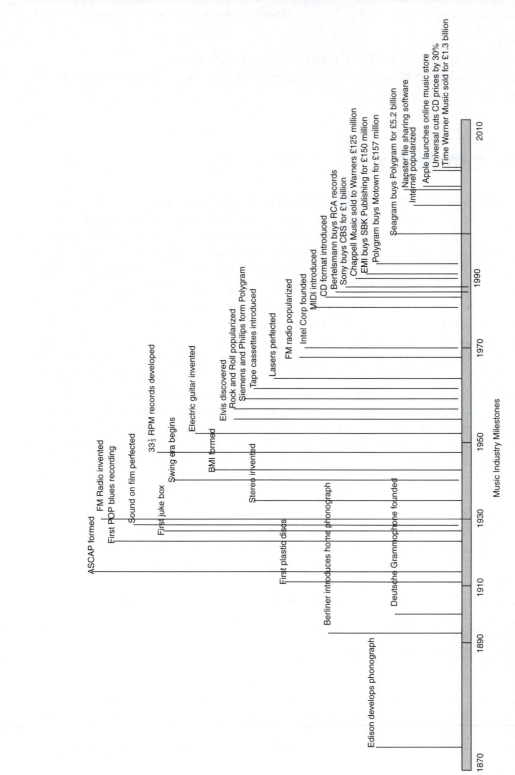

Figure 15.4   Music industry milestones
Source: Vogel (2007)

This inherent 'oil tanker' turnaround model of high fixed cost in marketing budgets can be seized upon and turned to the advantage of the more mobile entrepreneur with a close understanding of the market and audience for a particular act. Armed with this intrinsic information, more revenue streams can be created and capitalized upon with a clear understanding of the tastes and buying habits of a particular segmented musical audience.

Digitalization and new business models

So far, recorded music distribution has been the most disrupted aspect of the music industry, in part encouraged by the practice of magazine cover-mount CDs encouraging the public perception of 'music for free' that in turn encourages the culture of guilt-free computer piracy. Most surprisingly, in the four years up to 2003, music sales globally fell by almost a third; it is interesting to note that the film industry is currently considering the same methodology, and thus quite possibly is making the same psychological errors. As an entrepreneur entering this particular sector, one must understand the rapidly shifting scale of distribution and revenue streams. Among these are live concerts, brand sponsorships, merchandizing, publishing royalties and emerging mobile formats – led by the explosive ring-tone phenomena.

From a peak in the late 1990s when sales achieved a global record, sales of CDs have collapsed. This paradigm change (see Chapters 10 and 11) has given rise to the question: can the skies be tamed on digital distribution? The following quotes from the RIAA (an organization previously immersed in a war against online marketing of material, and central to the prosecution of illegal download activity) and the MPAA, give us some indication as to the level of understanding developing within the music industry.

- 'A vibrant online marketplace is taking root' (Mitch Bainwol, RIAA chairman).
- 'File sharing networks like BitTorrent and iMesh are showing that technology can be used legally' (Dan Glickman, MPAA chief executive).

Traditional business arrangements usually follow a similar model in every territory. Managers receive between 15–30 per cent of an artist's income; royalties are collected on an artist's behalf by collection agencies such as PRS (the Performing Rights Society) in the UK and ASCAP (American Society for Composers and Publishers) in the USA. Mechanical royalties are derived from a physical copy of an original work, either as sheet music or a musical artefact. Record labels provide up-front investment in the form of a recoupable advance (for this read bank loan), all of which may be spread over several releases by cross-collateralization. This approach is advantageous as it can spread risk for the new-label entrepreneur, with that difficult second album flop being subsidized by the large profit made on a new artist's first release. Major releases have recording budgets in excess of £100,000, with many far in excess of this figure; the producer is responsible for limiting any over-runs, and may indeed have to personally pay for any additional costs from his own advance. This acceptance of risk has led to many producers taking a more entrepreneurial approach, signing artists to a production deal and recording in home facilities before either going to market themselves – for example, Mike Batt and Katie Melua – or selling end products on to major companies like Stock, Aitken, and Waterman at much more favourable terms of royalty income. For a new label owner signing talent, the major points to be considered are:

- date of expiration of contract;
- number of albums and singles committed in this period;
- exclusivity;
- foreign release intentions;
- royalty rates;
- advances;
- recoupable items of costs;
- commitment to tour support;
- creative control;
- ownership of recordings;
- royalty deductions;
- joint and several arrangements with band members;
- period of accounting and hold-backs.

New business models

Sellaband.com, brainchild of Pim Betist and run by former head of Sony BMG, Johan Vosmeijer, offers the sort of industry connections most groups would die for. They have broken the traditional industry mould, with fans following a MySpace-type community model where fans literally buy futures in a band's success; i.e. fans own shares in the group's original recordings, and share in future profits. Currently over £250,000 is invested in unsigned acts on the site. The London-based band Second Person have just closed a £26,000 advance to record their first album, all funded by a 1,000-strong fan base who feel that they are intimately involved in the future success of the act.

Most music fans still collect their music for free from sites such as Limewire, and recent deals with BitTorrent appear largely superficial in nature. The most engaged music listeners, teenagers, are mostly disengaged from mainstream media outlets (in part evidenced by, for example, the extremely disappointing winter 2006 returns by HMV). Conversely iTunes has demonstrated the power of marketing synergies with a hardware product promoting a software delivery service, and micro-payment billing has been achieved after the music industry reluctantly opened up access to its intellectual capital, without the security advantage of digital watermarking.

Opportunities will always exist for the entrepreneur, as with Richard Branson and his first company, following a novel change in distribution patterns selling discounted albums through mail order. This highly successful format challenged the high street stores for the first time, and established Virgin Records as a successful brand. Kusek and Leonhard (2005) lay out another possible scenario where music, and potentially other aspects of the creative industry output, will be viewed as we do water – i.e. everyone uses, everybody pays a flat base fee. Indeed, at least in theory, the works of any creator and rights holder can be easily logged, used, and compensated for, if digital watermarking and DRM agreements are in place, or alternatively an extension of the blanket PRS licence. This would mean that emerging entrepreneurs would inevitably be seeking to invest in media searching, play-listing, recommendation or other digital marketing tools to capitalize on this new market in a model where end users pay flat fees according to level of service provided, and content is 'freely' added to the pool.

Technology in the music industry

Music production is easier than ever: computer-supported chord-recognition algorithms have been used in musicology to determine pleasing musical scripts and advances in music production, including the computer-enabled synthesizer (first typified by 'I Feel Love' by Donna Summer in 1977), has made it possible for even non-musicians to produce music, especially that with the insistent, robotic bass line characteristic of electronic disco.

Internet technologies and new file compression techniques make distribution easier than ever before – the important 'broker' role of the DJ has diminished rapidly since the 1960s and 1970s. The battle against P2P networks has been largely futile to date and the hope that music consumers can be retrained may be impossible, as the 'genie is quite firmly out of the bottle'. ISP charges are one possible answer, but may be commercially non-viable, and the debate over DRM (digital rights management) is currently gathering momentum. This means that music profits models are focusing less on the sale of the sound track itself and more on performance, merchandizing and image rights. Indeed, much music and video available on the Internet can be interpreted as the result of a pent-up demand for self-expression and much Internet uses music as a glue to keep virtual communities (e.g. the demise of the 'fan club' as such and its replacement by the Sellaband model – see above – and/or 'blogging') together in an age characterized by social networking, personalization and lack of physical community (see Chapter 5). This trend may mean a convergence between advertising, marketing and selling to the point where there is no meaningful difference. Points for the new entrepreneur to note include:

- Litigation will not deter music fans in the P2P marketplace, but simply drive them to untraceable sources (slyck.com reports that BitTorrent accounts for 60 per cent of internet traffic in downloads).
- Content is freely available (but not free) given ubiquitous coverage and a large number of entry points via fixed and mobile devices.
- Music file-sharers have always existed, the technology has simply changed.
- Compression technologies provide an inferior sonic product, and this needs to be highlighted in the battle for sales figures.

- These same file-sharers are trend makers, breaking new artists with little or no overt media support – for example, Clap Your Hands, Arctic Monkeys, Arcade Fire – giving an opportunity for new entrepreneurs to enter the traditional oligopolies.
- There is stiff competition for the entertainment dollar from emerging formats such as video games and movies, both of which have much larger marketing spends.
- The replacement cycle is over; digital does not wear out.
- It is now possible to select tracks individually and avoid inferior products, placing the emphasis on consistency. This has given a revival of the single as a format and diminished the importance of the album (LP) as a format.
- Mass-market retailers only carry chart material, with limited back catalogue.
- Very few initiatives are being generated from within the established music industry players, and most come from dynamic entrepreneurs outside the industry such as Steve Jobs (Apple) with the copyright deals that have enabled iTunes to develop their database and community.

Today emerging technologies allow new methods of listening and experiencing music, with the development of DVDA and SACD formats giving the general public surround mix possibilities via home cinema 5.1 systems, and once again the 'churn' or resale of back catalogue. Interestingly, resale of back catalogue has been a real lifesaver for many independent studios, as original masters are remixed for surround.

Chapter summary

The music industry is all about overcoming those knowledge barriers that separate those who are on the inside of the 'fence' and those who are on the outside. While artists focus less on technical mastery, the successful entrepreneur able to generate cost-effective surprises will find transient and possibly lucrative market niches. Plummeting barriers to entry combined with the deep-reaching paradigm change caused by new technology mean that it is more vital than ever that the entrepreneur keeps abreast of all initiatives. This highlights the extreme need for very intense networking in a milieu that is constantly shifting and redefining outputs and allegiances.

The 'big players' spread investments and release much more material than can be sold, but the new entrepreneur with a clear understanding of the tastes and buying habits of a particular segmented musical audience stands a better chance of success today than in the past few decades, especially in emerging mobile and electronic formats. Brand identity for labels tends to develop over time, and become a natural extension of the musical taste of the entrepreneur, rather than a market research-driven exercise, and *Zeitgeist* can be vital for the young entrepreneur.

Increasingly, the problems and solutions explored by the music industry will be mirrored by the broader entertainment industry, and encryption and copyright controls will determine the health of the larger organizations; eventually even the recent spate of take-overs will reach a natural end. Even companies of the size and financial muscle of Rupert Murdoch's empire require an engagement with digital communities that engender a sense of belonging, and inclusion in the product itself. As consumers, we still need to buy into the star system and recognize entertainment brands as consistent suppliers of quality work. This will always remain the challenge for anyone operating in the creative industries; increased access does not naturally supply increased quality, even if the historic gatekeepers may disappear.

References

Goodell, G. (1998) *Independent Feature Film Production*. New York: St Martins Griffin.

Kusek, D. and Leonhard, G. (2005) *The Future of Music: Manifesto for the Digital Music Revolution*. Berklee Press.

Vogel, H. L. (2007) *Entertainment Industry Economics: A Guide for Financial Analysis* (7th edition). Cambridge: Cambridge University Press.

Further reading

Aldrich, H. and Zimmer, C. (1986) 'Entrepreneurship through social networks', in D. Sexton and R. Smilor (eds), *The Arts and Science of Entrepreneurship*. New York: Ballinger.

Bacharach, S. B. and Lawler, E. J. (1981) *Bargaining Power Tactics and Outcomes*. San Francisco: Jossey-Bass.

Bainbridge, T. (1999) *Intellectual Property*. London: Sweet and Maxwell.

Buzan, T. and Buzan, B. (1995) *The Mind Map Book*. London: BBC Books.

Caves, R. E. (2000) *Creative Industries*. Cambridge, MA: Harvard University Press.

Harrison, A. (2003) *Music – The Business*. London: Virgin.

Kennedy, G. (1990) *Everything Is Negotiable*. London: Random House.

Sheridan, D. L. (1991) *Negotiating Commercial Contracts*. Maidenhead: McGraw-Hill.

Weinstein, K. (1995) *Action Learning*. London: HarperCollins.

Web links

Self-expression/fusion

http://myspace.com

www.hi5.com

www.orkut.com

www.youtube.com

Organizations and government agencies

http://www.access-funds.co.uk/

www.artscouncil.org.uk

(Continued)

www.creativelondon.org.uk

www.culture.gov.uk/about_us/creativeindustries

http://www.culture.gov.uk/NR/rdonlyres/08578764-31C2-4ADE-A0E4-8502A59B7743/0/Music MoneyMap_April07.pdf

www.nesta.org.uk

Music

Useful site for studying a range of options: http://www.dartingtonplus.org.uk/info_useful_websites.html

Premiere site for industry links and research databases: http://www.musictank.co.uk/about

Useful site for grant-funded aid: http://www.intute.ac.uk/artsandhumanities/cgi-bin/browse.pl?id=arti fact1230

Coalition of funding providers: http://www.onsong-festival.co.uk/partners.html

PRS Foundation initiative: http://www.prsf.co.uk/directory/resources.htm

Strategy site for creative thinkers: www.musicfuturist.com

Film

Skillset initiative: http://www.skillset.org/film/training_and_events/screen_academies/article_4190_1.asp

Coalition web site: http://www.korda.obs.coe.int/web/recherche_fonds.php

Regional funding: http://www.northernmedia.org/?pageid=9

UK film funding database: http://www.netribution.co.uk/funding/section.php?TYPE=contents

Suggestions for exercises

1 What do you understand by the term 'post-artisan market' and 'oil tanker turnaround model'?
2 Is YouTube a creative industry or an innovation in the form of an environment for the creators?

Acknowledgements

Figures 15.1, 15.2, 15.3, 15.4 and Tables 15.2 and 15.3 reprinted with permission from the author and Cambridge University Press.

Part V

Action

16 Growing the Venture

Robert B. Mellor

Introduction

Previous chapters have dealt with the principles, practice and context of entrepreneurship, as well as having given in-depth analysis of specialist areas studied by a wide range of students. In this chapter the threads are drawn together and the topic of actually running a new venture is addressed.

Innovative is attractive

For the reasons given in Chapters 1 and 2, many established organizations are interested in becoming more innovative or establishing innovative spin-off companies by a process of straightforward fission (establishing subsidiaries) or by intrapreneurship. The reason for this is that small innovative dynamic entrepreneurial companies, despite being high risk, can give very good returns on investment during the first five years of their life. Conversely they have difficulty holding their head above water during the last five years (Figure 16.1).

New entrants – should they survive – are the most lucrative portions of the market for the investor, which has given rise to the expression 'attackers' advantage, survivors' curse'. Although many are very young (e.g. Mark Zuckerberg was 23 when he was offered $500 million by Microsoft for just 5 per cent of his company, Facebook), the real winners are those individuals that have established credentials in the core competencies of the new venture, e.g.:

Bob Metcalf left Xerox to found 3Com.

Steve Jobs left Atari to found Apple.

Gordon Moore left Fairchild Semiconductor to found Intel.

Rod Canion left Texas Instruments to found Compaq.

Thus, it is not only that innovative start-ups are attractive investment objects and/or attractive acquisitions, but also that many established players in the market wish to exploit this effect, either by becoming more innovative, or by establishing innovative subsidiaries, or by exporting (e.g. franchising) their ideas to other countries where they may not yet exist in the same form.

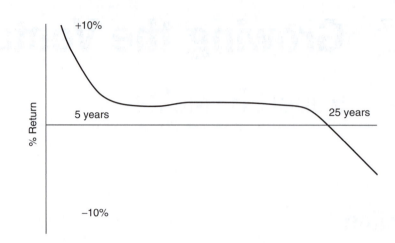

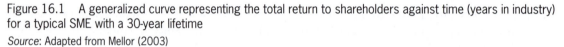

Figure 16.1   A generalized curve representing the total return to shareholders against time (years in industry) for a typical SME with a 30-year lifetime
Source: Adapted from Mellor (2003)

Establishing innovative subsidiaries could be by horizontal integration, e.g. line extensions like companies in the soft drinks sector may not only look at different soft drinks, but also look at beer, coffee, tea, snacks, etc. If any business idea is successful, then there is a good chance that it will quickly be replicated in other culturally aligned countries – in 2004 'smoothies' from the USA quickly sprang up across continental Europe by the process of 'creative imitation' (see Drucker, 1985, although his examples are Japanese cameras displacing Hasselblad, Leica, etc.). Many try to anticipate this by offering franchises.

Franchising

Franchising is a system of distribution in which the originator (the franchisor) agrees with many partners (franchisees) to handle specific products and/or services under certain mutually preferential conditions. These may include:

- the franchise fee, a one-off upfront fee;
- start-up costs, deposits on leasehold or buildings, inventory, deposits, etc;
- royalty fee, ongoing service fee, typically a fixed percentage of revenue;
- advertising fee, contributions to local or national advertising.

The first notable franchisor was Isaac Singer (of sewing machines fame), others include McDonald's and Subway. Franchising accounts for an estimated 40 per cent of total US retail sales, approx £500,000 million per annum!

Whether going down the franchise path or not, entrepreneurs in growth situations need to do the following:

- Understand capital management.
- Keep monitoring the market.
- Manage and monitor company politics.
- Build external relationships.

These will be discussed in the remainder of this chapter.

Business is about selling

Most specialist entrepreneurs are weak on the financial management side and this is especially the case for engineer entrepreneurs; however, managing your money cannot be abdicated to someone else, the responsibility is always yours. While it is difficult for most entrepreneurs to pay attention to the 'numbers', ignoring financial statistics can be costly. There are many key business indicators that small companies use to avoid the 'cash crunch'. Small companies are much more fragile and can fail on a relatively small cash deficiency. The key financial indicators all relate to 'liquidity' and include:

- *the financial indicators*: these are typically ratios such as the 'current ratio' (from the balance sheet); here are some: Current Ratio = Current Assets/Current Liabilities >2:1. Note that Current Assets are cash-in-hand plus others easily convertible to cash assets.
- *cash position*: these can be maintained by increasing current assets by long-term borrowing, by adding equity in the form of cash, or by ploughing back profits and not paying dividends.

Most small businesses derive their revenues from a very few major accounts; this puts them into jeopardy when one of these customers gets into trouble. Bad debts are real problems and in a successful business, there is no room for a 'soft touch' credit policy and the rule of thumb is that customers are not customers if they don't pay their bills. Extending credit is a crucial, yet delicate activity and while credit handling in a right way multiplies business many times over, casual treatment of business debts will bury the company. Everyone must accept that credit problems do occur and when they do, then one needs to act promptly and decisively, e.g. if an account is approaching 90 days overdue, then it should be turned over to a collection agency. You should never provide credit to friends and family (indeed avoid nepotism or other forms of favouritism, where it is not clearly in the company's interest) and always remember that providing 'loans' from your company to yourself is a criminal offence!

Banks are in the business of lending to people who pay back; they are not in business to put you out of business, so remember that the banker you deal with is a person too, s/he has the same fears and problems as you have. Select a banker who understands you and your business and involve the banker in your planning, don't give them any 'surprises' and generally try to build a relationship based on trust.

The leader of a small enterprise (you) should be able – at a pinch – to do all jobs and the most successful leaders know that this means staying on top of every task, keeping a cool head and being able to prioritize. Impatience and expectations can mount quickly; jumping the gun on any gradual process can seriously jeopardize its outcome. Another common mistake is counting the profits before a sale is made and making financial commitments on expected profits (i.e. believing the spreadsheet plan as if it has happened). This is particularly relevant to marketing and advertising.

Marketing and advertising in the small company

Small start-ups are normally strapped for cash and thus must adhere to the maxim: 'Marketing is an investment of limited size in one area, resulting in measurably higher income in another area' (Mellor, 2003). So the problem is not to set the ball rolling, but rather to design a marketing project which is affordable, and which contains sufficient realizable checks and feedback mechanisms to make it possible to calculate almost exactly how much revenue it has generated. This involves spending a lot of time researching the effectiveness of the effort. Every competitive business environment demands focused efforts, but it is very easy to get dragged into many diverse areas and end up not doing any very well. The marketing budget can easily become a bottomless black hole into which money can be poured in a seemingly endless stream. Abdicating this responsibility to 'The Agency' is not the answer either; I have always been surprised by how many apparently 'serious' marketers lack any kind of rational sense – they confuse familiarity with expertise, but these are not the same. This underlines the need for you to set budgets (see Chapter 5) quarterly and review success regularly.

Your marketing department should be able to answer these questions at short notice:

- What percentage of revenue is attributable to the top 10 and top 20 customers?
- What is the firms' current share of the most profitable customers?
- Does profit per customer increase after cross-selling?
- Are there any unprofitable customers, whose service costs outweigh revenue?
- What is the average lifetime and value of the customer base?
- What was the Return on Investment (RoI) for specific marketing campaigns?
- Do specific campaigns increase customer satisfaction and loyalty?
- Where are our customers located, and what else is known about them?

Leadership and the small company

Both start-ups and spin-offs are largely guided by the leadership personality, which can become a problem if the leader lacks experience. This is often reflected in lack of exercise of personal control; some forget they are the boss and try to become friends with their employees. However, the major symptom of trouble brewing is inflation of personal ego; absenteeism and arrogance, expensive cars and lavish shows of 'success'. Believing your own publicity is a particularly easy and usually fatal mistake. The 'ego' takes over and the entrepreneur begins really believe that s/he can do anything! One acid test is if the leader is still strong then they will be able to delegate properly, this is a sign of trust as well as being strong enough to be able to 'let go'.

The ability to delegate properly is a barometer of management competency

Delegation is being able to call upon an employee, explain what is wanted, and let them go – equipped with a reasonable budget and authority – to complete the task. Good delegation skills are a sign of mature authority. An early warning of bad management is bad delegation abilities, like giving a competent worker a badly thought-out task, no means to accomplish it, and a good thrashing when it doesn't work.

However, over-delegation is equivalent to absenteeism and choosing to be an 'absentee owner' is a sure way to invite employee fraud, theft, general carelessness, etc. Thus, when out of the office, leave clear instructions about where you are and how people can contact you when there is an important reason, leave a key person in charge during absences, build checks and balances to ensure that at least two people must 'collaborate' to do something wrong, and fire anyone who shows any dishonesty.

In addition to leading by example, building external relationships – a good network – is immensely valuable to a growing venture. The majority of the heads of industry get enormous salaries not because of what skills they have, but because of who they know. However, networking needs the same skills as good leadership. A leader who tells lies to the workforce and shrugs off their complaints will rapidly become unpopular and will not last long (the owner will go bankrupt or the best workers will leave, the same thing in the long run). This has led to the concept that the workforce works for you, and your network works for you. Both need the same approach. Your workforce does the things you can't do, or don't have time to do, and gets a financial reward – a salary – for this 'favour'. Your network also tells you the things you don't know (or don't have time to find out). Although network contacts don't (often) get cash rewards; even a little 'thank you' note is surprisingly powerful. The mention of networking may leave an unpleasant taste in your the mouth and conjures up images of Old Boys Club, people with funny handshakes and the Mafia. Common to all these phenomena is that the dead hand of monopoly lies over them. However, proper leadership techniques will enable budding entrepreneurs to build up an invaluable network of contacts, based on openness, use, challenge and mutual respect.

Your professional network

Most people have inhibitions when starting to network. Try phoning first to someone you have met personally, explain that you know they are probably not 'the person' you should talk with, but can they recommend anyone? You will be surprised how many people take it as a huge compliment to be phoned up and asked for their opinion. You will also be surprised how many are willing to give you the benefit of their experience. Of course, there is also a reverse side. At some point people will start ringing you. This may not be the same person you phoned, but this third person may have got your name from that person. Clearly, it may not be convenient to take the call there and then, but be courteous and arrange a mutually convenient time to ring back. Forgetting to reply can easily be taken as an insult. So forgetting to reply will quickly get you cut out of that person's network – including all those who know him/her.

How to develop a healthy blend of challenge and respect

1 Encourage people to challenge your ideas, practices and assumptions.
2 Don't take challenge personally. Be confident enough to relate to the challenge as an issue, where you and the other person solve it together.
3 Welcome challenge as an opportunity to learn, not as a competition to be won or lost.
4 If someone disagrees, check that they really do disagree, or if they are just addressing a different side of the same issue.
5 Develop decision-making skills and use notes so that you can easily justify your decision later.
6 Avoid dualistic, black-and-white thinking. There are always alternatives.
7 Try to understand emotional processes. Conflict management rests often on emotional management.
8 Seek to express yourself clearly and listen well to others, they may be trying to do the same, but they may not be as open or articulate as you – or perhaps you are not sufficiently articulate.
9 Focus on the issue, not the person. Be as specific as possible and be prepared to admit that you may be wrong, or that your anxiety is based on a hunch. Not admitting this will create further problems.
10 Never put anyone in a situation in which they cannot save face. Many will risk their life to avoid embarrassment. This is especially important in cross-cultural situations.

Entrepreneurial management

Although the above is rather practical advice, there are several abstract principles that typify innovative (and thus attractive) companies and differentiate them sharply from conventional management models. These are listed in Table 16.1.

Table 16.1   Some differences between innovative and operative organizations

	Operating organizations	Innovating organizations
Controlling expectations	Focus on short-term performance Watch costs	Set high long-term goals Focus on recruiting and developing human potential
Maintaining management	Hierarchy and control systems Stability and predictability Reward success and punish failure	Destroy to make room for innovations Accept ambiguities Tolerate honest failure

The innovative process involves first, increasing the field of vision by expanding business definitions, i.e. focusing on creating new business instead of just commercializing technology or developing products. Recognizing that only a small percentage of new projects will be successful, a strategy of 'try and prune' can be adopted; trying the market but cutting back rapidly if the expected results are not achieved. This is actually a consequence of the rule of listening to the customers and acting accordingly, this may open up to 'new' market groups (including new forms of delivery), but it is a risk, so you have to use entrepreneurial management – flexibility combined with quick pruning. The second step is to attract and motivate a team of exceptional performers with business-building experience, as well as recognizing the need for external networks. Both these attitudes involve radically changing some corporate assumptions (Table 16.2).

Certainly in e-business, examples like Amazon.com, which didn't turn a profit for over six years, illustrate that market value can be very significant before any earnings roll in the door!

Table 16.2   Contrasts in management and leadership assumptions between innovative and traditional organizations

Executives traditionally believe	Innovative mentality believes
One can judge market potential by analysis.	Markets are unpredictable, leading to customer-led flexibility and early confirmation.
It is best to put management talent into ventures that are big and successful.	New ventures need the best management. The initial business plan may turn out to be flawed, but a good team will learn and adjust course quickly.
The likelihood of success should be very high before investing.	The likelihood of success is very low, so pruning quickly is the key to success. If you must fail, fail fast, fail cheap and recover fast.
Shared ownership of ventures is an unacceptable risk.	Shared ownership expands the 'pie'.
New ventures should quickly produce earnings.	Market value can be significant before earnings are apparent.

Judge market potential by analysis

- In 1898, Commissioner of the US Patent Office, Charles Dell, wanted to close the office because everything that could be invented already had been invented.
- In 1943, IBM chairman Thomas Watson estimated that the global market for computers was around 'five or six' – and that with certainty no one would want one in their home.
- In 1962, the vice-president of Decca Records eyeballed four guys and pronounced 'Groups with guitars are out', so the Beatles left.

Source: Examples modified from Gundry and Kickul (2007)

There are certain other useful rules of thumb that have emerged from small business research in the past decade. These include:

- Concentrate on your core competencies (Chapter 7).
- Outsource everything else, trying to do everything will lead to you doing a bad job plus incurring large overheads as 'opportunity costs'.
- Minimize fixed outlays – if you incur costs, then preferably as variable costs.

Learning from failure

However, even the best-run ventures can fail and indeed many ultimately successful entrepreneurs have failed in earlier attempts at building and growing a business. There is always an element of uncontrollable risk – and therefore luck – in business. All is not lost providing you learn from failure and you diligently apply lessons learnt to the next endeavour. To put it succinctly; failing is acceptable, but not learning from failure is not acceptable. Entrepreneurship involves your personal style and this must include learning, critical evaluation, practice, enormous flexibility and resilience.

Chapter summary

Good leadership ethics and a healthy, honest and open style will enable the leader to manage both work (internal) and network (external) situations.

Cash flow is usually the major critical success factor in small firms. Controlling this involves anticipating financial problems (including costs and risks), closely monitoring both business trends and company performance while contrasting these to the business plan, as well as understanding the methods and alternatives available for resolving any problems.

References

Drucker, P. F. (1985) *Innovation and Entrepreneurship*. Oxford: Butterworth-Heinemann.
Gundry, L. K. and Kickul, J. R. (2007) *Entrepreneurship Strategy*. London: Sage.
Mellor, R. B. (2003) *Innovation Management*. Copenhagen: Globe.

Further reading

Bessant, J. (2003) *High Involvement Innovation*. Chichester: John Wiley and Sons, Ltd.
Bridge, S., O'Neill, K. and Cromie, S. (2003) *Understanding Enterprise*. Basingstoke: Palgrave.
Pettinger, R. (2002) *Introduction to Management*, 3rd edn. Basingstoke: Palgrave.

Web links

General information on many topics: www.webmergers.com

Help for new start-ups: www.shell-livewire.org

Low interest loans for young people with good ideas: www.princes-trust.org.uk

Suggestions for exercises

1 What do you understand by the expression 'attackers' advantage', survivors' curse'?
2 Google 'opportunity costs'.
3 Try to imagine what product could be cross-sold with your product.

Glossary

4Cs   Consumer wants, Convenience, Cost and Communication.

4Ps   The 4Ps of innovation: Product, Process, Position and Paradigm. Also, the 4Ps of marketing: Product, Place, Price and Promotion.

ACE-Chase   An action audit tool.

Adaption-innovation theory   A theory explaining consensus group formation and the exclusion of innovators.

ALUO (Advantages, Limitations, Uniqueness and Opportunity)   An evaluation tool for ideas.

backward compatible   New versions are still compatible with older versions.

business incubator   A shared facility where new businesses can start up for lower initial outlay.

Business angel   An individual investor.

cash cow   A mature product or service that generates unusually high profit margins.

convergence   Different types of technology evolving to perform very similar tasks, e.g. computer-mediated telephony.

creative destruction   The process of destroying the value of established companies by transforming a business area using radical innovation.

Creative problem solving   A thinking technique.

cultural intermediary   A go-between understanding 2 or more cultures.

liquidity   The amount of cash available.

Diffusion of innovations   A theory expressing in mathematical terms how innovations spread in a population.

Digital rights management (DRM)   Electronic protection of copyright.

disruptive technology   An improvement that sweeps away old technologies, e.g. GPS rendering map-reading obsolete.

early movers   Those trying to capitalize on 'First-mover advantage' i.e. the advantage gained by the initial occupant of a market segment.

ecopreneurship   Green entrepreneurship.

entropy   Defined in the second law of thermodynamics as a measure of the unavailability of a quantity of energy showing the possibility of conversion of that energy into work, i.e. the larger the entropy, the smaller the work potential.

fission   The process of dividing.

Generation X   Western generations born during the 1960s and 1970s. A numerically small generation following the 'baby boomers'.

goodwill   An intangible fixed asset, supposed to reflect the reputation and other positive characteristics of the business.

greenwashing   Non-green companies wanting to improve their green image.

Hewlett-Packard effect   Achieving a higher potential synergy by mixing technical and business people.

horizontal integration   Selling the same type of good in different markets.

HOTPLOT   An evaluation tool for ideas.

Initial public offering (IPO)   First flotation on a stock market.

Intellectual property rights (IPR)   Patents, trademarks, etc.

intrapreneur   The practice of entrepreneurial skills and approaches by or within a company.

Kondratieff cycle   Waves in the modern (capitalist) world economy of fifty to sixty years in length; the cycles consist of alternating periods of high sectoral growth and periods of slower growth, finally switching sector.

lateral thinking   Methods of thinking concerned with avoiding traditional step-by-step logic and about changing basic concepts and perceptions; reasoning that is not immediately obvious.

Mergers and Acquisitions (M&A)   A takeover (can be friendly or hostile).

Master of Business Arts (MBA)   A common business school degree.

outsourcing   Sub-contracting a process etc. to others.

PLC   Product life cycle (not to be confused with plc, public limited company).

Quality of Service (QoS)   How reliable an Internet connection is.

Research in Practice (RiP)   A knowledge exchange between universities and charities.

Return on investment (RoI)   The income an investment provides per year.

SEARCH (Scan, Expand, Adapt, Revise, Create and Harvest)   An evaluation tool for ideas.

Strategic Group Mapping (SGM)   An evaluation tool for market positioning.

social enterprise   Organizations driven by a social mission; trading in goods or services for a social purpose.

Social learning cycle (SLC)   An explanation of how knowledge moves in a cycle in a society.

Social, Legal, Economic, Political and Technological (SLEPT)   An evaluation tool for market positioning.

Small and Medium-sized Enterprise (SME)   Companies with 10–249 employees.

SWOT (Strengths, Weaknesses, Opportunities and Threats)   An evaluation tool for market positioning.

SWOTPLOT   An evaluation tool for ideas, a development based on SWOT.

syndication   Making products available to other retail or wholesalers, acting as a syndicate.

Triple Bottom Line (TBL)   Economic prosperity, environmental quality and social equity.

Trickle down theory   A theory explaining how innovations pass between socially super- and subordinate groups.

TQM (Total Quality Management)   A management tool.

TROTPLOT   An evaluation tool for ideas.

Time To Market (TTM)   Time needed before products can be sold, often a very diffuse measure.

USP (Unique Selling Proposition)   What your product has, that no-one else has, that makes the purchaser want to buy it.

value chain   An ordered chain of activities a product proceeds through resulting in the product gaining more added value than the sum of added values of all the individual activities.

Venture capitalist   A large corporate investor.

vertical integration   The degree to which a firm owns its upstream suppliers and its downstream buyers.

Voice over Internet Protocol (VoIP)   Internet telephony.

Appendix A
The Ten–Dimension
Rating Scale

Ideas harvested by lateral thinking and other techniques can be analysed by a variety of methods. The method explained below is reprinted by permission of David Saunders of the University of London at Royal Holloway. It is particularly applicable to technology-based ideas.

There are ten dimensions or criteria. The idea is held up against each of these in turn and given a rating on a scale of 1 to 5. Upon completion, the scores are added up and multiplied by 2 to give a percentage. The 10 dimensions are:

1   Uniqueness
2   Readiness
3   Value of the market
4   Gross profit margin
5   Competitive intensity
6   Competitive edge
7   Access to market
8   Customer conservatism
9   Commitment of team
10 Experience of team

1 Uniqueness of the technology

Score of 5:   for a family of patents, granted worldwide, which covers several interlinked aspects of the technology.
Score of 4:   for a single patent, granted worldwide, which covers the fundamentals of the technology, or for a very major suite of software which would take many man-years to duplicate.
Score of 3:   for a strong patent application, or for a significant suite of software.
Score of 2:   for smaller software suites, or extensive know-how.
Score of 1:   for an interesting research result that might be protectable.
Score of 0:   for a bare idea, with no evident uniqueness or protectability.

2 Readiness of the technology

Score of 5:   the technology is well proven and bug-free, and a process for volume manufacture has already been proven by manufacture of significant quantities (or is trivial, as for example, with software duplication).

Score of 4:   the technology has successfully completed beta-testing (i.e. field testing with real customers) and is thus relatively bug-free, and a small-scale manufacturing process has been demonstrated.

Score of 3:   the technology works well in the laboratory, but has not yet been tested by customers. Manufacture seems to be relatively straightforward in theory.

Score of 2:   the technology can be made to work sometimes in the laboratory, though there is still a considerable amount of 'black art' in doing it repeatedly. Not much thought has yet been given to larger-scale manufacture.

Score of 1:   closely related technologies have been made to work in this lab, and there seems to be no theoretical reason why this one shouldn't work too.

Score of 0:   the technology should work in theory, but hasn't yet been tried.

3 Value of the market

Score of 5:   the worldwide market for this product and its direct competitors is likely to be in excess of £20 million p.a.

Score of 4:   the worldwide market is likely to be £5–20 million p.a.

Score of 3:   the worldwide market is likely to be £3–5 million p.a.

Score of 2:   the worldwide market is likely to be £1–3 million p.a.

Score of 1:   the worldwide market is likely to be £250k to £1 million.

Score of 0:   the worldwide market is likely to be less than £250k p.a.

4 Anticipated profit margins (if considering a licence, the anticipated royalty rate)

Score of 5:   the gross profit margin per sale is likely to be over 70 per cent (royalty >7 per cent).

Score of 4:   the gross profit margin per sale is likely to be over 50 per cent (royalty >5 per cent).

Score of 3:   the gross profit margin per sale is likely to be over 30 per cent (royalty >3 per cent).

Score of 2:   the gross profit margin per sale is likely to be over 20 per cent (royalty >2 per cent).

Score of 1:   the gross profit margin per sale is likely to be over 15 per cent (royalty >1–2 per cent).

Score of 0:   the gross profit margin per sale is likely to be under 15 per cent (royalty <1 per cent).

5 Intensity of competition in the market

Score of 5:   this is a brand new market, and there are currently no actual or potential competitors.

Score of 4:   the market is relatively new, and the competitors are very small firms that have no current technological or marketing lead.

Score of 3:   the market is relatively new, and the competitors are still relatively small, though some may have a small lead in some areas, or have access to significant venture funding.

Score of 2:   the market is becoming established, and competitors have grown to medium size (£5m plus sales p.a.) and gained a reputation as market leaders.

Score of 1:   the market is well established, and the competitors are already substantial companies with the ability to quickly adopt or duplicate new technologies.

Score of 0:   the market is mature, and is dominated by a few multinational companies with major research capabilities, marketing reach and financial muscle.

6 Competitive edge of your product or service

Score of 5:   the product/service is several times as good as the competition in one or more customer-critical areas, and is not worse in any other areas.

Score of 4:   the product or service is significantly better than the competition in at least one customer-critical area, and is not worse in other areas.

Score of 3:   the product or service is marginally better (e.g. 25 per cent better in at least one customer-critical area), and is not worse in other areas, or is significantly better in one area, but has minor disadvantages in other less critical areas.

Score of 2:   the product or service is marginally better (e.g. 25 per cent better) compared to the competition in at least one customer-critical area, but has disadvantages in other less critical areas.

Score of 1:   the product or service has advantages over the competition in one or more areas, but they do not appear to be areas that are critical to the customer.

Score of 0:   the product or service has no evident advantages over the competition.

7 Ease of access to the market

Score of 5:   the potential customers worldwide have already been listed (or can very easily be listed) and sales contacts can be initiated as soon as the product is completed, or well-established worldwide distributors are enthusiastic.

Score of 4:   the potential customers or enthusiastic distributors can easily be listed in some territories, and it appears that with enough work, other territories can be brought up to the same level.

Score of 3:   the potential customers and distributors can be described in general, and there are no evident barriers to accessing them, though generating the lists would be significant work.

Score of 2:   it is still fairly unclear what the profile of the potential customers is, or the profile is clear but there are some significant barriers (e.g. regulatory approval) to reaching them.

Score of 1:   some potential customers can be described, but there are substantial barriers (e.g. regulatory approval) preventing short-term access to them.

Score of 0:   some potential customers can be described, but the barriers to reaching them are very substantial.

8 Customer conservatism

Score of 5:   the customer group is very innovative and experimental, buying new products or services just to try them out.

Score of 4:   the customer group is fairly innovative, and are willing to try out new products and services which seem to have some advantages.

Score of 3:   the customer group is not especially innovative, but is willing to give a fair hearing to any product or service which seems to offer clear advantages.

Score of 2:   the customer group is relatively conservative, preferring to stick to established methods unless new ones offer a strong advantage.

Score of 1:   the customer group is very conservative, tending to prefer 'tried and trusted' methods and resist new ones for years even, though they offer strong advantages.

Score of 0:   regulatory, legal, moral or religious reasons lead to new methods being rejected irrespective of their advantages.

9 Commitment of the team

Score of 5:   the inventors and other members of the team are glad to leave their current jobs, invest their life savings and mortgage their houses in order to see the commercial opportunity realized.

Score of 4:   the inventors and other members of the team are willing to take full-time leave of absence from their current jobs, and invest meaningful sums (e.g. 25 per cent or more of their annual salary).

Score of 3:   the inventors and other members of the team are willing to spend 50 per cent or more of their time on the commercial opportunity, on an agreed split with their current jobs, and to invest modest sums (over £1,000).

Score of 2:   the inventors and other members of the team are willing to take spend a small portion of their time (20 per cent or less) on the commercial opportunity, but are not willing to make even a modest investment.

Score of 1:   the inventors and other members of the team are willing to act as consultants, in addition to their normal jobs, providing they are paid consultancy fees, but are not willing to make even a modest investment.

Score of 0:   the inventors and other members of the team believe that their job is now finished, and are unwilling to spend any further time on the opportunity.

10 Commercial experience of the team

Score of 5:   the inventors and other members of the team have a previous, very successful, experience in the commercial exploitation of a new technology.

Score of 4:   the inventors and other members of the team have a previous, not very successful, experience in the commercial exploitation of a new technology, and feel that they have learnt to do it better this time.

Score of 3:   the inventors and other members of the team have worked for commercial companies in a management role, though this role was relatively narrow (e.g. managing a research team, rather than general management).

Score of 2:   the inventors and other members of the team have worked for commercial companies, though not in a management role, and have maintained good contacts with various commercial companies since joining the university.

Score of 1:   the inventors and other members of the team have not worked for commercial companies but have had regular contacts with a number of commercial companies through, for example, joint or sponsored research projects.

Score of 0:   the inventors and other members of the team have not worked for commercial companies and their university research has almost all been publicly funded.

Appendix B
Additional Case Studies

Technical innovation

Evolution on the net

From 1994 to today the Internet has not only grown enormously (in terms of technical progress, commerce, participants and social importance), but has also changed character with time, i.e. it has evolved. Many commentators agree on three phases:

1   The first phase – called the 'read' phase – concerns only finding information and lasted from around 1994 to 1998. Typical proponents include Yahoo and Google.
2   The second phase – called the 'buy/trade/talk' phase – concerns distribution and communication and lasted from 1998 to 2005. Typical proponents of this phase are Amazon, E-Bay and Skype.
3   The third phase – called the 'networking' phase – concerns publishing in the sense of peer-to-peer self-expression and started around 2005. Typical proponents of this phase are YouTube.com and MySpace.com.

Starting from a focused position as a search engine, Google has been able to follow these trends by developing advertising technology and communications (Gmail, Google Talk) into the second phase. Google has acquired 'third phase' presence through targeted acquisitions e.g. sketchup.com, vsocial.com, clipshack.com, hi5.com, orkut.com, MySpace.com and YouTube.com.

Yahoo started making money earlier than Google and has been subjected to 'attackers' advantage, survivors' curse' (Chapter 16). From a diversified position as a directory (rather than a pure search engine) Yahoo was able to sail through phase 2 with Yahoo Mail (and Messenger) as well as advertising. Yahoo has acquired 'third phase' presence through e.g. Flickr.com, del.icio.us, upcoming.org, Bix and Answers.

However, many observers feel that Yahoo spreads its efforts too thinly over its wide portfolio. Indeed, Yahoo has kept approximately the same market capitalization (between \$40 and 60 billion) since 2004, while Google – with perhaps a tighter follow-the-evolution policy – has risen from under \$10 to \$120 billion in 2007.

(*Source*: With thanks to Anil Hansjee, Director (EMEA) of Google.)

The biotechnology revolution

The technology that fizzled out

An ultracentrifuge is a fine and precise piece of engineering. The rotor is balanced on a cushion of air and intersecting a jet of compressed air with the outer surface induces the spin. The ultracentrifuge needs dependable vacuum and temperature controls as the friction between the spinning rotor and the atmosphere – even at reduced pressure – means that the power needed to drive the rotor increases rapidly with angular velocity, resulting in temperature rises. If the temperature rises too much, it can cause the substance in the tube to remix, disturb sedimentation and can even destroy biological specimens. This complex instrument, where the rotor can spin at 130,000 rpm, is a balancing act of fine engineering, electronic controls and the different systems, rotors, adaptors, etc. are the subject of many patents, the majority owned or filed by Beckman Instruments.

In 1934, Dr Arnold Beckman, a professor at the California Institute of Technology, invented the pH meter. Beckman's company (which also invented the spectrophotometer in 1941), later changed its name to Beckman Instruments, Inc. and in the 1950s acquired centrifugation technology by taking over Specialized Instruments Corporation (Spinco).

In the late 1970s and on the other side of the Atlantic Ocean, Kontron (founded in 1962) was looking for ways to gain a foothold in the biomedical instrumentation sector and had realized that the Beckman patents were reaching the end of their lifespan. Although Kontron had produced a computer in 1980, it became much better known for its Centrikon ultracentrifuge and its Uvicon spectrophotometer. The question was, could Kontron, without Beckman's massive development cost, split (or even conquer) the Beckman market? Could Beckman innovate to counter the threat?

With Kontron poised to step into Beckman's markets, a paradigm shift swept the biotechnology sector, catching both contestants off-balance. In the late 1980s and early 1990s, biochemistry was eclipsed by molecular biology and the massive shift in

(Continued)

focus away from macromolecules like proteins and carbohydrates and towards nucleic acid research left topics like the separation and analysis of sub-cellular particles largely high and dry. Ultracentrifuges, built ever bigger and ever more complex to separate ever finer particles, became a victim of this change. A small rump of activity was maintained, for example, for the preparation of large amounts of recombinant bacteria but once PCR came along, this too became virtually redundant.

The consequence was that Kontron was acquired by BMW and spun-out again in 1999. In 2002, it fused with a relatively new software company, JUMPtec AG (founded in 1991), to form Kontron Embedded Modules Gmbh. Today Kontron is a significant supplier of embedded computer technology, but makes no centrifuges or similar biomedical equipment.

Beckman Instruments, Inc. became a subsidiary of the global health care corporation SmithKline Corporation, and was later spun-out to trade as BEC. BEC acquired the Coulter Corporation in 1997 to form Beckman-Coulter, a major supplier to the clinical diagnostics and biomedical research sector – including a small range of ultracentrifuges.

Twenty years on and neither Beckman nor Kontron are the market leaders, indeed, the ultracentrifuge market is dominated by the Thermo Electron Corporation.

This is an example where the drive to develop a technology superseded the actual needs of most of the users. It created tunnel vision in the business strategies of the companies that were destroyed by a paradigm shift in the jobs that needed to be done by researchers. It is again an object lesson in looking for what is around the corner.

(*Source*: With thanks to Mr M. Henderson, Henderson Biomedical Ltd. London.)

Green, the ecopreneur and sustainable development

Green entrepreneurs USA: Patagonia

Patagonia is a company internationally recognized for the design of innovative and environmentally considered outdoor clothing. They have found unambiguous ways to couple their products' function and the brand's environmental values. Their business model raises major sums for environmental causes and their technological innovation reduces the environmental impact of their products.

Patagonia's mission is to 'build the best product, cause no unnecessary harm and use business to inspire and implement solutions to the environmental crisis'. Its turnover in 2005/2006 was US$240 million, and it has 1,200 employees.

Inspired by adventure climbing in Yosemite and the Patagonian Fitz Roy mountains, Patagonia was founded by Yvon Chouinard in 1973. The company came to Europe in 1987. Patagonia makes clear links between their products and the environment that the products help people enjoy, and they say their company mission statement gives them purpose and urgency.

The company's response to this has been to pledge at least 1 per cent of sales (or 10 per cent pretax profits, whichever is greater) to the protection and restoration of the natural environment. In 2005, this meant donations of US$2.1 million, bringing the total since 1984 to over US$20 million. This idea has become the '1 per cent For The Planet' business alliance (Article 13, 2006). These businesses are concerned with the social and environmental impacts of industry (1 per cent For the Planet, 2007).

Patagonia has an ongoing campaign called 'Big, Wild and Connected', which profiles different topics with stories in their catalogues, fundraising events and public outreach. It was Kris Tompkins, a former CEO of Patagonia, who approached the company with a plan to start a non-profit organization dedicated to buying, protecting and restoring land in the Patagonia region. The company assisted with the NGO start-up efforts, using their 'Creative Services' department to create, design and print all of their materials. In Europe, the company champions environmental causes relevant to Europe (Patagonia website, 2007).

The company also realized that if they could share profits, they could also supply time and muscle. The result was the Patagonia Employee Internship Program. Through the programme, employees can leave their jobs at Patagonia for up to two months to work full-time for the environmental group of their choice. Patagonia continues to pay employees' salaries and benefits while they're gone, and the environmental group gets them for free. More than 350 employees have worked as interns for groups worldwide since the program began in 1993 (Article 13, 2007).

References

Article 13 (November 2006). CRS best practice: Patagonia. Available at: www.article13. com

1 per cent For the Planet Business Alliance: www.onepercentfortheplanet.org.

Ottman J. A. (1998) 'Case Study: Patagonia: A deep-seated commitment to environmentalism', *Green Marketing: Opportunity for Innovation*, Booksurge, pp. 200–4.

Patagonia website 2007: www.patagonia.com.

STEP, 2007.

Enterprise in health and social care

Alternative high-street health

With a degree in food technology and engineering, Leicester-born Sanjay Bhandari worked all around the world in the cosmetics industry for 13 years before a major discontinuity – he collapsed from work-related exhaustion – forced him to reconsider his life (for the importance of discontinuities, see also Introduction). Learning from his own experience, he got together with his sister Meenu and started Farmacia Urban Healing (www.farmacia4u.com) in 1998, with the aim of providing an integrated health centre, offering counselling as well as both conventional and alternative medicines, for those suffering from stress and overwork. More recent innovations include the 'Walk-in' Doctor Clinic offering 'all that your would expect from your local GP except the three-day wait'.

Although the start was hard, they were fortunate that an influential magazine decided to publish a whole-page article featuring the company and after that, the business took off. Learning from this (see 'promotion', Chapter 5), Farmacia keeps up its public profile by being regularly featured in such newspapers as the *Sunday Times*, *Evening Standard* and *Metro*.

Today Bhandari employs 55 people in four stores (although the original store in Covent Garden was sold in 2004 to finance Farmacia's concession expansion) and has a turnover of around £5 million p.a.

(*Source*: Further researched from a case originally published in Bridge, R. (2006). *My Big Idea: 30 Successful Entrepreneurs Reveal How They Found Inspiration*. London: Kogan Page.)

Journalism and media entrepreneurs

Ethnic and back again

In 1994, BBC Arabic Television was launched by the BBC's commercial arm (BBC Worldwide) with financial backing from Orbit Communications Corporation, a subsidiary of the Saudi Arabian Mawarid Group. BBC Arabic Television aimed to establish a BBC Arabic-language TV channel available across the Middle East, North Africa and eventually Europe and the USA. The idea of the Arabic channel was conceived on the foundations and reputation of the BBC World Service Arabic radio service, which is widely heard and admired all across the Middle East. Unfortunately the service was closed down in April 1996.

Thanks to quick entrepreneurial thinking from those mostly involved, a new backer was found – Sheikh Hamad bin Khalifa, Emir of Qatar – and Al-Jazeera Satellite Television went on air at the beginning of November 1996, from its new location in Doha, staffed chiefly by former members of BBC Arabic Television.

After broadcasting TV in Arabic for a decade, Al Jazeera opened an English-language channel in November 2006. 'Al Jazeera English is the world's first global English language news channel to be headquartered in the Middle East' (www. aljazeera.net) and its reach rivals that of the BBC.

Music and the creative industries

Culture and music genre

As the well-known psychologist Maslow (Maslow, 1943) pointed out, human motivation comes from the desire of individuals to satisfy their needs. Maslow arranged these into a pyramid of needs, consisting first of a broad base; the basic physiological needs to satisfy hunger, thirst, etc. His theory, which is generally accepted, states that once satisfied, these needs are no longer seen to operate as primary motivators, but are discarded as menial and people concentrate on the next need in the hierarchy, which are the needs for physical safety and protection. Moving up the pyramid, these nutritional then physical needs are followed by the need to belong, then the need for esteem, followed finally – at the apex – by the need for personal growth, expression and development: self-fulfilment and self-esteem.

Obviously as sufficient individuals in a society progress up the pyramid to the apex, then their society inevitably progresses up too. Thus it may be that the USA is at the top of the pyramid because average individuals (or at least those prominent in the media) have transcended nutritional and shelter-associated deficiencies. In a depersonalized society the 'need to belong' is fulfilled by TV series like *Friends* and they are concentrating on the next stage: 'self-realization'. (Incidentally this may be why these countries may widely be regarded as 'decadent' by societies on a more survival level.) Being at this level on the Maslow pyramid, then, many people at the 'top of the pyramid' societies may think fulfilment and happiness are a 'right' they can demand (and possibly rebel – including seeking therapy – when it is not immediately forthcoming, see Furedi, 2004). This helps explain the 'feel good factor', including a pop music genre that features conspicuously over-consuming, rich, happy, successful, beautiful people writhing joyfully to pop music.

(Continued)

Should this be true, then Maslow's theory can be used in a predictive fashion. Could it be, for example, that certain genres of music that correspond to mid- or low-levels on Maslow's pyramid (e.g. the blues), are unlikely to become a mainstream phenomenon again? Could such a theory be used in other branches of the entertainment industry?

References

Furedi, F. (2004) *Therapy Culture*. London: Routledge.
Maslow, A. H. (1943) 'A theory of human motivation', *Psychological Review*, 50: 370–96.

Appendix C
Some Suggested Project Ideas

Euroflorida

Background

Increasingly, the 'grey gold' of north Europe (Scandinavia, Germany and the UK) are liquefying their assets and moving to south Europe. Their destinations are often Spain and south France. Indeed, in Spain a large building industry has started up building 'pensioner complexes' to cater for the market, similarly in the south of France, house prices are rising significantly. Smaller markets in the English-speaking Med (Gibraltar and Malta) have seen very dramatic rises in real estate value. However, Apulia (the 'heel' of Italy) is a relatively undiscovered region; prices are very reasonable and indeed, for a decade, Apulia was the poorest region of the (old) EU. The infrastructure, however, is excellent, with an airport at Bari, a motorway all the way to Vienna and the European net, excellent train connections within Italy and by ferry to Greece. Climatically Apulia is the second most 'blessed' region of the EU, after Portugal's Algarve. Temperatures are, however, not extreme and the landscape is lush, fertile and green. It is an area of small industry, as well as being extremely rich in culture and history.

The challenge

The project is to complete a feasibility study and business plan where the prime focus is to sell property in Apulia to North Europeans. While the client-facing system is probably going to be the Internet, the main challenge lies in the supply chain. In principle, the supply chain models could be, e.g.:

- The company buys, renovates and advertises the properties.
- The company enters into a joint venture with a large Apulia real estate agent.
- The company manipulates a network of smaller real estate agents.

As part of the 'package', essential services (plumber, electrician, etc.) should be included, so new immigrants – probably not speaking much Italian – are not left stranded. So the project may not be just to sell houses, but, rather, a lifestyle. In stages this could include keeping the new buyers in touch with each other (history club, cooking club?). Later it could include contact with the local Chambers of Commerce (remember the new inhabitants are also rich sources of knowledge and skills) and thus the challenge also includes usefully integrating the new inhabitants into the local culture: This should be the USP of the project.

Gnashes

Background

Private and cosmetic dental care are big business. However, prices for even standard procedures vary wildly between dentists. Unfortunately those giving 'better' deals are largely prevented from advertising. Conventional media, like UpMyStreet.com find it difficult to communicate fully why one artisan may justifiably charge more than another. This lack of market transparency means that consumers are unsure as to whether they are getting a good deal or not.

The challenge

The project is to design a website and describe a business model where consumers can locate dentists in their neighbourhood, showing formal details (address, telephone, etc.) and their clinical specialities. Upon clicking, the prices for various standard procedures will be revealed. There should also be a mechanism for comparing prices locally and across regions. Thus it is clear that the data supply and data quality aspects are central. How do you get dentists to contribute their data – especially if they are unduly expensive? How do you check that the data are up-to-date? Those dentists willing to contribute should be able to update and amend their data. Revenue streams should be taken into account; is it reasonable to expect dentists to pay a subscription? Do clients pay a fee? Are there chances of sponsorship or advertising (toothpaste companies, etc?) or strategic alliances with professional bodies or charities?

LP2CD

Background

Technology change has pushed the LP (vinyl) into the shade. However, many males around 50–60 years of age still treasure their LPs, many of which are not available on CD, and indeed the collectors market is expanding. LPs, however, are relatively rarely played in a normal household, due partly to the increasing value of the LP, as well as the convenience of CDs.

The challenge

The project is to design a 'box' which fits between the gramophone player and the amplifier of a 'classical' stereo system. This box could look in part like a stand-alone CD burner. LP owners can put the LP on the gramophone player, put a blank CD in the box and copy/record the LP onto CD while listening to the music. Thus owners will simply and easily have made a CD copy of the LP, and can safely store the LP away, playing the CD instead. Obviously there will be some technical problems, e.g.:

- Classical high-quality CD players play only files in CDA format, so the owner must be able to choose between CDA (default) and MP3 (if they have a newer MP3 player) format – perhaps also WAV.
- One big file – corresponding to a whole side of an LP – is not convenient, so different tracks on the LP must be recognized so the CDA files correspond to the right tracks.
- What happens when the owner forgets or is late in turning the LP over?

The assignment consists of several parts:

1 Writing a full business plan, paying special attention to a realistic market analysis and a detailed marketing plan.
2 Writing prototype software to take the above-mentioned problems into account and, on that basis, giving a detailed estimate of the hardware configuration and costs.
3 An analysis of IPR issues: patents, copyright (on the code) and design or other protection.

WFYK (Work For Your Kids) Holdings

Background

This example is rooted in a hypothetical university where retiring ex-staff represent a large loss of knowledge assets. Certainly other members of staff can, and must, take over their senior management responsibilities, but cuts in staff numbers means that these people will have less and less time to do so. To ensure the smooth running of the university, and to avoid abrupt changes in the university's relationships with the commercial sector, it makes sense to retain retiring knowledge assets as consultants on an ad hoc basis.

The challenge

Find out how to create a holding company called WFYK Holdings and how WFYK Holdings can create a daughter company 'Emeritus Consulting'. Emeritus operates with a list of university staff who have recently retired, are retiring, or who are taking early retirement. These people can operate as freelance consultants on an hourly basis at/for the university, or at/for the university's industrial partners, or with other contacts mediated through Emeritus Consulting. Revenues for the services rendered are paid to Emeritus Consulting, and at year-end, earnings rise up (tax-free) to WFYK Holdings. The consultant is not paid in cash, but rather in warrants for WFYK Holdings. Warrants are realized to non-voting stock at year-end. WFYK Holding guarantees to buy back stock at market price on demand whereupon monies are transferred back to the consultant. Alternatively, monies arising from outstanding stock are transferred to the consultant's estate seven years after death.

The project is to complete a feasibility study and business plan for the above, taking tax (corporation tax, income tax, inheritance tax), trust funds and other corporate legislation (holdings, stock, warrants, etc.) into account.

Index

Page numbers in *italics* refer to figures and tables.